RECKONING WITH HISTORY

RECKONING WITH HISTORY

UNFINISHED STORIES OF AMERICAN FREEDOM

EDITED BY

JIM DOWNS, ERICA ARMSTRONG DUNBAR,
T.K. HUNTER, AND TIMOTHY PATRICK McCARTHY

Columbia University Press

New York

Columbia University Press
Publishers Since 1893
New York Chichester, West Sussex
cup.columbia.edu

Library of Congress Cataloging-in-Publication Data
Names: Downs, Jim, 1973– editor. | Dunbar, Erica Armstrong, editor. |
Hunter, T.K., 1956–2018, editor. | McCarthy, Timothy Patrick, editor. |
Foner, Eric, 1943– honouree.
Title: Reckoning with history : unfinished stories of American freedom /
edited by Jim Downs, Erica Armstrong Dunbar, T.K. Hunter,
and Timothy Patrick McCarthy.
Description: New York : Columbia University Press, [2021] | Includes index.
Identifiers: LCCN 2020057629 (print) | LCCN 2020057630 (ebook) |
ISBN 9780231192569 (hardback) | ISBN 9780231192576 (trade paperback) |
ISBN 9780231549875 (ebook)
Subjects: LCSH: United States—Historiography. | Liberty—United States—
History. | History—Political aspects.
Classification: LCC E175 .R43 2021 (print) | LCC E175 (ebook) |
DDC 973.072–dc23
LC record available at https://lccn.loc.gov/2020057629
LC ebook record available at https://lccn.loc.gov/2020057630

Cover image: plainpicture / Marie Tercafs
Cover design: Lisa Hamm

FOR OUR PH.D. ADVISOR, ERIC FONER

CONTENTS

ACKNOWLEDGMENTS

Bridget Flannery-McCoy first saw the value of this volume and worked with us in developing the conceptual framework. Her keen editorial advice and steadfast commitment to this project made this book possible. After Bridget left Columbia University Press, Stephen Wesley became our editor. We were lucky to once again have a smart, energetic and enthusiastic supporter of our work. The final deadline for submission was during the height of the COVID-19 pandemic. Stephen was enormously patient and kind during this otherwise tumultuous and uncertain time.

Special thanks to Marisa Lastres and Christian P. Winting for their help with the manuscript as it moved through various stages at CUP. We are also deeply grateful to the production team for preparing the book for publication, most notably Ben Kolstad and his team of copyeditors.

Our beloved friend, brilliant classmate, inspiring colleague, and committed co-editor T.K. unexpectedly died before the publication of this book. She was working on her essay 48 hours before she transitioned. We decided to publish her essay as-is. We wanted not only to share with the world evidence of her most beautiful mind and capacious historical imagination, but also to create a permanent record of her words, hermetically sealed and permanently archived in the Library of Congress.

Finally, we would like to thank the contributors of the volume, who labored over the course of many years on their essays. They stuck with the volume because they wanted to offer a tribute to our mentor Eric Foner, who has profoundly shaped our lives in more ways than we know or would even wish to tally.

RECKONING WITH HISTORY

INTRODUCTION

JIM DOWNS, ERICA ARMSTRONG DUNBAR, T.K. HUNTER,
AND TIMOTHY PATRICK McCARTHY

Most people really don't know what historians do for a living, and for good reason. For many, the only introduction to history is a high school history class or maybe a course in college, and even then they are led to believe that history is simply about the memorization of dates with its focus on leaders, wars, and other important people and events. History textbooks unintentionally support these misconceptions by emphasizing coverage, the documentation of long periods that span centuries, in some cases millennia.

Few understand that history is actually the result of arguments and interpretation, and that it is not a defined story with a definite beginning, middle, and end but often an unfinished story, always designed to be rewritten and reconsidered.

What appears as a single sentence in a textbook often results from decades, even centuries, of various scholars' research. Take, for example, a line from Eric Foner's widely read history textbook, *Give Me Liberty!*: "Former slaves' ideas of freedom, like those of rural people throughout the world, were directly related to land ownership."[1] This simple statement resulted from decades of scholarship that can be traced to W. E. B. Du Bois's landmark study, *Black Reconstruction in America*, which was published during a time when leading historians portrayed formerly enslaved people as dependent, childish, and feckless. Du Bois challenged this interpretation by proving how formerly enslaved people were principal actors in the rebuilding after the Civil War of the nation. Although his view gained traction among Black readers and a few progressive white readers, leading white scholars in major universities dismissed Du Bois's interpretation for decades.

This began to change with the rise of the civil rights movement. After witnessing firsthand how Black people in the South strategically built a movement, scores of historians went to the archives in search of evidence about how freedpeople actually responded to the end of slavery. What they uncovered in military correspondences and government reports, in local and state archives, and in newspapers and manuscript collections across the country were endless accounts of formerly enslaved people articulating a claim to landownership.[2] These historians published their findings as articles, books, and dissertations.

This incalculable number of pages of historical analysis then led Eric Foner to declare in one sentence in one paragraph of a textbook, "Former slaves' ideas of freedom, like those of rural people throughout the world, were directly related to land ownership."

In this way a single, seemingly simple sentence can represent the often unknown process of how historical knowledge develops. Behind every textbook sentence, there can be a whole world of scholars who have researched, interpreted, and argued a particular point. And this sentence is also the result of a textbook author, in this case historian Eric Foner, who interpreted and synthesized the material to formulate his claim. In scholarly books, the process is similar but is more explicit due to the publication of endnotes and footnotes, which often don't appear in textbooks. The notes document the author's argument by including citations of both the primary and secondary research. The primary research can include archival records—which can range from newspapers and diaries to letters and government reports to a range of other surviving materials from the period under investigation. The secondary sources refer to what scholars have written on a particular topic.

The essays in this book, *Reckoning with History*, offer diverse insight into how historians work—how they develop their research projects; why and how they develop new interpretations; and how they make historical analysis available to the broadest audiences through films, museums, teaching and other public history endeavors.

As the contributors in this volume make clear, writing about the past is often tied to the present. In fact, when the first generation of historians began to write about the aftermath of the Civil War, they portrayed freedpeople as dependent and unable to be trusted with the rights to land, suffrage, and citizenship. According to Eric Foner, their analysis "was part of the edifice of the Jim Crow System. It was an explanation for and justification of taking the right to vote away from black people on the grounds that they completely abused it during Reconstruction. It was a justification for the white South resisting outside efforts in changing race relations because of the worry of having another Reconstruction."[3] When Foner's generation of historians rightly overturned this interpretation, they too reflected their historical moment: the power of the civil rights movement.

The authors in this book also have connections with the present, and they have often made those connections explicit rather than bury them in a footnote or not acknowledge them at all. While the chapters in this book span a range of periods from early America to the late twentieth century and encompass a diversity of subjects from enslaved people to gay activists, one of the central organizing principles is the focus on freedom, perhaps the paramount hallmark that defines the United States as a nation. In various iterations, the historians in this volume explore the dynamic ways that freedom has shaped the lives of Americans throughout history. But, as the essays in this book show, the promise of freedom remains "unfinished," and so then does its history.

To that end, the essays in this volume have also been written to appeal to a larger public audience. Unlike journal articles or academic monographs, the chapters that follow are meditations and commentaries, explications and reflections, designed to generate a productive conversation about how we, as a nation, reckon with our past.

There is another thread that connects the contributors in this volume. We all studied under Eric Foner at Columbia University. He was our main Ph.D. adviser on our dissertations. He taught us how to conduct research, how to interpret sources, how to develop an argument, how to craft a sentence, how to make history accessible to its widest audience, and, most of all, how to reckon with history.

And for that, we have assembled this book in his honor as a rather small token of our profound and deep gratitude.

NOTES

1. Eric Foner, *Give Me Liberty! An American History* (New York: Norton, 2020), 552.
2. In addition to landownership, they also found evidence of how formerly enslaved people fought for suffrage, citizenship, access to schools, better working conditions, and equal pay. See, for example, Ira Berlin, Barbara J. Fields, Steven F. Miller, Joseph P. Reidy, and Leslie S. Rowland, *Slaves No More: Three Essays on Emancipation and the Civil War* (Cambridge: Cambridge University Press, 1992).
3. Mike Konczal, "How Radical Change Occurs: An Interview with Historian Eric Foner," *Nation*, February 3, 2015.

PART I

ARCHIVES

1

LOOKING FOR ONA JUDGE

An Unfinished Story of Freedom

ERICA ARMSTRONG DUNBAR

I sat down at the microfilm reader and took a moment to catch my breath. I looked at my watch—I had exactly four hours to work through twenty microfilm reels before I made the mad dash through Philadelphia's Center City traffic to pick up my son from summer camp. Within sixty seconds the mental to-do list took control of my mind, persuading me to think about an upstairs running toilet, prescriptions that needed to be retrieved, and a fear that I hadn't left the chicken out on the counter to thaw. I stopped. No. This was not the place or time to think about those things. I was here for the work and everything else will have to wait.

I settled myself and engaged the calm and the quiet of the microfilm room. For many historians, it's the place where we encounter our subjects and spend hours piecing together lives and events—an act that often takes us down rabbit holes and fills our note-taking platforms with information that will never make it onto the pages of a book. But we can't help ourselves. We are in the archive for the hunt, a sport that requires years of practice before we can compete for what we believe to be the gold medals we seek: the publication of a monograph and tenure.

I exhaled.

My mission that day was straightforward: I needed additional information about everyday life in the 1790s, and newspapers would serve as my guides. Like a good historian, I had already accessed the archive's database and knew exactly what papers I would examine. I turned to my list, something that I had compiled over the course of two late evenings after the toddler was asleep and the dishwasher was humming. I walked to the metal shelves, located the reels, and returned to my seat, hoping to find the details I needed so that I could finally write that excited yet timid email to my editor. I began to craft the email in my mind: "Dear Christine, it is with great pleasure" . . . no, too grandiose. "Dear Christine, thank you for your constant support and guidance on this project. I'm delighted to attach the final draft of *A Fragile Freedom*." I stopped daydreaming and looked over at the stack of small, square, cardboard boxes in front of me.

I placed the film between the warm glass panes of the microfilm reader and began to advance the reel. I knew that my subjects would not immediately show themselves. As a scholar of Black women's history, I was accustomed to looking through multiple microfilm reels, journals, and diaries and walking away with only a few notes about Black women in the early republic. My generation of scholars took our cues from the pioneers who came before us: Evelyn Brooks Higginbotham, Darlene Clark-Hine, Deborah Gray White—Black women historians who refused to believe what their professors and publishers told them. They went on to build the field of Black women's history, elbowing their way into an academy that was overwhelmingly white and male. They taught me and other Black women historians that patience and fearlessness were ingredients for success. The architects of the field nurtured a generation of scholars who were committed to construction—each one of us laying the bricks of the building called Black women's history. There were so many stories that needed to be told, and as historian Thavolia Glymph once said, our subjects weren't hidden; they were simply waiting to be found. I prepared to go find them. Exhale.

Articles about political debates and concerns specific to the Philadelphia region filled the pages of *Claypoole's American Daily Advertiser*, a newspaper that ran from 1796 to 1800. I looked down at my watch again—thirty minutes until I had to pack up and run to my car. I came across a few mentions of Black women (always referred to as negresses or negro wenches), and, of course, their lives were told through runaway ads. Vague descriptions of clothing, the mention of a scar above the temple (most likely inflicted by the hands of a cruel enslaver), and suggestions about their possible destinations offered fragments of information about these women—women who were and always will be my subjects. Each time my eyes met with the familiar ads, a perverse excitement ran through my mind. I was thrilled to find evidence of these women in the archives and was simultaneously devastated by the terror and violence that marked their lives. The ads were never enough, serving as little more than proof of life, and they couldn't offer what I wanted. Who were these women? What evil made them finally abandon their homes and loved ones to seek what they believed was owed to them? Did they plan their escapes, and if so, who helped them? But the one question almost never answered was, did they win? Did they successfully escape and blend into the shadows of northern cities? Runaway ads tease the historians of slavery—they seduce us—but rarely leave us feeling satisfied.

It was time to stop for the day, but I kept reading—tempting fate, the Philadelphia Parking Authority, and evening traffic. I wanted to make it through the 1796 spring issues of *Claypoole's American Daily Advertiser*. I would stop at the end of May and continue reading the next time I returned to the archive.

My eyes focused on what appeared to be another advertisement for a runaway. But I quickly realized that I had stumbled across something that was quite different from anything I had read that day—or any other day I had ever been in the archives. The date of the advertisement was May 24, 1796, and I held my breath as I read through the text: "Absconded from the household of the President of the United States, on Saturday afternoon, ONEY JUDGE, a light Mulatto girl, much freckled, with very black eyes and bushy black hair—She is of middle stature, but slender, and delicately made, about 20 years of age."[1] I sat back from the microfilm reader, back erect and motionless. Had I just seen a runaway ad issued from the first president of the United States? And who was this Oney Judge? What happened to her? Why didn't I know any of this?

I quickly scanned the rest of the advertisement, made a photocopy, and exited the microfilm room. I walked with purpose toward my locker, trying to reconcile my excitement with the dread of possibly being late to pick up my son. I spotted my car, and the absence of a parking ticket confirmed what I already knew to be true: it was a special day. While I didn't know what the future held, my heart and head told me that my experience in the archive would lead me down a new path. For the next thirty minutes I thought deeply about what I had read and wished I could spend time simply looking at the photocopy of the advertisement. But I would have to put my excitement on pause and complete the tasks in front of me: pick up toddler, prepare dinner, start bath, and complete lengthy bedtime rituals. I switched from "scholar" to "mommy" mode and spent the rest of the evening checking off tasks, all the while thinking about this incredible find in the archives.

Spared from bedtime rituals by an always-supportive spouse, I hurried to my home office and laid my hands on the document I had been thinking about all evening. I read it over and over again, at least ten times, absorbing every piece of information that the short ad had to offer. In addition to the physical description of Judge, the advertisement issued a few clues about her life: "She has many changes of very good clothes, of all sorts, but they are not sufficiently recollected to be describe."[2] Having read through dozens of advertisements, I knew that this hint suggested that Judge had most likely been assigned to work within the household of the Washingtons. Both George and Martha Washington were acutely concerned with the presentation of their enslaved men and women, and I would come to learn that most of the enslaved people at Mount Vernon received yearly clothing allowances. An enslaved woman knew that her annual allowance included a petty coat, two shifts, one pair of stockings, and one pair of shoes. Her jacket or waistcoat would need to last more than a few seasons. Judge's extensive wardrobe and her presence in Philadelphia set her apart from the hundreds of enslaved people who worked on the president's sprawling estate, sometimes without shoes.

What intrigued me about this advertisement (and the many others that I had examined) was that it offered clues about the enslavers as well as the enslaved. It was clear from the wording of the ad that the Washingtons were surprised by Judge's actions—a baffling response by enslavers who had dealt with runaways in the past: "As there was no suspicion of her going off, and it happened without the least provocation, it is not easy to conjecture whither she is gone—or fully, what her design is."[3] I immediately thought about Stephanie Camp's groundbreaking text, *Closer to Freedom*, and its important argument and description of truancy. The Washingtons had no idea if Judge had permanently left the executive mansion in Philadelphia or if she would return in due time. If Judge was truant, it would be hard to remain hidden in Philadelphia for very long, especially after the runaway ads were printed. But the next sentence in the advertisement suggested that the Washingtons thought that Judge had run away for good: "but as she may attempt to escape by water, all matters of vessels and others are cautioned against receiving her on board, altho' she may, and probably will endeavour to pass for a free woman, and it is said has, wherewithal to pay her passage." Although I knew nothing about this woman or her escape, the evidence was clear: Judge had multiple sets of clothing and money, and she had no intention of returning to her enslavers.

And then I saw it—the price attached for Judge's capture: "Ten dollars will be paid to any person, (white or black) who will bring her home, if taken in the city, or on board any vessel in the harbor; and a further reasonable sum if apprehended and brought home, from a greater distance, and in proportion to the distance."[4] I tucked the photocopy back into my folder and placed it on my desk. It was midnight, and I knew that I needed to go to bed, but sleep would not come easy that night. I stared at the ceiling thinking about this woman that the Washingtons called Oney Judge. Earlier in the day I had been filled with excitement, wondering how I could include this piece of evidence in my manuscript. The advertisement might allow me to add more on fugitive status, and what better enslaver to include in a book about Black women during the early republic than George Washington? But by two o'clock in the morning my excitement had changed to anger. How could it be that I had never heard this story yet considered myself to be an expert in Black women's history during the eighteenth and nineteenth centuries? I immediately thought about the voluminous collection of texts that focused on the life of the Washingtons and knew that I would have to immerse myself in that scholarship. Someone must have written about Judge, I told myself, and I needed to find out what became of her.

Any thoughts I had about including Judge's story in *A Fragile Freedom* quickly vanished. In the matter of a week I located one published text that included a chapter about Judge and one M.A. thesis. Her name (which I came to understand was Ona, not Oney—the nickname given to her by her enslavers) appeared in a few additional sources, but there was little else. This was going to take time to unravel, and to include only a sketchy understanding of her life simply felt like a missed opportunity as well as historical malpractice. I knew that I had to complete my first monograph, as the project meant so very much to me. *A Fragile Freedom* would be the first monograph to focus on the lives of enslaved and free women in the urban North during the early republic and antebellum eras. This text was a contribution to the field of Black women's history—a cinderblock upon which others would build. From dissertation to published monograph, I had completed what many thought was an impossibility, and the decade of work would pay off in more ways than I had ever imagined. It never dawned on me that writing this first book would prepare me for the journey ahead.

I spent the next two years adjusting to the new demands that accompany tenure. Before the ink was dry on my tenure and promotion letter, I was inundated with service requests from administrators and scholars across the nation. I believe this to be the case for most associate professors, but for Black scholars the service work mushrooms beyond control. We are pulled from every direction and asked to serve on countless committees that need "diverse representation." Any marginal protections I may have experienced as a junior professor vanished with tenure. There was very little time for Ona Judge, and like other professors, I would have to rely on summers for research and writing. I resented the parceling of my time—feeling shortchanged and anxious about my inability to focus on Judge. She had become a central fixture of my life, and any stolen moment was dedicated to uncovering her story. Within a year of encountering that runaway ad, I decided that Judge's life would become the center of a new book project. At first, I worried about what appeared to be a thin trail of evidence. I allowed the voices of the past to give me pause, remembering the doubt and concern felt by all scholars of Black women's history, wondering if there was enough material for a book. I considered writing an essay about Judge, after which I would quickly find my way to a new project, one that had more readily available sources. This moment of concern passed swiftly, and I reminded myself that nothing would come quickly or easily in Black women's history. For those of us who have chosen the eighteenth and nineteenth centuries as our scholarly homes, fortitude and patience would always be required. To turn away from Judge would be cowardly and regrettable.

In time, I understood that a book about Ona Judge could be pivotal for Black women's history and for the history of the early republic. While Judge's incredible life story deserved a deep examination, I began to refashion my project, understanding Judge as a major intervention in late-eighteenth-century history. After reading dozens of texts about George Washington and other "founders," I soon realized that I was bored. I appreciated the historical contributions of biographers and scholars of the period, but it felt as though I was reading the same thing over and over again. So much of the historiography focused on white men—those who fought for America and for the British. These story lines had created the dominant narrative about the creation of the United States. Historians of women had made some progress by including the lives of white women who participated in the war effort in multiple ways. Scholars such as Benjamin Quarles had highlighted the contributions of Black men who fought in the Revolution for both the Americans and the British. But where were the Black women? Their stories were almost completely absent from the most well-read historical monographs—as if Black women simply didn't exist during the era of the Revolution or the early republic. I knew that Judge's story could trouble the tired and static historiography, and I soon knew that my book project would do two things: it would introduce readers to the incredible life of Ona Judge, but it would also serve as a history of the early republic that centered on the life of an enslaved and then fugitive woman.

In my book, the reader would follow Ona Judge from revolutionary Virginia to New York and Philadelphia—the largest northern cities of the early republic—to antebellum New Hampshire. As an enslaved teenager, Judge was involuntarily taken to the North, where she served Martha Washington in cities that had begun to dismantle the institution of slavery. It became clear that Judge's life would serve as what Isabel Wilkerson called an "x-ray of the country.[5]" By centering Judge's story, readers would be exposed to what lay underneath the ideals and practices of the "founders." Judge would be a portal into a world that had all too often been cast as white and male, and this history would explore the founding of the United States through the eyes of enslaved people.

The realization of what this book would and could be was simultaneously exciting and terrifying. I knew that there was an entire field of scholars who had spent their careers examining and revering George Washington and other early presidents. I was preparing to expose Washington, and I understood the politics behind my intervention. As a Black woman scholar, I was preparing to walk into spaces where I would be unwanted—spaces that very few Black scholars had infiltrated. I thought deeply about the kind of backlash that I might face. I was unbothered by the probable negative reviews and critiques from presidential historians or the scholars who squirrelled themselves away in ivory towers writing revelatory founding father monographs. Judge's story would provide an intervention—an insertion of Black women's lives into a space that had always been claimed by white male subjects and their authors. This kind of scholarship is political—no matter what the intention of the scholar is. The consequences could prevent future promotions and lock me out of the arena where I had fought to belong. In a moment of clarity, though, I realized that I just didn't give a damn. I was going to write the history that mattered most to me, and I would place my faith in the ancestors and the Black women scholars who had paved the way. I would be fierce. I would be patient.

My visits to libraries and archives were secretive. Unwilling to discuss my project with those outside my small circle of trusted friends and family, I offered very little information to librarians and archivists—all of whom were friendly and willing to offer assistance in any way possible.

I knew too much to show my hand. Stories of scholars who watched their book projects evaporate once a fast-paced writer or journalist caught wind of their great idea weighed heavily on my mind. I still couldn't believe that no one had written a full-length account of Judge's life, so I kept my library questionnaires vague. I told those who asked that I was working on a project regarding enslaved women, Virginia, and Mount Vernon and kept the details hidden.

But I was worried about more than thwarting a fast-typing journalist—I thought deeply about the backlash that would undoubtedly come my way. An avalanche of criticism found its way to scholar Annette Gordon Reed after she pulled back the sheets on Thomas Jefferson and Sally Hemings. While *The Hemingses of Monticello* won the National Book Award for Nonfiction, the Pulitzer Prize in history (she was the first African American ever awarded this prize), and many other awards, the public fury over the exposure of Jefferson's sexual encounters with the enslaved Sally Hemings was ugly. Few historians ever have to worry about threats of violence and personal harm upon the publication of a book. But for scholars who write about controversial topics, especially scholars who are women and people of color, the threat is very real. I remember having a dinner conversation with a well-known scholar and television personality who told me that she regularly received anonymous threats and one morning opened her front door to find a brown paper bag filled with excrement sitting on her front porch. This vile marker of intimidation was terrifying but not shocking. Black people have always lived with intimidation, and a connection to the academy will never shield us from the possibilities of violence.

Once I decided that I would write about the founding of the nation through the eyes of the enslaved and finished up most of my research, I sat down to write—a process that always made me feel uncomfortable. For most of my academic life, I had worked hard to write in a way that matched the long-held expectations attached to scholarly production. It was a skill that I learned how to employ, but one that I never liked. It felt unnatural—forced and ill-fitting. In the words of my grandmother, it was as if I were forcing Texas into Rhode Island. I wanted everyone with an interest to read this book, not only my colleagues in academia.

Judge's story was compelling, and I wanted to write a book for my peers, my family members, students, and book clubs across the nation. It was a gamble. I thought about promotion committees and the possibility of rejection. But could I really allow a small number of scholars, some of whom were not historians, to determine how I would write about Black women's history? The answer was a hard no. I would be fierce and I would be patient. I would tell Ona Judge's story in a way that would resonate with many, not a few.

I wrote a manuscript, refusing to share it with anyone. To move beyond the world of the academic press, I knew I would need an agent—a requirement that no scholar had ever discussed with me. I met my agent through a friend—someone who wrote children's books and had met with great success. She suggested that I call Laura Dail and feel her out. Before I knew it, I had sent Laura the manuscript, written an op-ed for the *New York Times*, and prepared to select an editor. My agent was honest and ethical, asking me about my hopes and dreams for my book. She listened and took notes and then finally asked the question for which I was completely unprepared: "Erica, would you prefer to work with an African American editor?" I paused. My agent, a blond-haired white woman, had surmised that this might be important to me. To be honest, I didn't even know it was an option. In academic publishing, there were no Black editors working at presses that were interesting to me. I didn't know the world of trade publishing and hoped that her question meant that this world might be different from academic publishing. I was wrong. She was honest and told me that there were very few Black editors in publishing but that she would do her very best to give me options.

In a few days' time I met with the woman who would become my editor and my "confidante." Dawn Davis was a powerhouse Black editor with her own imprint. She would call, I would talk, and she would listen. Her red pen was heavy but never controlling, allowing me to give voice to a woman who had been left in the margins of history. Davis offered me freedom from the confined world of academic prose, and for that I will always be in her debt.

Account logs, city records, correspondence, journal entries, and two interviews allowed me to breathe life into Judge's story. I filled in the gaps with suggestions—informed speculation based on the lives of the enslaved and free women who filled the pages of *A Fragile Freedom.* I offered the reading public the story of an enslaved woman, owned by the Washingtons, who gathered her nerves and grit and resisted the most powerful family in the new nation. Ona Judge was never free—she remained a fugitive for her entire life, a life that represented an unfinished story of freedom.

NOTES

1. "Ten Dollars Reward," *Claypoole's American Daily Advertiser*, May 24, 1796. (The advertisement was published on May 24, 1796, and appeared in the newspaper for several days.)
2. "Ten Dollars Reward."
3. "Ten Dollars Reward."
4. "Ten Dollars Reward."
5. Isabel Wilkerson, "America's Enduring Caste System," *New York Times*, July 1, 2020.

2

"LIKE PEOPLE IN HISTORY"

Why Social History Matters for the LGBT Community

JIM DOWNS

Before the Stonewall uprising in 1969, Craig Rodwell studied ballet but quit dancing to open the first-ever gay bookstore in the world. Barbara Gittings also loved books and set up a kissing booth at a national conference for librarians to bring attention to the lesbian novelist Alma Routsong's recently published book, *Patience and Sarah*. Harry Hervey wrote books about women traveling to faraway places and falling in love with gorgeous men, but he barely left his family's hotels in the U.S. South. William Dorsey Swann was born in the U.S. South as an enslaved person before the Civil War but has become known as the "First Drag Queen." Albert Cashier fought in the Civil War, dressed as a man, and remains the only Civil War veteran who has both a woman's and man's name listed on their tombstone.[1]

With few exceptions, many of these stories have largely not been told; their history is left mostly unread; their lives, even when they are documented, are left to the margins of most major U.S. history textbooks or do not even appear at all. This is not to undermine or even ignore the prodigious scholarship that many LGBT historians have put forward since the 1970s. There has been a great deal of scholarship conducted within the field among queer scholars that continues to grow and enrich our understanding of the past. My concern does not lie with them; in fact, they have often been laboring against many challenges, which I will explain. Rather, my criticism is aimed at the rest of the card-carrying members of the historical profession, who do not see LGBT history as fundamentally important to their interpretation of the past.

The writing of LGBT history, especially by queer scholars, cannot be divorced from the politics of the profession and the systematic homophobia that continues to harm or, at the very least, haunt many LGBT historians. Sadly, since the formal writing of LGBT history began in the 1970s, the historical profession has been largely unwilling to embrace gay history. In 2006, I began research for my book on gay liberation, and I met with Jonathan Ned Katz, whose pioneering book *Gay American History*, published in 1976, provided the first serious study of LGBT history. Katz's decision to write history had many inspirations. As an avid bibliophile and the son of political radicals, he often discussed history around the dinner table with his brother William and his father Bernard, a labor activist who took classes on Black history with the preeminent radical historian Herbert Aptheker. Due to Aptheker's influence, Katz and his father actually published books on slave resistance in the 1970s, in an effort to provide a historical context for the Black Freedom struggle, which was pioneering at the time.[2]

When modern gay liberation began to heat up in the early 1970s, Katz again turned to history for context. He began a massive research effort at the New York Public Library, reading newspapers, court cases, and other surviving materials to tell the history of gay people. At the time, Katz had also been in contact with two gay men who had been doing research on gay people in Berlin before Hitler gained power. They had uncovered a thriving gay culture in Berlin, which Hitler ultimately destroyed. That study became known as *The Early Homosexual Rights Movement (1864–1935)*.[3]

When I asked Katz directly about why he turned to history amid the political excitement of the queer revolution, he recounted a scene from *Life of Galileo*, Bertolt Brecht's short play about Galileo's imprisonment during the Inquisition. The Roman Catholic Church had imprisoned Galileo for his theory that the earth revolved around the sun and threatened to persecute Galileo if he continued to promulgate this claim. Galileo ultimately succumbed, Katz explained, but at the last minute he passed along his thesis notes to his assistant, who spirited them out of the country.[4] "I find it so moving," Katz said, "because that's the way we felt. This might be our only chance to sneak everything we learned into this book. This might be our only chance to sneak everything we learned into this book . . . passing on the information against the people who wanted to suppress it." He decided to become a historian to ensure that his people's history would not be forgotten.[5]

When I pushed Katz further on who might actually prevent gay history from being told or who might erase it, he looked up at me and said, "The AHA."[6] Katz was referring to the American Historical Association, which has been the leading American organization for historians since its founding in 1884. Not having a Ph.D. or even a college degree—Katz was a trained textile artist—he worried that the AHA's intellectual chauvinism and inherent homophobia would discredit and invariably erase gay history—similar to how the Nazis eradicated any trace of gay liberation and history in Berlin. That fear did not, however, stop Katz from continuing his research. He has published many books, devoted countless hours to creating online archives to preserve queer history, and remains a leading scholar in the field.[7]

In 1975, a year before Katz published his landmark book, historian Carroll Smith-Rosenberg, who earned her Ph.D. at Columbia University, published an article, "The Female World of Love and Ritual: Relations Between Women in Nineteenth-Century America," that provided proof of intimate relationships between women in the feminist scholarly journal *Signs: The Journal of Women in Culture and Society*. With the exception of her article, most of early gay history, as evidenced by Katz and many others, did not originate in the academy but began in the community.

Similar to the origin of Black Studies, the early practitioners and readers of gay history were not academics or scholarly audiences but people within the gay community who were hungry for history about their ancestors.[8] In fact, there was a convergence between Black activism and queer activism in 1974 when a group of Black lesbian feminists formed the Combahee River Collective, a political organization that took its name from Harriet Tubman's famous raid that freed 750 enslaved people in South Carolina. Barbara Smith, a leading member of the organization and a legendary activist, explained that she suggested evoking Tubman's raid because "it was a way of talking about ourselves being on a continuum of Black struggle, of Black women's struggle."[8] The organization led to a proliferation of publications that challenged the assumptions beneath categories of "man" and "woman" that historians took for granted and often viewed as natural. By pointing to the intersection of racial, gendered, and sexual identity, Black women activists compellingly revealed how the category of "woman" often implied white and heterosexual while the category of "race" often implied only Black men.[9] Theories about intersectionality now define many historians' analysis of the past, but these ideas originated among activists on the ground in search of a vocabulary and analytical framework that gave shape to their movements and a name to their identity.

Since the late 1970s and early 1980s, there has been a shift from the LGBT community as the primary sites of queer analysis to the academy—with the slight exception of trans identity, which has, in part, flourished more among activists and people in the trans community before being adopted and applied by scholars.[10] There has been, nonetheless, an increasing number of LGBT people who have earned doctorates in history, been members of the AHA, and worked as scholars, authors, and teachers, but they still voice concern about the treatment of LGBT history within the academy. In 1989, John D'Emilio, one of the most prolific and distinguished historians of gay history, wrote on the opening pages of *Journal of American History* that "to think—really to think—about gay history and gay historians in relation to the profession is to tap an interior well of pessimism, discouragement, despair, and exhaustion that shocks as well as frightens me."[11]

Over a decade later, in 2001, historian Marc Stein substantiated D'Emilio's concern with a study conducted by the Committee on Lesbian and Gay History, which is affiliated with the American Historical Association. According to Stein,

> the data suggests that despite a significant increase in the number of lgbtq history PhDs produced over the past decade, U.S. history departments have not made a commensurate increase in hiring such scholars to tenure-track positions. Unless change occurs, scholars completing

> PhDs on lgbtq history can expect to meet with some success in gaining part-time and temporary academic employment, but less success in gaining tenure-track or equivalent (TTE) positions.[12]

Then, in 2004, historian Jen Manion turned more directly to the actual practice of writing about LGBT communities by appealing to liberal historians in the article "Calling All Liberals: Connecting Feminist Theory, Activism, and History." Manion wrote, "The erasure of gay experience and the perpetuation of heterosexism" occur on many levels, "including individual, disciplinary, and institutional; in the production of scholarship, the selection of course material, and the classroom dynamic itself."[13] Five years later, in 2009, Manion furthered developed their analysis of heteroessentialism in an excellent comprehensive review of how many historians of early America failed to see how "the social, political, legal, and economic systems are rooted in and perpetuate heterosupremacy."[14]

In 2018, in the introduction to an anthology on queer history, historian Don Romesburg further echoed the concerns of LGBT scholars when he wrote,

> Those studying and teaching the queer past, especially as LGBTQ scholars, graduate students, and educators, continue to face discomfort, disregard, and at times outright discrimination from some administrators, colleagues, publishers, funders, politicians, and community members. Many of us do all sorts of labor, hidden and visible, on our campuses and off, to support LGBTQ students and faculty, students and faculty of color, women, immigrants, and others marginalized by the systems, structures, and interpersonal dynamics we unevenly face. We also push our institutions and communities toward more expansive potentialities under conditions that render the prospects of structural change daunting—and often make precarious our own employment, advancement, and security.[15]

Romesburg's assessment resonates with me on multiple levels, particularly at annual professional meetings of historians, where I often wonder how many scholars can name more than two queer people from the past—activists or thinkers or writers or ordinary people who lived, labored, and loved as queer before 1970. Can they even spout a paragraph about a queer historical episode other than Stonewall? Do they know of a queer history book other than *Gay New York*, which is an excellent book but not the only one? Often not being able to name LGBT history books means not being able to name LGBT scholars. And if LGBT scholars are not known and their books are not widely read outside of their circles, how can they and their expertise be considered valuable to departments, colleges, and universities when conversations about hiring take place? And for that matter, how many departments actually have positions designated for LGBT history? While there are some scholars who study gender and sexuality, that's not the same as from studying queer sexuality or even LGBT History.

In this chapter, I am fundamentally calling for history departments, American Studies programs, and other units to consider hiring scholars who identify as LGBT to teach LGBT history. While those are my hopes, this is an academic essay, not a note to Santa. And to that end, I want to frame my imperative within scholarly terms: to explore how social history can be used by nonspecialists as a way to teach LGBT history and how it can be a methodological choice employed by LGBT historians to further expand and develop the field.

Social history offers an analytical framework that privileges the everyday iterations of ordinary people, and in so doing it provides the most useful historiographical framework for making LGBT legible to nonqueer scholars. Social history—founded by the French annalists, practiced by British labor historians, and popularized by many legions of U.S. historians of slavery, immigration, and women—offers the most legible scholarly context for telling the stories of queer people of the past. Social history seeks to reclaim the lives of ordinary people, to recover buried subjectivities, and to center the marginalized. Its practice involves excavating the lives of people who often may only appear by name on a birth certificate, a tombstone, a census record, a bank account, a voting roll, or a property deed. Social history aims to understand the economic and political conditions that shaped their lives, the spiritual impulses and social forces that influenced their choices, and the cultural attitudes and personal decisions that gave their lives meaning. The objective of social history, nonetheless, means different things to its many practitioners, and even those who are often seen as its most prolific progenitors have been skeptical about efforts to define it, most notably the authoritative historian Eric Hobsbawm. "The term social history has always been difficult to define," Hobsbawm explained, "and until recently there has been no great pressure to define it, for it has lacked the institutional and professional vested interests which normally insist on precise demarcations."[16]

In the spirit of emphasizing the power of LGBT history and offering a clear method for historians to follow, I define social history (for the purposes of this essay) as a practice committed to excavating the lives of the dispossessed from the archives. This method of recovery had animated the pioneering days of many subfields within U.S. history, most notably women's history, African American history, and labor history. The practice of uncovering historical antecedents and ancestors and then unveiling those people and periods to a wider public constitutes, at its core, one of the most profound hallmarks of social history.

Social history gives insight into the everyday actions of the LGBT people who have crowded into urban apartments but slept alone or slept with their partner in lonely rural towns. In June 1969, for example, not more than two weeks before the Stonewall uprising, which was a critical turning point in the modern gay liberation movement, an eighteen-year-old college student from Allentown, Pennsylvania, wrote to Craig Rodwell, the gay activist who opened the first-ever gay bookstore in the world, The Oscar Wilde Bookshop, that he wanted to come to New York City to help advance gay liberation. Rodwell's bookstore served as a community and political hub, and news of it had reached this college student, hundreds of miles away in Allentown. Writing to Rodwell, the student wrote, "I am butch, I get along with all people, I am honest and I am creative. . . . I have ideas which I think may help our movement."[17] By placing ordinary people at the center of historical analysis, this college student's letter offers clues about the postwar history of queer migration within the United States, about how gay men conveyed information about moving to New York, about how they created political networks by mailing letters across state lines before Stonewall, and even about how this college student understood the meaning of "butch" identity. And the letter can also be read as an important artifact about Allentown and what it meant to be gay there, instead of centering on New York City as the epicenter of gay life.[18]

Within the field, however, there has been a tendency to move away from the social history of recovery and increasingly toward situating LGBT history "in the larger context of power, politics, and the state."[19] Building on Joan Scott's formulation of gender as a category of historical analysis, multi-award-winning historian Regina Kunzel states, "I consider historians' efforts to render sexuality a 'useful category of historical analysis,' an analytic optic that illuminates sexuality's association with power across a broad range of historical narratives and fields."[20] Since the 1970s, the field has, as Kunzel notes, "grown theoretically sophisticated, archivally rich and deep, and methodologically inventive, with the potential to transform other historical fields and to have a powerful impact on historical thinking and practice." Kunzel has done the field a great service by identifying these emerging developments, analyzing a range of books in twentieth-century U.S. historiography, and publishing her analysis in the *American Historical Review*, which provides essential credibility to LGBT history.

While the approach that Kunzel has identified has been very generative and led to the publication of compelling scholarship, have historians forgotten the "sex" in the history of sexuality? An approach that explains "sexuality's association with power across a broad range of historical narratives and fields" is an important part of the field but not the only one. This approach unwittingly creates portrayals of queer people that are both legible and, dare I say, acceptable to nonqueer academics, who can feel comfortable reading about other well-established historiographic subjects and narratives. For instance, historian Margot Canady's study, *The Straight State: Sexuality and Citizenship in Twentieth-Century America*, is a well-respected book that won multiple awards from many prestigious professional academic societies. By examining immigration, military, and other government records, Canady carefully explains how the enforcement of sexual norms emerged with the rise of the modern state. Canady places gay sexuality in conversation with a well-established history of the federal government, but what if this is the only book taught on gay history or the only book graduate students are required to read on LGBT history? Similarly, one would not just teach a book on *Brown v. Board of Education* to understand the Black community, Black culture, Black people, or even Black history. The *Brown* decision is a very particular kind of history that certainly imparts crucial details about Black people and activism, but it tells us more about the government, racism, and discrimination than about Black people. More to the point, a reasonable person would not expect one book on *Brown* to do the entire work of explaining a field, but this often happens in LGBT history.

Social history about the LGBT community can teach us about gay people, whereas a history about the state and a discriminated group often tells more about the state than the group. While both approaches are necessary, social history has the power to actually center queer people that often constitute the hallmarks that define the LGBT community. How might we emphasize specific questions that use queer sex, intimacy, and community as the central analytical questions of study?[21] How might these questions lead us to social histories on a range of topics, from pornography and sex workers to the leather community and sex clubs to polymorphous relationships and marriage to drag performers and lesbian comedians to LGBT sports leagues and gay religious groups to queer homeless youth and elderly gay populations to trans and intersectional histories to LGBT health and medicine? Consider the difference between writing an article about the LGBT community based on government records from the National Archives and writing an article based on the materials and manuscripts that queer people donated to the Leather Archives and Museum in Chicago.[22] As Joan Nestle, founder of the Lesbian Herstory Archives, astutely noted in 1981, "If we ask decorous questions of history, we will get a genteel history. If we assume that because sex was a secret it did not exist, we will get a sexless history."[23]

And yet, the politics of the profession, as well as scholarly standards, historiographic trends, and biases, cannot be divorced from research and writing on these subjects. Queer scholarship, particularly the books Kunzel cited, has largely been written by academics who have published with academic presses with academic audiences in mind. The pressure to succeed in the academy means that queer scholars often justifiably publish with university presses, where they are vetted by specialists, some of whom are not queer scholars. And they publish books that fit neatly into other historiographical debates. This process has made queer scholarship conform to a set of professional standards that departs from the standards of the founding generation of LGBT historians who first presented their research in their community—in bars, living rooms, bookstores, rented firehouses, and gay churches.[24] In 1972, a group of lesbians turned their apartment on Ninety-Second Street in the Upper West Side of New York City into the first lesbian archive. They collected photographs, T-shirts, buttons, candlesticks, letters, and other artifacts and stuffed them into shopping bags and went to lesbian bars and homes, where they taught audiences about the lesbian past.[25]

These women later founded what would become known as the Lesbian Herstory Archives, one of the few repositories in the world committed to the collection and documentation of a queer past. Reflecting on the origins of the Lesbian Herstory Archives, founder Joan Nestle explained, "Because of my own experience with the criminalizing 1950s, I felt that it was essential that the archives not become a hand-pick collection of respectable lesbian role models. . . . Yes, we wanted the papers of Samois, the first national public lesbian S/M group. Yes, we wanted the diary of a lesbian prostitute. Yes, we would cherish the pasties of a lesbian stripper. Yes, we wanted collections of woman-with-woman pornography."[26]

Nestle's inspiring statement makes me wonder: What have we lost in our effort to fit into the academy, which, by many metrics, remains at best reticent to engage LGBT history and at worst downright hostile to both the presence of queer scholars and their practice?

This is also not to suggest that writing social history for the community is a less intellectual enterprise than writing for the academy. In fact, the early practitioners of gay history were some of the sharpest minds in the twentieth century. Jonathan Ned Katz was not formally educated but spent many Saturday nights with a group of activists linked to the Gay

Socialist Activist Project, who read Marx in order to understand how power worked. In fact, Marxist analysis enabled them to think historically and to observe how the discrimination against queer people had to do with power exerted against them rather than with something innately wrong with them.[27]

For so long, gay people like Katz were made to believe that they were "sick," that homosexuality was an ailment and a deviance. By studying Marx's explanation of how power works, Katz realized that he was not, in fact, sick, that his understanding of himself resulted from those who had power to create a narrative about deviance and difference. Taking this theory and applying it to himself, Katz uncovered that at certain points in history those in power used their authority to define same-sex desire as aberrant, sinful, criminal, pathological, and deviant. History helped to elucidate how ideas about same-sex changed over time, and had more to do with those in power than with those marked as queer. Once he realized that same-sex desire was not innately wrong but rather was described as such by those with power, he (and others) could undermine those assertions cast against them and define same-sex desires as positive, revolutionary, and, most of all, historically situated. This framework served as the organizing principle for his anthology *Gay American History*. He grouped the documents he found in the archives according to how those in authority stigmatized gay people.[28]

Early LGBT history was, in turn, rigorous and smart; it combined Marxist analysis with social history sources to make sophisticated theoretical arguments accessible to a wider public.[29] LGBT history can return to its earlier roots of recovery and use social history as the professional framework to write more community-based histories for a larger queer public. Marc Stein's *City of Sisterly and Brotherly Loves: Lesbian and Gay Philadelphia, 1945–1972* and Marcia M. Gallo's *Different Daughters: A History of the Daughters of Bilitis and the Rise of the Lesbian Rights Movement* represent the best of this approach; newer work includes Julio Capó Jr.'s *Welcome to Fairyland: Queer Miami Before 1940* and Jen Manion's *Female Husbands: A Trans History*.

Nonetheless, the problem of actually identifying the historical actors that we might call LGBT often leads to a necessary if turgid theoretical discussion about identity. According to many leading historians, most notably Michel Foucault, the notion of sexual identity did not develop until the last quarter of the nineteenth century. During that period, biomedical authorities invented the categories of "homosexual" and "heterosexual." Prior to that there were people who engaged in same-sex acts and experienced same-sex intimacy, and they were punished as sinners, persecuted as criminals, pathologized as deviants, and hanged as sodomites, but it was not until the end of the nineteenth century that medical and scientific authorities invented the categories of homosexual and heterosexual that placed people into one of those groups. This is a thumbnail sketch of a far more complex theoretical argument, which has then led to even more interpretation and debate within the field, making it challenging for scholars to find queer people from the past.[30]

Consequently, since a theory has shaped the way scholars raise questions about the presence of queer people in the archives, there has been an emphasis on theory in the writing of LGBT history. Theory can be an enormously important tool in understanding the past; in fact, in my research on same-sex intimacy among enslaved men, theory provided the best way to conceptualize the past, to understand the power dynamics of the archive, and to recover the past.[31] However, theory has unwittingly led to more academic analysis and less recovery of actual people. Historians engaged in recovery will invariably be analytical in terms of their method, but when the theories of sexuality fill more of the textual space than the room allotted to the lives of the people we are investigating, something has been lost for the purposes of the social historian. In fact, this is not an entirely new conundrum. In the 1980s and 1990s, there was a debate between women's historians, who were "stuck in a descriptive rut, relegated to the limited byways of social history inquiry," and gender historians led by Joan Scott, who, according to historian Joanne Meyerowitz was "influenced by Derrida's deconstructionism and Foucault's formulation of dispersed power." Scott asked historians to "analyze the language of gender, to observe how perceived sex differences had appeared historically as a natural and fundamental opposition."[32]

Here, I am not calling to reinscribe this debate onto the LGBT field, but rather to use it as a way to possibly elucidate a set of practices and even priorities within the field. While Kunzel has smartly detailed the "power of queer history," attending to the analytical ways that power and politics intersect and inform sexuality, I am calling for a more direct recovery project: a social history excavation that does not dismiss theory or analysis but centers on the lives of people from the past.

While this pursuit risks getting labeled as amateurish, antiquarian, and even atavistic, my experience in writing for the public, serving as a consultant for the entertainment industry, and working closely with curriculum development—both as a former middle and high school teacher and an educational consultant—compels me to consider the need to have, dare I say, a pantheon of LGBT people from the past who could be easily added to curricula, taught to second graders, used as a way to teach the public, and serve as the subject of film, television, and other media. The values of social history also extend beyond scholarly discussions and have relevance for the increasing expansion of both gay public history and oral history.[33] The historical record is replete with LGBT people, but it takes a concerted effort to excavate them, as well as respect for those committed to this practice.

The emphasis on theory in the writing of gay history has also rendered queer history inaccessible to nonspecialists and those not familiar with sexuality or trained in the most basic tenets of gender and cultural studies. Framing LGBT history as a continuation of the social history project of the 1970s and 1980s offers a clear entry point to those wanting to add queer history to their curricula. One can also remember that the origins of social history can be traced to Marc Bloch, a historian who during World War II became a member of the French Resistance and who penned sections of *The Historian's Craft* about how to write about the everyday actions of ordinary people while being imprisoned in a Nazi prisoner of war camp.[34]

Social history allows one to revel in the recovery of archival sources and to celebrate the discovery of the ordinary details of an anonymous person's daily life. Professional historiography often skims over reference to these records and takes them for granted. With few exceptions, the discovery of surprising sources has been muted and relegated to footnotes, while the main text continues to engage in a historiographical debate.

Consequently, to find a queer person in the archives is a remarkable achievement. Traditional archives before the 1970s did not catalogue or classify queer people as a distinct culture worthy of bibliographic citation. The Dewey Decimal System had labeled "homosexuality" as criminal and aberrant, saying nothing of the writers, people, communities, cultures, and movements that had self-identified as queer. Appearing within traditional repositories as pathological or criminal was, nonetheless, a recognition of their existence in the face of mountains of paper that refused to say their name. According to the logic of library classification, queer people did not exist. In the 1970s, however, Barbara Gittings worked with the American Library Association to reclassify queer subjects.[35]

LGBT people have been the leading and often exclusive archivists of their own history; beginning in the 1970s and continuing until the present, community centers in cities like Chicago, New York, and Philadelphia have been home to large collections of gay records. In fact, in the 1990s, as an undergraduate at the University of Pennsylvania, I volunteered at the William Way Community Center, where gay people had left brown paper bags filled with old newspaper clippings, letters, and other ephemera that had then been stored in the center's attic before being formally catalogued years later. Efforts are just beginning to collect and to preserve LGBT history in mainstream archives and libraries, and even these collections, with few exceptions, emphasize the late twentieth century. The ONE National Gay and Lesbian Archives at the University of Southern California now has the largest collection of LGBT records in the world.

Therefore, before we interpret how a document supports our own arguments or upends a historiographical debate, we ought to first hold that document in our hand and be in awe of its survival, of its ability to withstand the efforts to erase and hide any reference to queer life, an evisceration process not only enacted by homophobic individuals but even, at times, committed by gay people against themselves. There were those who purposely burnt their own letters, hid any reference to their intimate lives, or purposely distorted the official records in order to avoid notice.[36] We, in turn, ought to celebrate that record. Promulgate it.

Tell its story and, like the early pioneers of the Lesbian Herstory Archives, bring it to a bar to show gay communities.

LGBT historians can borrow and build on the ways in which historians of women and African Americans framed their discovery of lost subjectivities in order to place these documents within a scholarly conversation. In African American history, the field of slavery and emancipation grew out of the discovery of government documents housed at the National Archives, known as the Freedmen's Bureau records. This led to a robust scholarly project that in 1976 began to transcribe the sources, organize them according to subject, and then publish these records as part of a multivolume series that remains in print today. Sources, not just historiographical trends, drove historical analysis. Furthermore, the emergence of African American Studies as an interdisciplinary field benefited enormously from the discovery of over two dozen books written by Black women in the nineteenth century. Known as the Schomburg Collection, this series of books, which included scholarly analysis in the introductions to each volume, not only provided students and the reading public with a range of new primary sources to learn about the past but also became the basis for many scholarly monographs, articles, and dissertations. In both cases, the recovery of these sources informed scholarly examination. Scholars valued the sources as central components to their analysis. Today, a similar scholarly tradition continues in African American history. Erica Armstrong Dunbar's discovery of a runaway slave ad in an eighteenth-century newspaper provided evidence of how one of George Washington's enslaved people, Ona Judge, had successfully escaped from slavery. Dunbar foregrounded the sources that were recovered as part of the stories she narrated. They are not just shoehorned into the endnotes but part of the story that she tells.

Recovery also has the added advantage of facilitating another emerging direction within the broader historical profession: narrative history. Practiced by an increasing number of historians, most prominently Jill Lepore, the art of storytelling presents the possibility of reaching broader audiences, bridging the divide between the academy and the public, and making history more accessible to students.[37] Narrative history amplifies the people and places, the artifacts and archives, the events and episodes that define social history. It provides a framework that turns a document's setting, plot, characters, theme, and conflict into the structure of the story. It assigns meaning to the details within a document that often are omitted from a historian's analysis. It demands a closer inspection of the record.

To be clear, I am not calling for an abdication of scholarly standards but rather a realignment of points of scholarly engagement. For instance, within the broader field of historical practice, there has been attention to the "archival turn," a move to consider how the process of recordkeeping has its own history, persuaded by its own political orientations and ideological commitments. This emerging development offers a productive, rich, and compelling framework for examining the discovery of queer sources.[38] In a special issue of the *Radical History Review*, Daniel Marshall, Kevin P. Murphy, and Zeb Tortorici inaugurated this discussion for LGBT history by offering a brilliant analysis of "queering the archive."[39] This endeavor, which they describe as "recalling and renewing the historical imperative to apply critical pressure to the type of knowledge we inherit in relation to sexuality and gender and the manner through which we inherit it," provides an excellent framework for underscoring the project of recovery.[40]

Located with the National Archives, far removed from the hustle-bustle of Washington, DC's queer community, Albert Cashier's pension record, for example, can be requested by filling out a simple form.[41] Cashier's pension record offers a fascinating glimpse into their life and provides bona fide evidence of a person changing gender during the Civil War. But the history of Cashier does not end with the information listed on the surviving record. There is a story about the very discovery of the document, its preservation within the federal archives, and its place among military records. While the National Archives are full of service records from the War of Independence to the Vietnam War, Cashier's record cannot be handled with the same assumptions. It is an extraordinarily rare document that needs to be rigorously interrogated based on a range of factors, including most fundamentally the building that houses it.

This document within the National Archives cannot treated like the millions of other nineteenth-century wartime records; it must be contextualized within the broader, more complicated history of how any queer records have survived from the past. Unlike a diary that offers a passport to a person's life or a newspaper that serves as an artifact of a forgotten time, government reports are purposely dull and standardized, formatted to not capture feeling but to collect facts. Thus, to find evidence of a person changing gender in this context adds further layers for the investigation of those who lived and labored in the United States before the twentieth century. Placing it in this context allows us to narrate its recovery as central to the history it imparts.

The story of Cashier resonates on many scholarly levels, but it also offers ample opportunities to be adopted in elementary, middle, and high school curricula. Fortunately, some schools have begun to formally incorporate LGBT studies into their curriculum. They need digestible, easily understandable historical details—people, places, and events that can be adopted into a curriculum. Recently, when I served as a consultant to one of the nation's largest school districts, I was tasked with coming up with historical material for students from first grade to high school. While my bookshelves are teeming with smart LGBT books, anthologies, and articles, I found very little material that could be adopted into the curriculum. The school district developed the idea of using biographies and a few scattered terms as the organizing principles for each unit. This led me to do more social history research into the lives of many LGBT people from the past.

A social history of queer people enabled me to develop sophisticated lessons that drew on advanced scholarly arguments while simultaneously offering compelling but powerful thumbnail profiles of queer people from the past for elementary school. These profiles were like those in other units that celebrated historical figures. Working with this school district reminded of the power of social history, as well as how urgent it is that historians mine through the archives to find more people, places, and events to populate these curricula.

Furthermore, when I am interviewed by a journalist to historically situate a particular crisis surrounding queer issues or when I am writing my own essays for the popular press or serving as a consultant for the entertainment industry, I find that nonspecialists best understand the significance of LGBT history when I can explain a particular theory or make an argument by pointing to a flesh-and-blood person from the past. Journalists can better visualize the past, get a grasp of the nuances, understand the texture of the period, and grapple with the complexities and conflicts when they learn about a particular person, community, or group. Social history has the power to furnish this evidence and to illustrate this history.

I borrowed the title of this essay from Felice Picano's novel, *Like People in History: A Gay American Epic*, which I had read when I had just graduated from college in 1995. I remember seeing the jacket of the book in a gay card and gift shop that was adjacent to a gay coffeeshop and a few doors away from a gay gym in Philadelphia. The image on the jacket enchanted me. It was a drawing of an apartment building that featured three men looking out their windows—one was in a tank top and jeans, looking flirtatiously out the window. The one above him was shirtless and gawking at the stud below, and the third was daydreaming, hand on his head, either looking at the guy in the tank top below or frustrated by the spectacle of the other two. Until now, I never really thought about whom I identified with most—maybe all of them, maybe none of them.

It was the book's title splashed across a familiar urban setting, evoking for me Gloria Naylor's *The Women of Brewster Place*, that made the jacket enchanting. I do remember thinking at the time that we—gay men—were "like" people in history, and at twenty-three years old that felt reassuring and comforting. It made me feel less alone, less unmoored to any tangible queer tradition. It was the 1990s, when gay politics shrouded its radical edge to pave the way for marriage equality and Supreme Court employment protections. It was a time for me to feel that I had a history, because despite attending an Ivy League university, two decades after Stonewall, there were few references to gay people in my entire academic study of dispossessed and marginalized peoples. A novel in a card and gift gay store—another relic of a lost time—became a portal to a past that had no name. The use of the term "like" in the title of the book evoked the possibility of a queer past, but I didn't know if that past was actually historically accurate or just the author's imagination. But I did know that I reached for the novel because I wanted to hold my history in my hand, and I did sense that many other gay people were deciding to pick up a novel in the 1990s because they too were hungry to know about our history.

I forget the plot of the novel. I do remember refusing to read the final twenty pages for months because I didn't want the portal to the gay past to suddenly close. It would take ten years for me to return to that neighborhood in Philadelphia, which had then been affectionately dubbed the "gayborhood." The card and gift shop and café closed, but the gym was still there, and so was the Gay Community Center, which had moved to a more spacious location. I had just defended my dissertation under the direction of Eric Foner on the untold history of epidemics that devastated formerly enslaved people during the Civil War and Reconstruction. I was told during my dissertation defense to take a year off, to let the ideas marinate so that I could revise my dissertation into a book. I, however, took the time to return to the William Way Community Center in search of queer people in history.

What I found led to my book, *Stand by Me: The Forgotten History of Gay Liberation*, which includes only a fraction of the dazzling if dizzying number of sources that I uncovered. In the William Way Community Center, I read through old issues of *The Advocate*, the leading gay national newspaper, and stumbled upon articles about an arson attack on a gay bar in New Orleans in 1973. In 2005, when I was doing this research, the Internet was in its early days of including historical data, and I had no way of verifying this event. I spent years reading through more gay newspapers to piece together the entire story, which I found no reference to in gay history books. Having sown together the main plot points of the story, I remember distinctly having a conversation with my father and telling him that there was no police or fire report, which I concluded was a result of homophobia because the gay press documented how the police, fire department, and local media downplayed the fire and actually used it to ridicule gay people. My father, while sympathetic to my claim, assured me that if the fire trucks rolled down the street in the French Quarter there would be a report; I just had to find it.

In 2008–2009, librarians and archivists in New Orleans told me that Hurricane Katrina had wiped out many of the city records. Colleagues who worked with twentieth-century municipal reports warned me that police records are often unorganized, uncatalogued, and inaccessible to researchers. I then turned to the gay community in New Orleans for any clues. They sent me down a rabbit hole that led me to San Francisco and then back to New Orleans, where I came in contact with an artist, Skylar Fein, who had curated a spectacular exhibit on the history of the arson attack. He had actually found a copy of the fire department's report and stowed it away under his name at the Historic New Orleans Collection Museum. In a private box in a plush decorated room, I finally found the names of the gay people who died in what was then the largest massacre of gay people in the United States.

Based on this finding, I worked with *TIME* magazine to publish the story on the fortieth anniversary of the fire in 2013, which predated the publication of my book. I wanted to do this even if it meant spoiling the launch of my book three years later. My colleague and friend, historian Catherine Clinton, explained to me that tying a historical event to an anniversary was my best shot at getting this history published in a revered, noteworthy national magazine. I took her advice because I wanted the history of the gay people who died in the fire to appear in print in *TIME* magazine—to ensure that gay history would be remembered and documented. Katz's warning that gay history could be erased stuck with me.

Drawing on newspapers, I found other compelling evidence about gay liberation: of how gay people organized a movement against mass incarceration in the 1970s, how they developed their movement in response to the Black Freedom struggle, and how stories of Black activists Joan Little and Assata Shakur appeared in gay newspapers; in fact, the gay press actually republished an article that Shakur wrote for *The Black Scholar*.[42] I found evidence of how gay people, much to my surprise, created a global religious movement, founded organizations like Dignity for gay Catholics and Integrity for those in the Episcopal Church, how they fought for the ordination of gay men and women, and how they even established their own church, known as the Metropolitan

Community Church (MCC). I soon learned that the arson attack on the gay bar in New Orleans was actually an attack on a meeting of the New Orleans chapter of MCC. The media reported that gay men were killed in a gay bar, but they failed to state that it was actually during a gay church service that the fire bomb was detonated.[43]

Social history archives opened a world to me that I had not known. When my book was reviewed, many LGBT periodicals and even mainstream papers, like the *San Francisco Chronicle*, gave it glowing reviews. But there were murmurs among LGBT scholars in the academy, critiques that they fired off in academic outlets, that indicted the book, particularly along lines that it did not engage issues of race and gender.[44] On the surface, one can easily accept those critiques and fault the book for those shortcomings, but a closer examination reveals less about my shortcomings and more about the content of gay social history archives.[45] During the course of my research, I did my absolute, honest best to find any representation of Black people in the gay archives. When I couldn't find them, I realized that it was more about the organization of the archive and whose history got recorded. I noticed that in 1969 the gay liberation movement was diverse, populated by women, trans people, and many people of color, but by the end of the decade the movement and the archive had become lily white. I, therefore, purposely ended the book with a chapter that analyzed how gay liberation became both white and male by the decade's end, which influenced the content and character of the surviving archive.

Furthermore, while conducting research I had a couple of working theories about the absence of Black men in the archives. First, I read through texts by James Baldwin, likely the most prolific Black queer male writer of the twentieth century, and he left very little archival trace of being queer or details about the Black gay community. In his gay novel, *Giovanni's Room*, he purposely created white gay male characters, which suggests something about how he understood gay desire. In a telling interview in 1984, Baldwin explains how the term *gay* does not apply to him. "The word gay has always rubbed me the wrong way. I never understood exactly what is meant by it. I don't want to sound distant or patronizing because I don't really feel that. I simply feel it's a world that has little to do with me, with where I did my growing up. I was never at home in it."[46]

Baldwin further articulates how his racial identity trumped his sexual identity. "The sexual question comes after the question of color," Baldwin explained. "I think white gay people feel cheated because they were born, in principle, into a society in which they were supposed to be safe. . . . Now that may sound very harsh, but the gay world as such is no more prepared to accept black people than anywhere else in society. It's a very hermetically sealed world with very unattractive features, including racism."[47] Given this direct statement about racism in the white gay community, it is no wonder Baldwin refused to identify as gay, which at the time seemed only to be the province of white men.[48] If Baldwin can be seen as a proxy for Black gay men, it is not surprising that there is a limited archival record that annotates their experience, since the very formulation of gay identity constituted a form of epistemic violence that did not say their name.[49] His iconic quip, "I Am Not Your Negro," could be read as a posthumous rebuttal of efforts to place him within a pantheon of Black queer icons from the past. Additionally, As Kwame Holmes brilliantly theorizes, Black Gay Social History, was informed largely by gossip, which resisted visibility and challenged the liberation discourse that defined gay life in the twentieth century. While Holmes focuses mostly on the 1980s and HIV, his move toward gossip helps to expose the politics that led to the formation of the archive and the silences in the written records.[50]

To that end, during the research for my book I became intrigued by the gay religious community but soon realized that religious faith and spiritual practice had different meanings for white people than for Black people, creating a disjuncture within the archive. White people might establish their own gay churches, prayer groups, and other associations attached to major denominations, but Black people may have viewed their faith as conflicting with their sexuality or not found refuge, as white gays did, in makeshift religious communities, or they may not have been willing to give up the Black church in ways that white people did. Thus there are reasons for the absence of Black gay religious men in the gay social history archives.[51]

My critics instead imagined what was in the archives and then criticized me for not including something that they invented. Their critiques overlooked the politics of gay archives and the polemics surrounding the mere survival of any queer source. It's a miracle that gay records even about the 1970s, a period not too long ago, survived. It's a miracle that a gay artist had the good sense to deposit a fire department report in a private collection under his name to ensure that it would not be destroyed. It's a miracle that gay newspapers, still in their infancy in the 1970s, sent reporters on a shoestring budget to write an article about the death of thirty-two gay people in a city that laughed about their mortality and wished that the fire would have killed more gay people. It's a miracle that community centers, in their fight for funding to keep their doors open so they can accommodate lobbies packed with homeless teens, actually find room to store dusty old newspapers. It's a miracle that gay community centers, whose resources are stretched to organize HIV testing, to host self-help support groups, and to keep their eye on local, state, and national politics—all the while trying to be a social hub for the community by hosting drag queen bingo, events for the elderly, and food drives for the sick—manage to also have libraries that preserve the queer past. It's no wonder that many gay archives in big cities are only open for researchers one night a week for a few hours.

Writing about gay people is not like writing about other well-established topics. LGBT documents are not naturally in these community centers by a decree of the gods, but they are there because of a deep political investment to preserve gay history. To be able to write a book drawn exclusively from these records is a testament to gay community center archives and the scores of volunteers who staff them. But my book, like any study, including this chapter, aims to generate a conversation, and for me, that discussion is less about quibbling about the thesis and more about engaging in a robust discussion about LGBT records—their discovery, survival, and importance—a discussion about gay archives exemplifies the power and promise of social history.

Social history offers a framework that can tell the history of LGBT people. We do not need to simply rely on novelists to imagine the past for us. We can also see it, if we start looking.

NOTES

1. On Rodwell, see Jim Downs, *Stand by Me: The Forgotten History of Gay Liberation* (New York: Basic, 2016). Because of homophobia, Routsong initially published her novel under the pseudonym Isabel Miller. (See "Barbara Gittings and Isabel Miller Kissing at the "Hug a Homosexual" Booth, ALA," New York Public Library Digital Collections, accessed October 30, 2020, http://digitalcollections.nypl.org/items/510d47e3-960e-a3d9-e040-e00a18064a99.) On Hervey, see Harlan Greene, *The Damned Don't Cry—They Just Disappear: The Life and Works of Harry Hervey* (Columbia: University of South Carolina Press, 2017). On Swann, see Channing Gerard Joseph, "The First Drag Queen Was a Former Slave," *Nation*, January 31, 2020. On Cashier, see John J. Kim, *Tombstones of Albert Cashier*, http://digitaledition.chicagotribune.com/tribune/article_popover.aspx?guid=f7e8c822-83d5-4923-ae47-aa5453fec8fc.
2. Downs, *Stand by Me*, 89–112.
3. The groundbreaking study was John Lauritsen and David Thorstad, *The Early Homosexual Rights Movement (1864–1935)* (New York: Times Change Press, 1974). Scholar/activist Jim Steakley also wrote about this history in the 1970s in the popular newspaper *The Body Politic*, which I describe more in my book, *Stand by Me*. For a more contemporary analysis of gay life in Berlin, see Robert Beachy, *Gay Berlin: Birthplace of a Modern Identity* (New York: Knopf, 2014).
4. Downs, *Stand by Me*, 92–112.
5. Downs, *Stand by Me*.
6. Jonathan Ned Katz, interview with Jim Downs, New York City, May 29, 2012.
7. See, for example, Jonathan Katz, *The Invention of Heterosexuality* (New York: Dutton, 1995); Katz founded outhisorty.org.
8. Martha Biondi, *The Black Revolution on Campus* (Berkeley: University of California Press, 2012).
9. As quoted in Duchess Harris, *Black Feminist Politics from Kennedy to Trump* (Cham, Switzerland: Springer International, 2019), 114.
10. Gloria T. Hull, Patricia Bell Scott, and Barbara Smith, eds., *All the Women Are White, All the Blacks Are Men, but Some of Us Are Brave: Black Women's Studies* (Old Westbury, NY: Feminist Press, 1982).
11. Jen Manion, *Female Husbands: A Trans History* (Cambridge: Cambridge University Press, 2020), 11.
12. John D'Emilio, "Not a Simple Matter: Gay History and Gay Historians," *Journal of American History* 76, no. 2 (1989): 435.
13. Marc Stein, "Committee on Lesbian and Gay History Survey on LGBTQ History Careers," June 2001, http://clgbthistory.org/resources/reports/lgbtq-history-careers.
14. Jen Manion, "Calling All Liberals: Connecting Feminist Theory, Activism, and History," in *Taking Back the Academy! History of Activism, History as Activism*, ed. Jim Downs and Jen Manion (New York: Routledge, 2004), 145.
15. Jen Manion, "Historic Heteroessentialism and Other Orderings in Early America," *Signs: Journal of Women in Culture and Society* 34, no. 4 (2009): 998.

16. Don Romesburg, *The Routledge History of Queer America* (New York: Routledge, 2018), 4. In 2015, the AHA created a task force that surveyed queer members of the organization and provided various recommendations. "LGBTQ Task Force Final Report (2015)," American Historical Association, https://www.historians.org/about-aha-and-membership/governance/reports-of-committees-and-divisions/lgbtq-task-force-final-report-(2015).
17. E. J. Hobsbawm, "From Social History to the History of Society," *Daedalus* 100, no. 1 (Winter 1971): 20–45, 20–21.
18. Collin Charles Schwoyer to Craig Rodwell, June 19, 1969, Box 1, "Professional and Political Correspondence, 1963–1970," Craig Rodwell Papers, New York Public Library.
19. There has been an encouraging, growing trend among historians to not use major cities as the exclusive sites of LGBT history. See, for example, Colin R. Johnson, *Just Queer Folks: Gender and Sexuality in Rural America* (Philadelphia: Temple University Press, 2013).
20. Regina Kunzel, "The Power of Queer History," *American Historical Review* 123, no. 5 (2018): 1562.
21. Kunzel, "The Power of Queer History," 1563.
22. A number of scholars have been raising these questions, but their research has not gotten the attention, outside of LGBT circles, that it adequately deserves. The lack of recognition, I believe, results from both homophobia within the academy and an intellectual chauvinism that no longer validates the significance of gay social history. Excellent gay social histories include but are not limited to: Katie Batza, *Before AIDS: Gay Health Politics in the 1970s* (Philadelphia: University of Pennsylvania Press, 2018); Kevin Mumford, *Not Straight, Not White: Black Gay Men from the March on Washington to the AIDS Crisis* (Chapel Hill: University of North Carolina Press, 2016); Daniel Winunwe Rivers, *Radical Relations: Lesbian Mothers, Gay Fathers, and Their Children in the United States Since World War II* (Chapel Hill: University of North Carolina Press, 2015); Phil Tiemeyer, *Plane Queer: Labor, Sexuality, and AIDS in the History of Male Flight Attendants* (Berkeley: University of California Press, 2013); and Karen Christel Krahulik, *Provincetown: From Pilgrim Landing to Gay Resort* (New York: New York University Press, 2005).
23. On the leather community, see, for example, Alex Ellis Warner, "Where Angels Fear to Tread": Feminism, Sex and the Problem of SM, 1969–1993" (Ph.D. dissertation, Rutgers, The State University of New Jersey, 2011). On sex work, see, for example, Joan Nestle, "Lesbians and Prostitutes: A Historical Sisterhood," in *Sex Work: Writings by Women in the Sex Industry*, ed. Frédérique Delacoste and Priscilla Alexander (San Francisco: Cleis Press, 1998).
24. Joan Nestle, *A Fragile Union: New and Selected Writings* (San Francisco: Cleis Press, 2018), loc. 784 of 2641, Kindle.
25. See Downs, *Stand by Me*, 100–12.
26. Jim Downs, "How Gay History Came Out of the Closet," *Vice*, August 9, 2016.
27. Jim Downs, "The Education of Jonathan Ned Katz," *Chronicle of Higher Education*, February 21, 2016.
28. Nestle, *A Fragile Union*, loc 794–95 of 2641 Kindle. For an excellent analysis of what constitutes an acceptable queer archive, see Marc Stein, "Canonizing Homophile Sexual Respectability: Archives, History, and Memory," Radical History Review 2014, no. 120

(Fall 2014): 53–57; and Leah DeVun and Michael Jay McClure, "Archives Behaving Badly," Radical History Review 2014, no. 120 (Fall 2014): 121–30.

29. Downs, *Stand by Me*, 89–112; Jonathan Ned Katz, *Gay American History: Lesbians and Gay Men in the U.S.A.* (New York: Avon, 1976).
30. Marc Stein has smartly examined the limitations of Katz's approach and the ways in which Katz and others "did not address the homophile movement's sexual radicalization." See Stein, "Canonizing Homophile Sexual Respectability," 55.
31. Michel Foucault, *The History of Sexuality* (London: Penguin, 1992); Siobhan B. Somerville, *Queering the Color Line: Race and the Invention of Homosexuality in American Culture* (Durham: Duke University Press, 2000); Jonathan Ned Katz, *The Invention of Heterosexuality* (Chicago: University of Chicago Press, 2007); David M. Halperin, *Saint Foucault: Towards a Gay Hagiography* (New York: Oxford University Press, 1995).
32. Jim Downs, "With Only a Trace: Same-Sex Sexual Desire and Violence on Slave Plantations, 1607–1865," in *Connexions: Histories of Race and Sex in North America*, ed. Jennifer Brier, Jim Downs, and Jennifer L. Morgan (Champaign: University of Illinois Press, 2016), 15–37.
33. Joanne Meyerowitz, "A History of 'Gender,'" *American Historical Review* 113, no. 5 (2008): 1347.
34. Great examples include, but are not limited to, Don Romesburg, "Presenting the Queer Past: A Case for the GLBT History Museum," Radical History Review 2014, no. 120 (Fall 2014): 131–44; Kevin P. Murphy, "Gay Was Good: Progress, Homonormativity, and Oral History," in *Queer Twin Cities: Twin Cities GLBT Oral History Project*, ed. Kevin P. Murphy, Jennifer L. Pierce, and Larry Knopp (Minneapolis: University of Minnesota Press, 2010); and Stephen Vider, curator, "AIDS at Home: Art and Everyday Activism," Museum of the City of New York, May to October 2017. Jennifer Brier has spearheaded a range of public history initiatives in Chicago; see, for example, Jill Austin and Jennifer Brier, *Out in Chicago: LGBT History at the Crossroads* (Chicago: Chicago Historical Society, 2012); and Eric Gonzaba, "Wearing Gay History" (a digital mapping project that charts LGBT people through T-shirts), https://wearinggayhistory.com/about.
35. See Mike Dash, "History Heroes: Marc Bloch," *Smithsonian Magazine*, November 10, 2011; and Carole Fink, *Marc Bloch: A Life in History* (New York: Cambridge University Press, 1989).
36. Jim Downs, "Before Stonewall, There Was a Bookstore," *Atlantic*, June 27, 2019.
37. Estelle B. Freedman, "'The Burning of Letters Continues': Elusive Identities and the Historical Construction of Sexuality," *Journal of Women's History* 9, no. 4 (1998): 181–200.
38. See, for example, Jill Lepore, *The Secret History of Wonder Woman* (New York: Vintage, 2015).
39. Ann Laura Stoler, ed., *Haunted by Empire: Geographies of Intimacy in North American History* (Durham, NC: Duke University Press, 2007); Carolyn Steedman, *Dust: The Archive and Cultural History* (Manchester, UK: Manchester University Press, 2001); Saidiya Hartman, "Venus in Two Acts," *Small Axe* 12, no. 2 (2008): 1–14; Marisa J.

Fuentes, *Dispossessed Lives: Enslaved Women, Violence, and the Archive* (Philadelphia: University of Pennsylvania Press, 2018).

40. Daniel Marshall, Kevin P. Murphy, and Zeb Tortorici, eds., "Editors' Introduction: Queering Archives: Historical Unravelings," Radical History Review 2014, no. 120 (Fall 2014): 1–11. Also see Lachlan Glanville, "Queering Archives: Historical Unravellings, Radical Histories Review Special Issue," *Archives and Manuscripts* 47, no. 2 (2019): 280–84.
41. Marshall, Murphy, and Tortorici, "Editors' Introduction," 3.
42. On Cashier's record, see DeAnne Blanton, "Women Soldiers of the Civil War, Part 2," *Prologue Magazine* 25, no. 1 (Spring 1993); National Archives Record Group 15: Records of the Department of Veterans Affairs, 1773–2007; Series: Case Files of Pension Applications Based on Service Completed in the Years 1817 to Approximately 1903, ca. 1935–ca. 2002; File Unit: Approved Pension File for Private Albert D. J. Cashier, Company G, 95th Illinois Infantry Regiment (XC-2573248), https://catalog.archives.gov/id/36605129.
43. Assata Shakur, "Women in Prison: How It Is with Us," *Join Hands* 14 (April–June 1978), originally appeared in *The Black Scholar* (April 1978). Downs, *Stand by Me*, 143–68.
44. Downs, *Stand by Me*.
45. Emily Hobson, review of Jim Downs, *Stand by Me: The Forgotten History of Gay Liberation*, and Timothy Stewart-Winter, *Queer Clout: Chicago and the Rise of Gay Politics*, in *H-Net Reviews*, February 2017, http://www.h-net.org/reviews/showrev.php?id=46435; Alison Lefkovitz, "Many Roads Led to Gay Rights: Place, Activism, and the Church," *Reviews in American History* 44, no. 4 (2016): 629–35.
46. I should mention that I am trained as a historian of African American history; published a book, *Sick from Freedom: African-American Illness and Suffering During the Civil War and Reconstruction*; and, more to the point, devoted my publishing career to writing articles on how to actually *find* Black people in nineteenth-century archives. See Jim Downs, "Emancipating the Evidence: The Ontology of the Freedmen's Bureau Records," in *Beyond Freedom: Disrupting the History of Emancipation*, ed. David W. Blight and Jim Downs (Athens: University of Georgia Press, 2017); Jim Downs, "With Only a Trace: Same-Sex Sexual Desire and Violence on Slave Plantations, 1607–1865," in Brier, Downs, and Morgan, *Connexions*; Jim Downs, "#BlackLivesMatter: Toward an Algorithm of Black Suffering During the Civil War and Reconstruction," *J19: The Journal of Nineteenth-Century Americanists* 4, no. 1 (Spring 2016): 198–206; Jim Downs, " 'Who Got Bloody?': The Cultural Meanings of Blood During the Civil War and Reconstruction," in *The Cultural Politics of Blood, 1500–1900*, ed. Kimberly Anne Coles et al. (London: Palgrave MacMillan, 2015), 210–28; Jim Downs, "Harriet and Louisa Jacobs: 'Not Without My Daughter,' " in *North Carolina Women: Their Lives and Times—Volume 1*, ed. Michele Gillespie and Sally G. McMillen (Athens: University of Georgia Press, 2014), 117–32.
47. *The Village Voice* reprinted a 1984 interview with Baldwin in 2018. See "James Baldwin on Being Gay in America," *Village Voice*, June 22, 2018.
48. "James Baldwin on Being Gay in America."
49. The idea that *gay* means only "white" illustrates what historian Evelyn Brooks Higginbotham has defined as the "metalanguage of race." Evelyn Brooks Higginbotham,

"African-American Women's History and the Metalanguage of Race," *Signs* 17, no. 2 (December 1992): 251–74.

50. A few weeks after I published my book in 2016, Kevin J. Mumford published his excellent history of Black gay men, which focuses more on leading gay men from the twentieth century, like Baldwin and Bayard Rustin. Mumford's important contribution confirms my findings that there are not major, copious archival repositories on Black gay men in the 1970s. Kevin J. Mumford, *Not Straight, Not White : Black Gay Men from the March on Washington to the AIDS Crisis* (Chapel Hill: University of North Carolina Press, 2016). The archival collections on gay Black men become more voluminous due to the outbreak of HIV in the early 1980s, which provided a rhetorical mechanism to capture the everyday lives or ordinary Black men. See, for example, Dan Royles, T*o Make the Wounded Whole: The African American Struggle against HIV/AIDS*, (Chapel Hill: University of North Carolina Press, 2020).
51. Kwame Holmes, "What's the Tea: Gossip and the Production of Black Gay Social History," *Radical History Review*, no. 122 (May 1, 2015): 55–69.
52. As for the criticism of not including women, I focused only on men for two reasons. First, in LGBT history, some books often separate men from women and women from men based on how the archives and the movements differed. Similar to acknowledging racism, I also actually explained throughout my book how sexism splintered gay liberation. More to the point, I focused only on men because I had argued that the outbreak of HIV in the early 1980s had the inadvertent effect of turning the 1970s into a decade purely about sex in order to rationalize the spread of HIV. Journalists, doctors, public health officials, the media, and even white gay men were terrified and confused about how HIV had emerged and rapidly decimated the gay population. Many then pointed to the sexual liberation movement to rationalize the outbreak of the epidemic. In their telling of the 1970s, it was just one big orgy, with no gay men attending church, being murdered in a fire, or fighting alongside Black people against mass incarceration. I focused on men to undermine the hypersexualized caricature that had dominated the discourse and that I feared would soon infect the historiography.

PART II

REVISIONS

3

AMERICAN FOUNDERS RECONSIDERED

The Case of Thomas Jefferson and Henry Christophe

ASHLI WHITE

The phrase *American founders* evokes the group of men who were instrumental in fighting the American Revolution and establishing the U.S. republic—men like Washington, Adams, Jefferson, and Hamilton. But what if we think about the American founders in the more eighteenth-century sense of the term *American*, which referred to people born not just in North America but also in South America and the Caribbean? While we have been quick to consider U.S. founders alongside European contemporaries, we have been reluctant to discuss them as a part of a hemispheric cohort. To some extent, this disinclination is a result of timing: the wars of independence in Latin America, for example, began about four decades after the U.S. revolution concluded. However, almost all of the U.S. founders witnessed the Haitian Revolution, which started in 1791 as a slave rebellion in the French Caribbean colony of Saint-Domingue. Over the next decade, it became a revolution that abolished slavery, extended citizenship to freed men, and resulted, in 1804, in the founding of Haiti, the second republic in the New World.

The leaders of Haiti's revolution—Toussaint Louverture, Jean-Jacques Dessalines, and Henry Christophe, among others—were men of African descent. Given the rampant racism of the time, it is not surprising that U.S. revolutionary leaders resisted seeing their Haitian counterparts as peers.

President John Adams made a diplomatic deal with Louverture in the late 1790s, and in the nineteenth century, some publications referred to the general as the "black George Washington." But U.S. founders did not incorporate Haitian founders into their intellectual and political circles to the same degree that they did European revolutionaries.[1]

And neither, tellingly, have we—a sign that nineteenth-century attitudes still exert a powerful influence over the types of histories that we are able to imagine and accept. To be sure, in recent decades, scholars have done vital work reappraising the U.S. founders and their relationship to slavery. But we continue to neglect the possible parallels between them and their contemporaries in the Caribbean and Latin America, even though they grappled with similar problems of breaking free from European imperial rule, creating new national institutions and identities, and setting the boundaries of freedom and order.[2] While race as a category of analysis remains an essential tool for understanding this era, it has prevented us from thinking about the founders across the Americas as sharing key attributes: most notably, their standing as members of a property-holding elite that wielded political power in their new nations.

This essay considers what an American, hemispheric perspective might reveal about U.S. founders and the ways we are (and are not) willing to view them. For a case in point, I bring together Thomas Jefferson and Henry Christophe. Admittedly, they were very different. Jefferson fought for independence with his pen, and Christophe did so with his sword. Jefferson could not conceive of a workable abolition for the United States, and one of Christophe's main goals was preserving the liberty of formerly enslaved people in Haiti. That said, each man knew of the other, especially in the early nineteenth century, when they became the leading political authorities of their respective countries and worked to secure their new nations' standing in the wider world.

Christophe and Jefferson also shared an important pet project: architecture. Both men, more than any other founder in Haiti or the United States, supported bold building campaigns. They designed remarkable residences for themselves as well as notable public buildings: in Jefferson's case, the state capitol in Richmond, Virginia, and the University of Virginia, among others, and in Christophe's case, a cathedral, hospitals, schools, and a series of forts.[3] At first glance, architecture might seem a trivial point of comparison for two revolutionary leaders. But Christophe and Jefferson were acutely aware that architecture was a powerful means through which to communicate their ideals to the broader world. As Jefferson enthused, the right architecture could "improve the taste of my countrymen, . . . increase their reputation, . . . reconcile them to the rest of the world, and procure them its praise."[4]

Nowhere is the application of this tenet better seen than in both men's houses. Just as Jefferson lavished attention and resources on his Virginia home, Monticello, Christophe was deliberate in the creation of his estate, Sans Souci, a magnificent structure built between 1810 and 1813 near the village of Milot in northern Haiti. Even today, we cannot think of Jefferson without Monticello, and Sans Souci is as central to histories of Henry Christophe and early national Haiti. As tourist attractions and UNESCO World Heritage sites, Monticello and Sans Souci are places where the public continues to interact with these men and their pasts. Then and now, Monticello and Sans Souci help to explain the visions of the men who inhabited them, and by extension, the revolutions and nations they led.

Monticello and Sans Souci, however, have been made to tell different stories in the United States. Jefferson's Monticello was, and still is, lauded for its studied combination of elements. Borrowing from antiquity as well as au courant European modes, Jefferson created an architectural style befitting an American republic. Christophe, too, incorporated European design features in the architecturally innovative Sans Souci, but it has not been celebrated in the same terms. According to firsthand accounts, Sans Souci was reminiscent of the official seats of seventeenth- and eighteenth-century European monarchs. Its "Old World" influences were so striking that visitors claimed that Christophe had named his estate after Frederick the Great's renowned palace in Potsdam. As this attribution suggests, Sans Souci's European qualities were sometimes treated as mimicry rather than originality—a pale imitation in an effort to assert legitimacy.[5] When the house fell into disrepair with Christophe's death in the 1820s, some commentators took it as evidence of the folly of the owner's ambitious aesthetic and political choices.

The grandeur of Sans Souci and its unapologetic appropriation of European aesthetics remain problematic in the present, as they sit uneasily with current narratives about the Haitian Revolution. Scholars have struggled to reconcile Sans Souci's "Old World" opulence with the Haitian Revolution's radical insistence on liberty and equality. Further complicating interpretations, Sans Souci was, like Monticello, constructed by forced laborers (although not technically enslaved), a practice that defied what postrevolutionary Haiti was supposed to represent.[6]

The disparity in interpretations of Jefferson's and Christophe's architectural decisions stems from a general tendency to emphasize the contrasts between these two men, in terms of their racial identifications and their views on slavery. These differences are crucial, but they do not explain everything. Motivated by racism, Jefferson and others like him disavowed any commonalities between the Haitian and U.S. political projects: the goals of a "black king" could, from his perspective, share nothing with his "empire for liberty" for white men. But Sans Souci and Monticello demonstrate similar preoccupations about social status, political legitimacy, and the display of "civilization" in new nations. In so doing, they shed light on elite power and how it challenged the application of republican ideologies in both places.

Both Monticello and Sans Souci were entirely new constructions, and as such, they reflected the aspirations of their owners—aspirations that were social and political. Their houses announced the status of their owners and argued for a respected position for each man's nation among, as Jefferson put it, "the powers of the earth." That said, the unique biography of each man and the unique trajectory of each revolution shaped each house and what people thought about it.

Jefferson began work on Monticello in 1768 as a plantation home that would exhibit his particular aesthetic preferences, yet the purpose of the project—building a fine house—was commonplace for elites throughout the Atlantic world. Jefferson came from a wealthy family that afforded him all sorts of privileges in Virginia society. Around the time that he started Monticello, Jefferson, then in his mid-twenties, was set on making his own mark by launching his public career in earnest. Inspired by the works of Andrea Palladio, James Gibbs, and Robert Morris, Jefferson's Monticello was a fusion of ancient, Renaissance, and contemporary designs—a bravura display of the maker's intellectual and economic resources. This vision took a while to come to fruition, however, and Monticello was under construction throughout the colonial crisis and the Revolution.[7]

With U.S. independence and the founding of the republic, the style of the house developed political as well as personal importance for Jefferson. He saw Monticello as one physical manifestation of his idea of American-ness: an architectural expression of what enlightened men in the United States could achieve. For over five decades, Jefferson reworked his designs for the house, rebuilt it in light of new plans, and constantly spent money to remodel and furnish Monticello in an attempt to fulfill his aesthetic and political principles.

While Monticello was extraordinary in many ways, the endeavor itself was recognized as within the scope of a man of Jefferson's stature. The same cannot be said for Henry Christophe. By eighteenth- and early-nineteenth-century standards, he should not have had the capacity—neither economic nor intellectual—to create and construct Sans Souci. Yet Christophe was acquainted with the form of such an estate. Elite residents in Saint-Domingue had built extraordinary homes, complete with luxurious furnishings, splendid gardens, and breathtaking vistas, and they were regular sights in the eighteenth-century landscape for free as well as enslaved residents.

Born in Grenada in the 1760s, it is thought that Henry Christophe traveled as a cabin boy and arrived at the port city of Cap Français (also called Le Cap), Saint-Domingue, sometime in the 1770s. Unlike most black men in the French colony who toiled on plantations, Christophe was, according to one biographer, hired out as an artisan. One early-nineteenth-century account claims that he worked at a Le Cap hotel known as the "Crown," a name suspiciously prescient for a future king. Other reports place him among the Chasseurs-Volontaires de Saint-Domingue, a unit of black and colored soldiers who fought in the American Revolution at the battle of Savannah in 1779.[8]

While the details of his youth are murky, Christophe was a free man by the time the revolt began in Saint-Domingue in 1791. The revolution of which Christophe was a crucial part stemmed from both internal and external factors. Although economically flourishing, eighteenth-century Saint-Domingue was socially unstable, with a large enslaved majority who resented their condition and with a free population divided by class antagonism (between wealthy and poorer whites) and by racial animosity (whites versus free people of African descent, some of whom were affluent landowners and slave owners). The fall of the Bastille in 1789 provided the tinder that sparked unrest among the already discontented free population in Saint-Domingue. Political disputes often erupted into violence, and enslaved people on the northern plain of the colony took advantage of this discord and rebelled in the summer of 1791.

Henry Christophe joined the insurrection early on and quickly rose through its ranks, as the rebellion spread to other regions of the island. During the Jacobin phase of the French Revolution, officials adopted a new approach to the discord in Saint-Domingue. Fearful of losing the colony to invading British forces and counterrevolutionary locals, republican authorities turned for help to the rebelling enslaved people, who had organized into well-disciplined and effective military units under charismatic leaders like Louverture, Dessalines, and Christophe. In 1793, French commissioners on the island offered enslaved people freedom in exchange for military support, and in February 1794 the National Assembly in Paris broadened this measure by abolishing slavery in the French colonies and granting citizenship to black men. For the rest of the decade, revolutionaries in Saint-Domingue fought to make French republican decrees a reality on the ground, driving out homegrown and foreign enemies. But in 1802 Napoleon Bonaparte sought to reinstate slavery in French possessions and sent an expedition of over 15,000 soldiers to carry out his plan. At this point the war in Saint-Domingue became one for independence.

Christophe was one of the generals who coordinated the military campaign against the French, and he and his counterparts emerged victorious in the late winter of 1803. In January 1804 Dessalines, the recognized leader, declared the colony independent with a new name, Haiti (the indigenous term for the island). But Dessalines's rule soon fell apart, as his heavy-handed measures alienated the population. In 1806, on his way to quell an uprising in the south, he was ambushed and killed.[9] In the political vacuum that followed, Haiti split in two, with Henry Christophe ruling the north and Alexandre Pétion the south.

Jefferson monitored the unfolding of the Haitian Revolution carefully and had some knowledge of Christophe's role. Throughout the 1790s, Jefferson feared what the "bloody scenes" in Saint-Domingue portended for the future of slavery in the U.S. republic and looked for ways to "try to avert them."[10] In the early 1800s, Bonaparte's representatives requested support from the United States for the reconquest of the island, but President Jefferson demurred, worried that the French leader might use Saint-Domingue as a stepping-stone for colonial aspirations in North America. His stalling paid off. When Haitian forces won, Napoleon's fantasy of an expanded American empire evaporated, and he offered to sell the Louisiana Territory to the United States. As Alexander Hamilton pointed out, one of Jefferson's crowning achievements was only possible thanks to "the courage and obstinate resistance made by [Haiti's] black inhabitants."[11] While Jefferson disdained such an acknowledgment, his success as a president and as a founder depended, in part, on Christophe's military and political victories in Haiti.

Christophe's Sans Souci was built in this complicated revolutionary context of Haiti and the broader Atlantic world. The stakes at Sans Souci were greater than those at Monticello because Sans Souci was not just Christophe's estate; it was also the center of political life. Northern Haiti was a kingdom, and Sans Souci was the place where Christophe held court. The differences in political systems have obviated comparisons between the United States and Haiti; but it's worth remembering that, although not a republic like the United States, northern Haiti was free of the tyranny of slavery, which the United States, for all its pretentions to liberty, was not.

Political systems aside, both Jefferson and Christophe faced the same problem: to establish their nations on equal footing with other states.

This agenda informed Jefferson's Monticello. During the late 1790s and early 1800s, Jefferson, as vice president and then president, looked to wrest the country from Federalist policies. At the same time, he embarked on his most grand renovations for his home. Having visited several pioneering buildings when in Paris in the 1780s, Jefferson sought to apply some of their sensibilities—attention to light and flow between rooms—to Monticello.[12] In 1796 he demolished and remodeled the second story to include the now-iconic dome, and a few years later, he added the north and south terraces and dependencies. In 1806, the same year that Christophe became king, Jefferson began work on the north pavilion, which was finished two years later, and then he revamped the south pavilion. On a practical level, the timing of this architectural transformation at Monticello reflected the fact that it was less tedious to embark on massive changes when he was not living there full-time. But it also coincided with his political agenda—the "Revolution of 1800," which sought to put the country on what Jefferson considered a proper republican course and to make that position clear to the rest of the world.

Christophe's, and by extension, Haiti's, circumstances were much more difficult in this regard because of attitudes toward Haitian independence and toward Christophe as a ruler, and these conditions influenced Sans Souci. Christophe felt he needed the palace to look a certain way to fulfill two interrelated goals that were fundamental to the longevity of his regime and, he surmised, to Haiti's future: formal diplomatic recognition from other nations and legitimate commercial ties with them.[13] Official recognition remained elusive during his reign. Since France refused to accept the independence of its former colony, other states were reluctant to do so. Jefferson, throughout his presidency, turned a blind eye to Haitian independence, and subsequent administrations did the same until 1862.

Isolationist policies were effective only up to a point, however. Merchants from European nations and the United States were willing to trade with Haiti, and so Christophe's second aim—to promote legitimate commerce—saw some success. Sans Souci was about twelve miles from Cap Henry (now Cap Haitien), the major port of northern Haiti, and this location signaled Christophe's desire to be close to the main artery of trade. As one Virginia newspaper put it, "Christophe is a merchant as well as King," and at Sans Souci, the king met face-to-face with importers and exporters, settled disputes among consuls and traders, and corresponded with foreign dignitaries to broker deals.[14] One account maintained that, looking out from his palace, the king could see the flag of every boat that sailed to the coast.[15]

Some commentators complained that the king had too tight a hold on trade, but more often articles described him as a shrewd yet fair negotiator, committed "to court the commerce and friendship of all nations."[16] Proponents emphasized the personal and financial safety of foreign merchants in Cap Henry, as well as their "most perfect confidence in [the king's] promises."[17] In light of persistent racialized fears about Haiti, Christophe worked hard to craft an image of his nation as safe and open for business.

But given the fact that Saint-Domingue's plantation economy had collapsed with the revolution, what did northern Haiti have to offer Atlantic markets? Just as Jefferson had an agrarian vision for the United States, Christophe imagined a Haitian economy rooted in agricultural commodities that would be sent to Europe in exchange for manufactured goods. To a certain extent, Sans Souci served as a testament to Haiti's economic potential in people and products. Viewed from the road leading to the residence, the palace demanded attention as it sat nestled among the mountains that rose behind it.[18] Clearly, both Christophe and Jefferson had a penchant for dramatic locales, which gave Sans Souci and Monticello the ambiance of "splendid retreat[s]." More importantly, these mountaintop settings accentuated their owners' ability to command the laborers necessary for the arduous undertaking.[19] Labor was also critical to the realization of Sans Souci. To build Monticello, Jefferson had an arsenal of workers at his disposal. He employed white artisans as well as enslaved laborers for everything from clearing the land and felling trees for the structural timber, to making the bricks, erecting the walls, and finishing the interior woodwork.[20] It was a colossal, multistory, stone and brick structure, and a visiting English merchant claimed that "the whole of the materials for building which could not be obtained on the spot, were carried from other parts on the shoulders of the people, and Christophe compelled blacks and browns, young and old, boys and girls, of all ages and denominations of citizens, to perform that labour."[21]

While the presence of slavery at Monticello attracted some commentary by observers, at Sans Souci the conversation about laborers was different. Throughout the Atlantic world in this period, abolitionists and proslavery advocates argued about the sustainability of postemancipation economies and societies, and both sides looked to Christophe's northern Haiti as an example. Racist postrevolutionary reports decried the supposed laziness of the black population and emphasized the coercion necessary for Christophe to see results. They then concluded that slavery was the only means for securing economic success in the Caribbean and the United States.[22] Meanwhile, abolitionists glossed over accounts of compulsion and celebrated Sans Souci as an extraordinary feat that recently freed Haitians had accomplished on their own.[23] Although abolitionist and proslavery camps disputed workers' willingness, both understood that Christophe's grandiose building was a clear sign that he had control over a sizable workforce, ready for mobilization in the broader Atlantic economy.

A key element of the interiors at Sans Souci reinforced Christophe's Atlantic-oriented economic plans. Almost every traveler marveled at the extravagant use of mahogany in the palace: the floors, the wainscoting, and the ceilings were fashioned from this expensive wood.[24] Usually harvested by enslaved laborers in the tropics, mahogany was a prized material reserved for the finest applications.[25] At Monticello, Jefferson used it for the window sashes and for select pieces of furniture. But the lavish display of mahogany at Sans Souci demonstrated Christophe's understanding of this wood's privileged status in Atlantic hierarchies of value and taste. The sheer amount of it at the palace—the fact that Christophe had the audacity to walk on it—affirmed that Haiti had more than enough capacity, in terms of trees and labor, to supply external markets.[26]

While Sans Souci showcased local resources for trade, visitors were most struck by its appropriation of European aesthetics and luxury goods. For some white observers, the adoption of European stylings by a black man was troubling. They saw Sans Souci as an indication of Christophe's presumption to place himself on a level with white rulers.[27] Moreover, they refused to give him, and Haitians more generally, credit for the design of the elegant edifice. The English traveler James Franklin noted, "The Citadel Henry, or Fort Ferrier, . . . was not constructed from the design of a Haytian, but from the plan of a British officer, from whom it takes one of its appellations, Ferrier. The same thing is true with respect to the palace Sans Souci."[28]

Franklin's specific attribution is suspect: Le Pic des Ferrières, or Laferrière, was the long-standing name of the mountain upon which the Citadel, a fortress neighboring Sans Souci, stood.[29] Prejudice—and a heavy dose of English ethnocentrism—inform his assessment of the Citadel and Sans Souci, yet his urge to deny Haitian achievements also highlights the indisputable magnificence of the palace. Most observers hailed its overall effect as "spacious and handsome" and compared its grandeur to that of the Louvre, Versailles, Windsor, and St. James—sometimes evoking the French and English examples in the same line.[30] Like its European and North American counterparts, Sans Souci's architecture stressed symmetry on a massive scale, inside and out, and its rooms included rich architectural features like marble columns, mosaics, and crystal chandeliers. Enormous mirrors, some of which measured six by twelve feet, reflected light and helped to illuminate rooms—a trick that Jefferson employed at Monticello, having seen it at work in Paris.[31]

These interior finishes set off stylish imported furnishings. By all accounts, Sans Souci was "sumptuously" decorated with luxuries from across Europe: beautiful draperies, table accoutrements, and of course, mahogany furniture.[32] Jefferson, too, was attentive to how furnishings enhanced his architectural designs, and he sourced many from Europe. In London, Jefferson indulged in the "splendor of their shops," buying reading lamps, dinnerware, and scientific instruments, among other items, for Monticello.[33] Lafayette chided Jefferson for his English purchases, seeing them as impolitic, but Jefferson pleaded otherwise and made up for it with a spending spree in Paris. When Jefferson left that city in 1789, he shipped eighty-six crates of furniture, art, accessories, and books to Monticello.[34]

Christophe also turned to European goods for specific reasons, and as with Jefferson, their point of origin had political significance at Sans Souci. Consider some of the goods from Britain. In 1816, Christophe ordered his state carriage and equipage from a London firm, which displayed it in its workshop before shipping it to Haiti.[35] British and American newspapers detailed the carriage's exceptional features: the "nouvelle" shape of the body, intended to maximize shade; the upholstery of "finest velvet" embroidered with gold; and the emblems of Christophe's kingdom that ornamented the coach. It was "one of the grandest specimens of art and elegance ever combined in one piece of work of the kind," costing, by some estimates, $18,000.[36]

Along with his carriage, Christophe commissioned from British artisans other material manifestations of his rule, such as his crown and regalia. Some scholars have interpreted these purchases as evidence of Christophe's Anglophilia and as an attempt to repudiate French cultural precedents.[37] But his ambitions were greater: as one article noted about the crown, "It remains to be seen whether our Government will recognize the Sovereign whom it thus allows to be crowned."[38] As British artisans crafted luxury items for Christophe's state and as they were discussed in the press and even seen by curious Londoners, these goods argued for the legitimacy of Christophe's rule and coaxed Britons to acknowledge the independence of Haiti. By importing the trappings of his sovereignty from Britain, Christophe attempted to draw that empire more firmly and more formally into his own and Haiti's orbit.

Christophe's French material goods resonated differently from his English ones. On one level, it is surprising that Christophe sought out items from France. The Haitian Declaration of Independence cast the French as the inveterate enemies of the Haitian people and affirmed that the survival of the new, free republic depended on their expulsion: "Let them tremble when they approach our coast, if not from the memory of those cruelties they perpetrated here, then from the terrible resolution that we will have made to put to death anyone born French whose profane foot soils the land of liberty."[39] This ethos pervaded the remainder of the Napoleonic era, and the restoration of the Bourbon monarchy in 1814 did little to better relations between France and its former colony.

Louis XVIII schemed to reinstitute French control in Haiti, including slavery, and sent emissaries to the Caribbean to that effect. After uncovering the motivations for the French king's intrigues, Christophe resisted his agents' overtures and tried to reassert Haitian independence.[40]

At this tense moment in French-Haitian relations, Christophe decided to make a large purchase of French goods for his palace. In the winter of 1818 he refurbished "the grand hall of audience and state" with over one million livres' worth of furniture from Paris.[41] Although we do not have an inventory of his acquisitions, we do know that they stood at the spatial center of Christophe's rule, the room where he conducted public ceremonies of state. But why place the material culture of one's enemy at the heart of one's government? Some insight comes from a brilliant interpretation about the name of the estate. The anthropologist Michel-Rolph Trouillot has called into question the idea that Christophe borrowed the name Sans Souci from Frederick the Great's palace. Trouillot draws out the story of Sans Souci the man, an officer in Louverture's army, whose execution, at Christophe's order, occurred near to the spot where Christophe later erected his official seat. Trouillot sees Christophe's choice of the name Sans Souci as an Afro-Haitian appropriation, a way to subsume the power and neutralize the legacy of his one-time challenger.[42]

Perhaps in a similar dynamic, Christophe sought to incorporate the power of his and Haiti's ultimate rival, France, by using its vaunted material culture for his own and his kingdom's benefit. The display was meant to speak to Christophe's counterpart in southern Haiti as well. Pétion, the president-for-life of southern Haiti, had died in March 1818, a few months before Christophe's significant purchase. While ill, Pétion had named his successor, the general Jean-Pierre Boyer, and no doubt Christophe intended his acquisitions for Sans Souci to send a signal to his new adversary about the impressive scope of his dominion.

With Sans Souci, Christophe broadcast that under his reign, Haiti was poised to participate as an equal partner—economically, politically, and intellectually—in the Atlantic world. Jefferson's Monticello sent the same message, demonstrating what North Americans could achieve now that they had thrown off the onus of colonial rule. Both houses made the case that with such men at the helm, how could their nations go astray?

Christophe and Jefferson died within years of each other, leaving their houses to uncertain fates. Ailing and facing increasing military pressure from Boyer's sympathizers, Christophe committed suicide in 1820 in his beloved palace, just before a group of armed men stormed it. Finding their target already dead, the soldiers seized his family members and set about ransacking Sans Souci. Many items were destroyed in the fray. But in subsequent weeks, reports stated that soldiers spent their time pilfering and hawking the palace's valuables, even "stripping [Sans Souci] of its rich mahogany floors, wainscotings and ceilings, and selling them for whatever they would fetch."[43] They, too, recognized the literal and figurative value of the material culture within the palace's walls. An earthquake in 1842 further compromised the building, reducing it to a shadow of its former glory.

Jefferson met his end, famously, on July 4, 1826, and Monticello and its contents were soon sold. Since Jefferson was over $100,000 in debt (in part because of his lavish spending on Monticello), his heirs were forced to auction almost all of the furnishings, farm equipment, and enslaved people in 1827. A few years later, the house and 552 acres were sold for only $4,500. Over the next several decades, Monticello was a site for failed experiments in sericulture, was seized and sold by Confederates, and was given to the federal government, which refused to accept the terms of the bequest. While the house did not fall into complete ruin like Sans Souci, it was far from prized. Not until the early twentieth century was the estate preserved by a foundation dedicated to memorializing its original owner.

For all of the important differences between Henry Christophe and Thomas Jefferson, this comparison of their renowned houses has described their similarities to reveal how racial ideologies have obscured possible connections, then and now. Most of this work has involved reinterpreting the significance of Sans Souci, to contest the assumptions that have surrounded it. After Christophe's death white observers turned his Sans Souci into, as one palace visitor put it, "a melancholy emblem of the downfall of ambition and power."[44] Certainly, Christophe used

Sans Souci as a vehicle for consolidating his personal authority, as did Jefferson at Monticello. But to see it only as a project of self-aggrandizement risks perpetuating early-nineteenth-century racist readings about Christophe's presumption to "overstep" his bounds. Rather, Christophe's aesthetic choices at Sans Souci demonstrate how well he understood and created meaning through Atlantic material culture, even its most "European" elements—a capacity that is, historically, often denied people of African descent.

Sans Souci made elites like Jefferson uneasy because it challenged expectations. White leaders throughout the Atlantic world feared that Christophe's main export would be an antislavery agenda, even though the king repeatedly vowed to avoid meddling in slave regimes elsewhere. With its prominent display of luxury goods and use of coerced labor, the palace stood as a testament to Christophe's willingness to work within well-established networks, rules of trade, and standards of taste dictated by white Atlantic elites. Yet his status as a black man and black ruler made his appropriation of these norms radical, at least in racial, if not in class or gender, terms. Christophe claimed his right not only to consume such items (something refused under slavery), but also to embody the social and cultural values these objects denoted: refinement, discernment, and rank, among others. Jefferson and others repudiated Christophe not simply because he was a black ruler, but because he was a black man who exhibited an extraordinary knowledge of and ability to employ the highest forms of European culture. In a sense, Christophe had beat Jefferson and his U.S. counterparts at their own game.

The case of Jefferson and Christophe shows us how and why we have neglected their provocative points of intersection and calls on us to reappraise North American founders in light of other founders. It reveals the contradictions—in both countries—between principles of freedom and equality, on the one hand, and the formation of a postindependence elite, on the other. It also underscores that the fragile and fraught process of establishing states was shaped not just by developments within the confines of each emerging nation, but also by events in and engagement with the wider hemisphere. The commonalities shared by Christophe and Jefferson allow us to appreciate the difficulties of achieving an enlightened republic in a world rife with social inequalities and racial hierarchies. And, perhaps most significantly, the legacies of this moment continue to animate both Haiti and the United States—and their relationship with one another—today.

NOTES

1. Matthew Clavin, *Toussaint Louverture and the American Civil War: The Promise and Peril of a Second Haitian Revolution* (Philadelphia: University of Pennsylvania Press, 2010); Ronald Angelo Johnson, *Diplomacy in Black and White: John Adams, Toussaint Louverture, and Their Atlantic World Alliance* (Athens: University of Georgia Press, 2014); and Ashli White, *Encountering Revolution: Haiti and the Making of the Early Republic* (Baltimore: Johns Hopkins University Press, 2010). For the ties (and their limits) between the United States and the Latin American wars of independence, see Caitlin Fitz, *Our Sister Republics: The United States in an Age of American Revolutions* (New York: Liverlight, 2016).
2. One recent exception is David A. Bell, *Men on Horseback: The Power of Charisma in the Age of Revolution* (New York: Farrar, Straus, and Giroux, 2020).
3. Gauvin Alexander Bailey, *The Palace of Sans-Souci in Milot, Haiti, ca. 1806–1813: The Untold Story of the Potsdam in the Rainforest* (Berlin: Deutscher Kunstverlag, 2017), 25, 29.
4. Quoted in Richard Guy Wilson, "Thomas Jefferson's Classical Architecture," in *Thomas Jefferson, the Classical World, and Early America*, ed. Peter S. Onuf and Nicholas P. Cole (Charlottesville: University of Virginia Press, 2011), 102. Doris Garraway shows how this impulse influenced Haitian writers during this period. Doris Garraway, "Print, Publics, and the Scene of Universal Equality in the Kingdom of Henry Christophe," *L'Esprit Créateur* 56, no. 1 (2016): 83.
5. On the architectural innovation of Sans Souci, see Bailey, *The Palace of Sans-Souci*, 25, 31, 113–37.
6. Doris Garraway, "Empire of Freedom, Kingdom of Civilization: Henry Christophe, the Baron de Vastey, and the Paradoxes of Universalism in Postrevolutionary Haiti," *Small Axe* 16, no. 3 (November 2012): 1–21.
7. Susan R. Stein, *The Worlds of Thomas Jefferson at Monticello* (New York: Harry N. Abrams, 1993), 14–15.
8. Karl Ritter, *Naturhistorische Reise nach der westindischen Insel Hayti* (Stuttgart, 1836), 69.
9. Laurent Dubois, *Haiti: The Aftershocks of History* (New York: Metropolitan Books, 2012), 44–51.
10. Thomas Jefferson to James Monroe, July 14, 1793, *The Papers of Thomas Jefferson*, ed. John Catanzariti (Princeton, NJ: Princeton University Press, 1995), 26: 503.
11. Quoted in "Hamilton and the Louisiana Purchase: A Newly Identified Editorial from the New-York Evening Post," *William and Mary Quarterly* 12, no. 2 (1955): 274.

12. Stein, *The Worlds of Thomas Jefferson*, 19–20; Henry Adams, "The Architectural Jefferson: The Draftsman and His Ideals," in *The Private Jefferson: Perspectives from the Collections of the Massachusetts Historical Society* (Boston: Massachusetts Historical Society, 2016), 39–40.
13. John Candler, *Brief Notices of Hayti: With Its Condition, Resources, and Prospects* (London, 1842), 37. Julia Gaffield, *Recognition After Revolution: Haitian Connections in the Atlantic World* (Chapel Hill: University of North Carolina Press, 2015).
14. Quotation from *Alexandria Gazette* (Virginia), October 4, 1816. See also *American Beacon* (Norfolk, VA), July 31, 1818; *Independent Chronicle* (Boston), August 21, 1815; and Jonathan Brown, *The History and Present Condition of St. Domingo* (Philadelphia, 1837), 2: 215.
15. Ritter, *Naturhistorische Reise*, 77.
16. Quotation from *Morning Post* (London), August 13, 1816; see also *American Beacon* (Norfolk, VA), July 31, 1818.
17. *Caledonian Mercury* (Edinburgh), December 3, 1818.
18. Candler, *Brief Notices of Hayti*, 29.
19. *Hillsboro Telegraph* (Amherst, NH), June 23, 1821. Adams, "The Architectural Jefferson," 44.
20. Lucia Stanton, *"Those Who Labor for My Happiness": Slavery at Thomas Jefferson's Monticello* (Charlottesville: University of Virginia Press, 2012), 12–13, 64–65.
21. James Franklin, *The Present State of Hayti, with Remarks on Its Agriculture, Commerce, Laws, Religion, Finances, Population, etc. etc.* (London: John Murray, 1828), 214. On the landscape overhaul at Sans Souci, see J. Cameron Monroe, "New Light from Haiti's Royal Past: Recent Archaeological Excavations in the Palace of Sans-Souci, Milot," *Journal of Haitian Studies* 23, no. 2 (Fall 2017): 6.
22. Franklin, *The Present State of Hayti*, 6–7.
23. Similar debates surrounded Christophe's fortress: La Citadel. Dubois, *Haiti: The Aftershocks of History*, 53–54.
24. *Newburyport Herald* (MA), June 5, 1821; see also *Rhode Island American* (Providence), June 8, 1821. Bailey, *The Palace of Sans-Souci*, 97.
25. Jennifer Anderson, *Mahogany: The Costs of Luxury in Early America* (Cambridge, MA: Harvard University Press, 2012).
26. Dubois, *Haiti: The Aftershocks of History*, 65–68.
27. Dubois, *Haiti: The Aftershocks of History*, 63–64.
28. Franklin, *The Present State of Hayti*, 214.
29. Bailey, *The Palace of Sans-Souci*, 13; Earl Leslie Griggs and Clifford H. Prator, eds., *Henry Christophe and Thomas Clarkson: A Correspondence* (Berkeley: University of California Press, 1952), 50.
30. Brown, *The History and Present Condition of St. Domingo*, 2: 187 [Louvre], 213 [St. James]; *American Commercial Daily Advertiser* (Baltimore), February 5, 1816 [Windsor, Versailles]. For a critique of the façade, see Candler, *Brief Notices of Hayti*, 29.
31. Hérard Dumesle, *Voyage dans le Nord d'Hayti, ou Révélations des lieux et des monuments historiques* (Aux Cayes, 1824), 226; Brown, *The History and Present Condition of St. Domingo*, 2: 187; Candler, *Brief Notices of Hayti*, 29–30; *Newburyport Herald* (MA),

June 5, 1821; also *Rhode Island American* (Providence), June 8, 1821. On Jefferson and mirrors, see Stein, *The Worlds of Thomas Jefferson*, 20, 23, 26.

32. Quotation from Candler, *Brief Notices of Hayti*, 29; on the impressive furnishings, see *Lancaster Gazette* (UK), November 24, 1821; W. W. Harvey, *Sketches of Hayti: From the Expulsion of the French to the Death of Christophe* (1827; reprint London: Frank Cass, 1971), 134; Ritter, *Naturhistorische Reise*, 78–79; Griggs and Prator, *Henry Christophe and Thomas Clarkson*, 48–49; Monroe, "New Light," 17, 23.
33. Stein, *The Worlds of Thomas Jefferson*, 27.
34. Stein, *The Worlds of Thomas Jefferson*, 11, 23.
35. On Christophe's other English purchases, see Tabitha McIntosh and Grégory Pierrot, "Capturing the Likeness of Henry I of Haiti (1805–1822)," *Atlantic Studies* 14, no. 2 (2017): 13–14; Rosalie Smith McCrea, "Portrait Mythology? Representing the 'Black Jacobin': Henry Christophe in the British Grand Manner," *British Art Journal* 6, no. 2 (Autumn 2005): 66–70.
36. Quotation from *Morning Chronicle* (London), November 1, 1815; *Columbian* (New York), February, 22, 1816.
37. Karin Racine, "Britannia's Bold Brother: British Cultural Influence in Haiti During the Reign of Henry Christophe (1811–1820)," *Journal of Caribbean History* 33, nos. 1 & 2 (1999): 125–45; and Paul Youngquist and Grégory Pierrot, "Introduction" to Marcus Rainsford, *An Historical Account of the Black Empire of Hayti* (Durham, NC: Duke University Press, 2013).
38. *Morning Post* (London), November 28, 1811.
39. The Haitian Declaration of Independence, January 1, 1804, reprinted in Laurent Dubois and John D. Garrigus, *Slave Revolution in the Caribbean, 1789–1804: A Brief History with Documents* (Boston: Bedford/St. Martin's, 2006), 189.
40. Garraway, "Empire of Freedom," 11–12; Jean-François Brière, *Haïti et la France 1804–1848: Le rêve brisé* (Paris: Karthala, 2010); Griggs and Prator, *Henry Christophe and Thomas Clarkson*, 56–61; Dubois, *Haiti: The Aftershocks of History*, 76–84.
41. *Caledonian Mercury* (Edinburgh), December 7, 1818.
42. Michel-Rolph Trouillot, *Silencing the Past: Power and the Production of History* (Boston: Beacon Press, 1995), 31–69.
43. Quotation from *Newburyport Herald* (MA), June 5, 1821. For accounts of other palace valuables being sold, see *Franklin Gazette*, November 23, 1820; *Lancaster Gazette*, November 24, 1821.
44. *Newburyport Herald* (MA), June 5, 1821.

4

THE CIVIL WAR, SLAVERY, AND THE PROBLEM OF NEUTRALITY

APRIL E. HOLM

We must always take sides. Neutrality helps the oppressor, never the victim.

—ELIE WIESEL, "NOBEL ADDRESS"

Elisha Phelps was deeply troubled. It was December of 1860, and he had just returned to Virginia from the annual convention of lay leaders in the Baltimore Conference of the northern Methodist Church. The meeting had convened in an atmosphere of excruciating tension. For one thing, nobody in Baltimore had been able to ignore the crisis unfolding to the south. In Charleston, South Carolina, another convention was gathered to consider a plan of immediate secession that would protect the institution of slavery in that state. Conflict over slavery had riven the Baltimore convention as well. Earlier that year, after decades of evading the issue, northern Methodist leaders had formally condemned slavery as evil. This presented a problem for Phelps and his peers. The Baltimore Conference was part of the northern Methodist Church, but it drew members from Maryland and Virginia—both slave states.

Tempers flared. Many delegates in Baltimore were ready to sever their connection with the northern church. They condemned Methodist leadership for taking an explicit stance on the "vexed slavery question." It made evangelism in slave states impossible. "The hearts of the people are closed," the delegates wrote in a formal protest; "the church is in perpetual agitation." They wanted the condemnation of slavery retracted, not necessarily because they supported the institution themselves, but because it was the only way to "preserve our unity" and to continue mission work with "some measure of peace and quiet."[1]

With the Baltimore Conference teetering on the brink of separation from the northern Methodist Church and the state of South Carolina one day away from issuing a declaration of secession, Elisha Phelps was distraught. He wrote to a friend to vent his concern that northern and southern "politicians in church and state" would drive the conference (and the nation) apart. Phelps was confident that he himself had made a noble "effort to maintain the unity of the church." Thinking of those who pressed the issue of slavery, he noted, "I thank God that I am not responsible for the state of things existing."[2]

Reflection on the moral dimensions of slavery itself was strikingly absent from both Phelps's letter and the resolutions drafted at the Baltimore Conference. Phelps worried more about how Virginia Methodists would react to the condemnation of slavery than he did about slavery itself. In his letter, he detailed a plan to "prevent extreme action" among congregants: he would excise any mention of the church's denunciation of slavery from local church publications—in other words, do his best to avoid the subject entirely. Likewise, the resolutions left the question of slavery's sinfulness untouched. The great wrong they focused on was local "agitation" and the likelihood that pews would empty in response to the church's stance on slavery.[3]

To Phelps and his fellow delegates, both secessionists and abolitionists fractured the nation and threatened the church. They, and not slavery itself, were to blame for the unrest in Virginia's white churches. In contrast, Phelps viewed his own attempts to preserve unity as a principled stand against forces of destruction. He sought, above all, a "compromise," one that would appease both sides and safeguard a unified church despite the explosive slavery debate and the secession crisis.[4] He did not want to take sides.

We are accustomed to thinking of the Civil War in terms of stark opposition: North versus South, Union versus Confederacy, freedom versus slavery. This framework, however, obscures people, like Phelps, who longed desperately to remain neutral in the conflict. A moment's consideration, however, tells us that they must have been there, and in great numbers, just as they have been in other moments of national crisis. The impulse toward neutrality arises time and again in moments of political and moral conflict. Those who called for neutrality in 1860, however, did not leave the same lasting impression as other actors, such as fire-eating secessionists and radical abolitionists.

Moderates often fade from view because, as the case of neutral clergy in the Civil War illustrates, maintaining neutrality usually proves futile. People who do not take sides end up on one side or the other anyway. Still, neutrality's lure is hardly difficult to understand. The greater the degree of local conflict—of people directly confronting one another over slavery, and later secession—the more people caught in the middle sought to escape their individual agonies. Neutrality offered a way out of the personal upheaval that would follow from taking sides. Then, as now, personal crises loomed larger for most people than did more abstract moral quandaries. Neutrality not only offered a way to sidestep difficult choices, but it also acquired its own patina of morality. It made sense to blame both sides for agitation and assure oneself that real virtue lay in avoiding controversy.

As this essay will show, moderates felt that they themselves were the victims of the crisis over slavery and secession. Clergy throughout the border states employed the same rationale as Elisha Phelps. First, a movement for change took shape—in this case, mounting opposition to slavery within the northern Methodist Church. As Phelps and his peers noted, the most immediate consequence of rising antislavery sentiment in their denomination was chaos and upheaval in Virginia's congregations. They therefore blamed abolitionists, not the institution of slavery itself, for destroying the harmony in their churches. This was not a phenomenon unique to the Civil War era. Martin Luther King Jr., writing from his Birmingham jail cell a century later, eloquently described the thought process of the moderates who urged civil rights activists to "go slow." Those, he wrote, who "have not suffered unduly from the disease of segregation" continuously urged activists to "wait." "This 'Wait,'" King observed, "has almost always meant 'Never.'" King correctly identified the concerns of the moderate, "who is more devoted to 'order' than to justice; who prefers a negative peace which is the absence of tension to a positive peace which is the presence of justice."[5]

White clergy who resided in the broad border region—Maryland, Kentucky, Missouri, and portions of all surrounding states—were particularly prone to seek King's "negative peace": order over justice. Crisis and controversy came to clergy sooner than it did to other Americans, not only because slavery was a moral issue, but also because evangelical denominations were among the few national organizations that drew members from across the nation and from slaveholding and free states.[6] Clergy in the border region, in particular, were at the center of a long struggle over slavery, sin, and politics that consumed individual congregations and entire states. It was in the border region that the slavery debates and, later, the secession crisis had material consequences.

By the time the war came, churches were no strangers to sectional tension. Several decades earlier, the three largest evangelical denominations (Methodists, Baptists, and Presbyterians) had divided over the sinfulness of slavery.[7] These schisms resulted in the creation of northern and southern branches of each denomination. In each case, conflict over the morality of slavery precipitated the split.[8] National denominational divisions wreaked havoc in the border region, and border congregations fought fiercely over their sectional affiliation. Individual congregations fractured, and congregants turned upon each other, and on ministers—sometimes with violence. In one northern Virginia congregation, a mob drove a minister out of town over his antislavery views, but only after congregants who supported him clashed violently with his detractors during a calamitous Sunday sermon.[9]

Meanwhile, the national leaders of each sectional branch attempted to shore up the allegiance of local congregations and influence local decisions. In response to this pressure, many border evangelicals turned to a doctrine called "the spirituality of the church." Spirituality was a theologically grounded and politically expedient argument that secular affairs should be kept completely separate from religious practice.[10] This idea allowed border evangelicals to define the discord within the churches as a battle over the role of politics within religion and reject arguments for an antislavery church on the grounds that slavery was a purely political concern and not a moral one. They cast themselves as morally superior to those engaged in "political" disputes over slavery. John Stevens, a Cincinnati Baptist, advised coreligionists to "let the subject of slavery entirely alone" and to "act, as nearly as possible, as if there were no such institution in being."[11] Border-state evangelicals clung to the hope that political neutrality and spirituality could prevent the division of God's kingdom in the United States.

The doctrine of spirituality was an extension of the conservatism that characterized residents of the border, and evangelicals in particular; they were keen to protect the church from what they saw as corrupting fanaticism originating in both the North and the South. In addition, border moderates argued, dividing national denominations expressly violated the biblical injunction against the sin of schism. Seen through this scriptural lens, slaveholders and abolitionists were both potential sinners who threatened to undermine Christian unity.[12] Moral equivalence of this sort—placing equal blame on "both sides" of a public controversy—reinforced the argument that neutrality or moderation was the morally superior position. Clergy who dismissed opposition to slavery as purely political controversy, no matter what their private beliefs were, were proslavery in effect.[13] Classifying slavery as a political issue warded off antislavery challenges to the institution.

In order to maintain ties with their members in the border, northern church leaders avoided any outright condemnation of slavery during the antebellum denominational schisms. "Nonpolitical" border evangelicals welcomed this discretion. In consequence, most border churches, like Phelps's Baltimore Conference, remained affiliated with northern branches in the years between denominational schism and the Civil War. However, their allegiance proved short-lived.[14]

When the war came, northern denominations responded to secession in a markedly different way than they had responded to the slavery debates. Instead of the cautious approach taken during the schisms over slavery, northern evangelical leaders leapt enthusiastically to the defense of the Union, associating it with God's cause.[15] In contrast, many border evangelicals argued that direct support for the Union was, like the slavery debates, another instance of politics in the pulpit. They wanted to weather the war, as they had the slavery debates, as neutral parties. The onset of war further threatened the viability of the neutrality strategy. Unlike during the slavery debates, however, northern evangelical leadership did not condone neutrality. Nor did secular authorities.

Both demographics and location made the border region a crucial battleground in the contest between the North and South. The white population of the border slave states alone totaled 3,408,837. In addition, the southern regions of Ohio, Indiana, and Illinois boasted a white population of 2,629,699. This amounted to nearly a million more people than the white population of the entire Confederacy. Little wonder that Lincoln remarked, early in the war, "I think to lose Kentucky is nearly the same as to lose the whole game."[16]

Even after political and military maneuvers secured the upper tier of slave states for the Union and border states no longer threatened to secede, civilian loyalty remained a concern.[17] The Union army, the federal government, and unionist citizens kept a watchful eye on the activities of border residents. Any member of the local clergy who professed neutrality aroused particular suspicion. And, for clergy in the border, expressions of neutrality were by no means uncommon. They possessed a host of theological, practical, and political justifications for remaining neutral.[18] As Elisha Phelps knew, congregants on the border watched clergy closely for signs of the political partiality that religious and secular leaders demanded. During the Civil War, a Baptist minister in Missouri began to anticipate the approach of Sunday with "anxiety and some dread." Each week he fretted that a new provocation—the singing of "My Country, 'Tis of Thee," an announcement about a citizens' defense organization—would prove the rock upon which his congregation would split.[19] Elsewhere in Missouri, Union authorities banished a Methodist minister not just from his pulpit, but from the entire state after unnamed congregants reported him for a lack of patriotism and loyalty.[20]

Secular demands for overt loyalty to the Union only intensified the border commitment to "spirituality." One Missouri minister explained his strategy for weathering the sectional crisis as follows: "My own course has been, and will continue to be, to avoid entirely the discussion of political questions." He argued that taking sides in the war was sinful and a moral failing. He predicted it would "rend asunder the church . . . and, in trying to save the country . . . inflict an irreparable injury upon the kingdom and cause of our Lord Jesus Christ."[21] Union authorities were unpersuaded by such arguments and insisted that clergy should use their influence to assist the war effort. One general, for instance, told a recalcitrant minister, "You ought to preach union forever!"[22]

As this general's admonition suggests, the Civil War was a time of unprecedented federal involvement with clergy and churches. Union authorities went to great lengths to ensure the loyalty of border evangelicals. Federal agents policed the behavior of ministers by demanding prayers for Union victory, administering loyalty oaths, closing newspapers, and banishing suspected disloyal ministers. Under federal orders, unionist clergy also took possession of southern-sympathizing churches. In each case, neutral clergy increasingly felt like victims of overreaching federal power.[23] They did not blame their predicament on the actions of proslavery secessionists. Meanwhile, many border evangelicals continued to argue that direct support for the Union was, like the slavery debates, another instance of politics in the pulpit.

By the time hostilities ended, government involvement in border churches and northern evangelical patriotism had eroded the border brethren's tenuous claim that slavery was a purely political issue. This fiction had allowed them to claim neutrality, both on the question of slavery and in the matter of secession. But neutrality—and the pretext it was built upon—could not survive the end of the war. The Confederate defeat altogether eliminated the possibility of neutrality for border clergy. Rather than ending internal conflict, the war's conclusion led to a final rupture between northern-affiliated clergy and their border brethren. Attempting to remain neutral regarding slavery, even after it was abolished, placed these neutral clergy in the awkward position of defending the now-defunct institution of slavery.

Once Union victory was ensured, secular authorities, for their part, no longer concerned themselves with ministerial loyalty. Northern church leadership, however, stepped in to monitor the border. Northern denominations required their members to provide proof of loyalty to the federal government. And, after slavery had been destroyed in a bloody war, these denominational leaders publicly demanded that all members denounce slavery as a sin.[24] "God be thanked that the day of compromise with slavery is over," read an editorial in Kentucky's pro-Union *Danville Quarterly Review*. "There are but two parties in our country," the editorial asserted, "that which is for its preservation and that which is for its destruction; and all men must range themselves on the one side or the other."[25] Such demands eliminated the possibility that any member of the northern denominational branches could continue to profess "neutrality" in regards to slavery. They also compounded the grievances of border clergy, who again blamed northern leadership—not secessionists or the institution of slavery—for their predicament.

Border clergy dug in to their position of political neutrality. A Kentucky Presbyterian explained that ministers on the border should not be "politicians, nor preachers of politics." Rather, they "ought to be men of common sense who know how and when to conciliate." The editor of the *Missouri Baptist Journal* agreed. "The end of the war should have brought peace," he wrote, but "the spirit of exultation, national pride, sectional superiority, and bitterness toward the Christians of other sections, is higher than ever before." A Kentuckian remarked, "By our superior moderation [we] put ourselves clearly in the right."[26] Superior moderation, however, had lost its currency with northern evangelicals in the wake of the Union victory.

In contrast to northern political and religious authorities, southern church leaders retroactively downplayed the role of slavery in their own support for the Confederacy during the war. "Slavery was not, in any proper sense, the cause," of antebellum schism, two southern Methodist bishops asserted in 1869.[27] This shift made the northern denominations appear more radical and punitive than their southern rivals.

Angered by secular loyalty tests during the war and still claiming that the abolition of slavery was a purely political, not a moral issue, border clergy felt victimized. Rather than hold secessionists and slaveholders accountable for their difficulties, they blamed the northern churches, thus cementing border sympathies with the section they perceived as least radical: the South.

Claiming to possess a spiritually pure faith governed "simply by the word of God," border evangelicals turned away from northern denominational branches.[28] Wartime experience had led them to the conclusion that, by embracing the Union cause and rejecting slavery, northern churches had lost their spiritual purity. Border evangelicals pointed to pervasive Unionism and antislavery sentiment to justify leaving northern churches and uniting with southern denominations. Southern evangelicals castigated the northern churches for condemning slavery as a moral wrong even though, by 1866, it had been legally abolished. Even then, critics of slavery were seen as "politico-religious fanatics" who brought politics into a spiritual realm.[29] Religious realignment coincided with a broader postwar trend of border-state residents identifying with the Confederacy.[30]

Border grievances proved a boon to southern evangelicals, who themselves were attempting to rebuff reunion overtures from northern brethren. Southern churches emerged from the war weakened. Both of the institutions they had defended—slavery and the Confederacy—had been destroyed. The border's history of spirituality and claims to neutrality gave southern evangelicals precisely the justification they needed to remain separate even after slavery was abolished. Border history helped to bolster claims that the churches had divided, not over slavery, but over theological differences regarding the role of politics in the church. A southern Presbyterian pamphlet insisted that their branch "had never, in any form, entangled itself with the state . . . on the contrary, it . . . separated from the Northern church in order to escape these political complications."[31] These protests made no mention of the fact that the southern branches had defended slavery and the Confederacy. Writing slavery out of their origin story allowed southern evangelicals to successfully perpetuate denominational branches formed to defend that very institution. The end of the nineteenth century saw these denominations more divided than they had been at the close of the Civil War.[32]

This outcome—in which neutral clergy aligned themselves with the South (and with a defense of slavery) after the war—highlights the problem with the neutrality strategy in response to the moral conflicts of the nineteenth century. By the end of the century, the border experience—of being chastised for neutrality—was used to justify separate sectional faiths. It became part of the history of the southern branches, and therefore part of a frequently rehearsed catalogue of wartime Yankee abuses. This was an ironic turn, given that it was the border evangelicals who first opposed division over slavery and initially prioritized the preservation of church unity.

In their opposition to division and conflict within the church, border evangelicals had embraced a theology of spirituality and political neutrality. Border moderates were profoundly disturbed to see debates over slavery and secession break up their churches and institutions. As a result, they came to view the debates—instead of slavery itself—as the most pressing problem their churches faced. Within this context, attempting to remain neutral was not just appealing—it acquired a patina of virtue. Moderate white border clergy believed that eschewing "politics" was taking the moral high road. They did not acknowledge that remaining neutral meant valuing church unity over the freedom of millions of enslaved African Americans. They could not see that the ability to dismiss the slavery debate as a purely political matter was an option not available to everyone. (African Americans, of course, had no such luxury.) In fact, as pressure to declare loyalty increased and the possibility of remaining neutral dwindled and disappeared, neutral evangelicals began to perceive themselves as victims of "great public crimes" and "atrocities" by Unionists and opponents of slavery.[33] This sense of persecution led them away from the northern churches. They began to affiliate, instead, with southern churches, which continued to defend slavery even after it had been abolished. Neutrality regarding slavery ultimately led to membership in proslavery denominations.

Abolitionists within the church, of course, recognized why neutrality was appealing and why border clergy so often opposed the shift toward an antislavery stance in the northern denominations. Abolitionists sought an end to slavery, even if it meant disruption. During antebellum slavery debates, one Methodist abolitionist asked, "Are there no interests to be consulted besides the peace of the Church?"[34] As the nation teetered on the brink of war, another antislavery minister expressed his frustration with his peers on the border who refused to denounce slavery or secession on the grounds that doing so was too political. Neutral clergy, he said, threatened to "involve us in permanent trouble for the sake of temporary triumph—to sacrifice principle and position to gain quiet for a brief space."[35] His complaint was echoed one hundred years later in Martin Luther King Jr.'s famous letter in which he castigated moderates who were "more devoted to 'order' than to justice."

Time and again, moderates sought to use the strategy of neutrality to avoid the discomfort of conflict during moral crises. As King noted, many Americans responded to demands for black equality during the civil rights movement by advocating for a "go slow" approach—one that would ensure a "negative peace which is the absence of tension" rather than bring about justice. When violence erupted, the moderates blamed activists for pushing too hard, for wanting too much, too fast, and for instigating unrest. As King wrote, however, their blame was misplaced: racism, white supremacy, and segregation were the source of conflict in the South: "We who engage in nonviolent direct action are not the creators of tension. We merely bring to the surface the hidden tension that is already alive."[36] Just as moderates on the border blamed abolitionists rather than slavery, so too did civil rights moderates blame activists rather than the institutionalized inequality of the Jim Crow South.

The consequences of adopting the strategy of neutrality have also reverberated in more recent debates. People who take this position in the face of intensely charged conflicts come to feel that they occupy the moral high ground and that they themselves are victims. This response could be found among the opponents of affirmative action in the late twentieth century who proposed that "color blindness" could be a solution to racism and structural inequality. Advocates of "color blindness" criticized affirmative action, rather than racism, for generating racial antagonism. One study of popular opinion about affirmative action revealed that white respondents frequently "portrayed themselves as victims" of the policies.[37] Choosing to be "color-blind" offers a reason to remain silent about the realities of racism in the United States—an outcome that benefits the white majority at the expense of people of color.

The strategy of neutrality was also on display in responses to the Black Lives Matter movement of the early twentieth century that asserted, "All Lives Matter." Like claiming "color blindness," this stance is only available to people who are not, themselves, victims of discrimination and racism. These responses might feel like solutions—a way to weather a moral crisis unscathed—just as they did to clergy who embraced neutrality on the slavery issue. However, the only thing they really resolve is discomfort. They allow people to avoid confronting a moral crisis and to avoid going through what King called "a necessary phase" of discomfort that accompanies "the transition from an obnoxious negative peace . . . to a substantive and positive peace, in which all men will respect the dignity and worth of human personality."[38] As the experience of border clergy showed, when "neutral" parties were called to task for abetting racism and segregation, they themselves felt persecuted. Their sense of victimhood, in this case, led them into churches that defended slavery even after it was abolished. This, then, is ultimately the problem of neutrality in the face of a moral crisis: neutrality itself cannot be neutral.

NOTES

The epigraph by Elie Wiesel is from "The Nobel Address," in *From the Kingdom of Memory: Reminiscences* (New York: Random House, 1990), 233.

1. "Another Church Separation," *Daily Dispatch* (Richmond, VA), December 8, 1860.
2. E. P. Phelps to Matthew Simpson, December 19, 1860, Matthew Simpson Papers, Library of Congress Manuscript Division.
3. E. P. Phelps to Matthew Simpson.
4. E. P. Phelps to Matthew Simpson.
5. Martin Luther King Jr., "Letter from Birmingham Jail," in *Why We Can't Wait* (New York: Signet, 2000), 64–84.

6. Amanda Porterfield, *Conceived in Doubt: Religion and Politics in the New American Nation* (Chicago: University of Chicago Press, 2015); Theda Skocpol, Marshall Ganz, and Ziad Munson, "A Nation of Organizers: The Institutional Origins of Civic Voluntarism," *American Political Science Review* 94, no. 3 (2000): 527–46.
7. These were the three largest evangelical denominations in the antebellum United States. Over 1.7 million Americans (nearly 70 percent of the Protestant population) were members in full standing of one of them, amounting to nearly 70 percent of the Protestant population. See Mark A. Noll, *America's God: From Jonathan Edwards to Abraham Lincoln* (New York: Oxford University Press, 2002), 166; Richard Carwardine, *Evangelicals and Politics in Antebellum America* (Knoxville: University of Tennessee Press, 1997), 5.
8. James Moorhead, "The 'Restless Spirit of Radicalism': Old School Fears and the Schism of 1837," *Journal of Presbyterian History* 78 (Spring 2000): 29; Nathan Hatch, *The Democratization of American Christianity* (New Haven, CT: Yale University Press, 1989), 196; Carwardine, *Evangelicals and Politics*, 166–67; Timothy Wesley, *The Politics of Faith During the Civil War* (Baton Rouge: Louisiana State University Press, 2013), 13.
9. Matthew Simpson Diary, December 26–29, 1852, Matthew Simpson Papers, Library of Congress Manuscript Division. See also Charles Elliott, *History of the Great Secession from the Methodist Episcopal Church in the Year 1845* (Cincinnati: Swormstedt and Poe, 1855), 592.
10. Jack P. Maddex, "From Theocracy to Spirituality: The Southern Presbyterian Reversal on Church and State," *Journal of Presbyterian History* 54 (1976): 446. See also Preston Graham Jr., *A Kingdom Not of This World: Stuart Robinson's Struggle to Distinguish the Sacred from the Secular During the Civil War* (Macon, GA: Mercer University Press, 2002).
11. John Stevens, *Brief Historical Sketch of the Western Baptist Theological Institute* (Cincinnati, 1850), 62.
12. Christ prayed of the churches "that they might be one; as thou, Father, art in me" (John 17:21). Neander Wood, "Our Redeemer's Prayer for Christian Unity," in *Southern Presbyterian Pulpit: A Collection of Sermons* (Richmond, VA, 1896), 128.
13. This was the case even when individual men styled themselves as antislavery moderates. Luke Harlow traces a transformation from "conservative antislavery" to "proslavery unionism" in the fifteen years before the Civil War. See Luke E. Harlow, *Religion, Race, and the Making of Confederate Kentucky, 1830–1880* (New York: Cambridge University Press, 2014), 76–106.
14. It is impossible to determine how many of those who professed neutrality did so out of religious conviction, how many supported slavery or harbored racist fears about emancipation, and how many were motivated by both reasons. See Wesley, *The Politics of Faith*, 94–104.
15. See George Rable, *God's Almost Chosen Peoples: A Religious History of the American Civil War* (Chapel Hill: University of North Carolina Press, 2010), 51–68. Harry Stout argues that clergy, North and South, were "virtually cheerleaders all" for the war. The response of border clergy complicates this claim. See Harry Stout, *Upon the Altar of the Nation: A Moral History of the Civil* War (New York: Viking, 2006), xvii.

16. W. M. Brewer, "Lincoln and the Border States," *Journal of Negro History* 34 (January 1949): 46–72; William C. Harris, *Lincoln and the Border States: Preserving the Union* (Lawrence: University Press of Kansas, 2011), 3.
17. In April 1861, irate Maryland Confederate sympathizers attacked Union soldiers and destroyed railroad bridges and other infrastructure to isolate Washington, DC, occasioning the Union's first application of martial law. Mark E. Neely Jr., *The Fate of Liberty: Abraham Lincoln and Civil Liberties* (New York: Oxford University Press, 1991), 4; Harris, *Lincoln and the Border States*, 42–158. See also Louis Gerteis, *Civil War St. Louis* (Lawrence: University Press of Kansas, 2001), 5; Thomas C. Mackey, "Not a Pariah, but a Keystone: Kentucky and Secession," in *Sister States, Enemy States: The Civil War in Kentucky and Tennessee*, ed. Kent T. Dollar, Larry H. Whiteaker, and W. Calvin Dickinson (Lexington: University Press of Kentucky, 2009), 33.
18. For a more detailed discussion, see Wesley, *The Politics of Faith*, 94–104. See also Marcus McArthur, "Treason in the Pulpit: The Problem of Apolitical Preaching in Civil War Missouri," *Journal of Church and State* 53 (2011): 545–66. A number of them privately supported the Confederacy. Others favored the Union cause but subscribed to the doctrine of spirituality. A third group, often affiliated with northern Democrats, opposed the war and viewed both sides as equally blameworthy. One such Kentucky Baptist vented his frustrations in his journal, condemning "rebels and traitors" along with "Radicals and abolitionists." In this conflict, he believed, "both [are] wrong and their sins cry to Heaven" (Samuel Haycraft, September 27, 1863, "Transcribed Journal of Samuel Haycraft Jr.," Filson Historical Society). This language echoes earlier arguments against political agitation that were used during antebellum slavery debates.
19. Jonathan B. Fuller to "Dear Father," June 20, 1861, and July 18, 1864, Western Historical Manuscript Collection—Kansas City.
20. Berry Hill Spencer, Oath of Allegiance, Lincoln County, Missouri; Berry Hill Spencer to "My dear Wife," February 5, 1863, Berry Hill Spencer Correspondence, Missouri Historical Society. See also Marcus McArthur, "'Sent into a Land of Strangers': The Banishment of Reverend Berry Hill Spencer," *Missouri Historical Review* 106 (2011): 14–31.
21. W. W. Whipple to "The Rev. Secretaries," September 16, 1856, American Home Mission Society Papers, Missouri, Library of Congress Manuscript Division.
22. Jonathon Palmer Finley Diaries, December 25, 1861, Presbyterian Historical Society, Philadelphia, PA.
23. Patrick Lewis, "'All Men of Decency Ought to Quit the Army': Benjamin F. Buckner, Manhood, and Proslavery Unionism in Kentucky," *Register of the Kentucky Historical Society* 107 (2009): 513–49. See also Harlow, *Religion, Race, and the Making of Confederate Kentucky*, 157–85.
24. Robert Andrew Baker, *Relations Between Northern and Southern Baptists* (Ph.D. dissertation, Yale University, 1948), 91–92; Ralph E. Morrow, *Northern Methodism and Reconstruction* (East Lansing: Michigan State University Press, 1956), 53; and Lewis G. Vander Velde, *The Presbyterian Churches and the Federal Union, 1861–1869* (Cambridge: Oxford University Press, 1932), 265.

25. "Slavery in the Church Courts," *Danville* (KY) *Quarterly Review*, December 1864, 516.
26. "The Presbyterian's Correspondent in South-Western Kentucky," *Louisville True Presbyterian*, March 31, 1864; "Spiritual Ruin," *Missouri Baptist Journal*, February 19, 1866; Stuart Robinson, "To the Presbyterian People of Kentucky," *Pamphlet* [1865], Filson Historical Society.
27. R. Paine and H. N. McTyeire, "To the Bishops of the Methodist Episcopal Church," *Western Christian Advocate* (Cincinnati), May 19, 1869.
28. James H. Brookes, "Introduction," in William Leftwich, *Martyrdom in Missouri* (Saint Louis: S. W. Book, 1870), 2:16.
29. Leftwich, *Martyrdom in Missouri*, 2:26–27.
30. Aaron Astor, *Rebels on the Border: Civil War, Emancipation, and the Reconstruction of Kentucky and Missouri* (Baton Rouge: Louisiana State University Press, 2012), 4. See also Jacob Lee, "Unionism, Emancipation, and the Origins of Kentucky's Confederate Identity," *Register of the Kentucky Historical Society* 111 (2013): 199–233; Jacob Lee, "'Between Two Fires': Cassius M. Clay, Slavery, and Antislavery in the Kentucky Borderlands," *Ohio Valley History* 6 (Fall 2006): 50–70; Anne Marshall, *Creating a Confederate Kentucky: The Lost Cause and Civil War Memory in a Border State* (Chapel Hill: University of North Carolina Press, 2013).
31. *Reunion Overture of the Northern General Assembly to the Southern Presbyterian Church, Considered* (Jackson, MO: Clarion Steam Printing Establishment, 1870), 55.
32. Luke Harlow, "The Long Life of Proslavery Religion," in *The World the Civil War Made*, ed. Gregory Downs and Kate Masur (Chapel Hill: University of North Carolina Press, 2015), 132–58.
33. E. M. Marvin, "Prefatory Note," in Leftwich, *Martyrdom in Missouri*, 1:6–7.
34. Orange Scott, "Address to the General Conference of the Methodist Episcopal Church by the Rev. O. Scott, 1836," in *The History of American Methodism*, ed. Emory S. Bucke (New York: Abington Press, 1964), 30.
35. R. Ricketts to Matthew Simpson, March 19, 1861, Matthew Simpson Papers, Library of Congress Manuscript Division.
36. King, "Letter from Birmingham Jail," 73.
37. Charles Lawrence III and Mari J. Matsuda, *We Won't Go Back: Making the Case for Affirmative Action* (New York: Houghton Mifflin, 1997), 84, 72.
38. King, "Letter from Birmingham Jail," 73.

5

HISTORIANS, LINCOLN, AND "THE RUINING OF AMERICA"

MATTHEW TAYLOR RAFFETY

Like many historians of nineteenth-century America, I feel the looming shadow of Abraham Lincoln everywhere. Anyone who teaches U.S. history at any level must grapple with the complex legacy of Lincoln, both within and beyond the classroom. By now, though, I really ought to have ready some bon mots, wise adages, esoteric arcana, or even a trenchant critique or two for the students, parents, passersby, people on the barstool next to me, other delayed passengers at Terminal 6 at LAX, or just about anyone else I foolishly tell I am a historian. When they find out what I do, they inevitably want to ask an "expert" about Lincoln or share their own Lincoln stories.

My struggles with Lincoln are somewhat more personal, however. They began in high school, when my history class attended a dinner theater production of a one-man play on the life of Lincoln, performed by an earnest and historically-minded soap opera star.[1] After the play, the dessert course was given over to a question-and-answer session. In class, we had been reading the work of Richard Hofstadter, among the first modern historians to approach Lincoln with a critical eye. Hofstadter describes Lincoln as a self-aggrandizing political maneuverer rather than the unambiguously heroic savior of the republic. During the dessert course, I raised my hand and impertinently outlined Hofstadter's portrayal of Lincoln as a "self-made myth."[2] Still in character, "Lincoln" rose up to his full height, gripped the lapels of his black frock coat with both hands, and leveled his gaze at me. "I'm not familiar with Dr. Hofstadter's work," said this approximation of the sixteenth president of the United States, "and I don't really think I'd like to be." The crowd went wild. Dinner theater denizens whooped and applauded. My classmates fell out in hysterics. I was the anti-Lincoln jerk, hell-bent on ruining America, one dinner theater at a time. But my showdown with Lincoln did force me, for the first time, to think of Lincoln not only as an artifact of the American past but also as an ongoing presence, as alive in the wider culture as the actor was up there on the stage. Indeed, we're all still facing a living Abraham Lincoln, and, with no disrespect meant to the daytime Emmy hopeful performing that night, one related in complex, attenuated, and bizarre ways to the original.

For historians as well as the wider public, Lincoln presents a paradox. Compared to other presidents, Lincoln left a relatively brief written record, yet he is the most written *about* president. A list compiled before World War II of books on Lincoln runs more than 1,000 pages; today, Amazon pulls up over 66,000 books at least in part about Lincoln.[3] By one reckoning, on average, we've been churning out Lincoln biographies at the rate of "around two a week, since the Civil War."[4] As a result, he represents a peculiar challenge to historians who want to engage thoughtfully with the sixteenth president and his legacy. The abundance of secondary sources on Lincoln is daunting. Trying to parse the way Lincoln is interpreted and deployed quickly overwhelms even the most diligent scholar. Of course, there's also an upside to the perennial public fascination with Lincoln. The Civil War (especially Lincoln's role in it) serves as a job creation program for historians. No one goes broke writing about Lincoln, it seems, even in so crowded a market.

Literary scholar Fred Kaplan states that "our 16th president is often either vilified or deified,"[5] but Kaplan's dichotomy is too limited, leaving out the many different visions of what was good or overrated about Lincoln. He also leaves out the far bigger, vaguer, but enormously powerful presence of the pop-culture, "folk" Lincoln, who impacts far more people than even the most public-facing scholars will ever reach. Although all kinds of interpretations abound, in the end, for a historian, there are really three broad approaches one can take in the study of Lincoln (personally, I'm torn between them): (1) the fan: Lincoln was awesome; (2) the critic: Lincoln was overrated; and (3) the ironic pose, which sees Lincoln as a subject of morbid curiosity and kitschy roadside tourism.

GOOD LINCOLN

The fan sees Lincoln as inherently great and indisputably important. Such is the Lincoln of my dinner theater nightmares, and it is the oldest, and still most popular, historical interpretation. The Great Man School began to form at the instant of Lincoln's death. At the moment of Lincoln's passing, Secretary of State William Seward got the canonizing rolling by saying of his recently deceased commander in chief, "now he belongs to the ages" or "now he belongs to the angels." Historians still debate which of these he actually said and what the political message was. In a 2007 piece in the *New Yorker*, essayist Adam Gopnik explores the ideological debate behind the angels/ages divide. Since politicians and historians of all stripes seek to lay claim to Lincoln, Seward's mumbled one-liner of a eulogy set up a political division. Liberals like Doris Kearns Goodwin see Lincoln as the hero of "a brand of American neoclassicism," whose legacy is in his words and deeds. Conservative scholars like Jay Winik and James L. Swanson prefer "angels," which they see as in keeping with Lincoln's and Stanton's devout faith and as an illustration of Lincoln as the Christian martyr for a Christian nation.[6] Whether he belongs to the angels or the ages, this ongoing debate illustrates the problem with the Great Man School. It is long on festive decoration and short on coherence.

At its worst, the Lincoln hagiography is trite and reductive, creating a single false hero totally devoid of any actual content. Immediately upon his assassination, Lincoln was transformed from an embattled president who saw the Union divide and fought bloodily (and some argued incompetently) to keep it together, who suspended habeas corpus in Maryland, and who ushered in the draft and the income tax, to an unalloyed hero of epic proportions. In an address at Harvard not long after Lincoln's death, James Russell Lowell called him our "Martyr-Chief,"[7] and that Christ-like image has only grown in fervor and breadth.

Lincoln has become all (good) things to all people. Lincoln is praised as a self-made man and as the archetype for the American dream, capable of bridging personal success with personal morality. Lincoln is regularly touted as the "Great Emancipator," who, as Gary Wills argues, "cleansed" the Constitution of the grievous stain of slavery. Lincoln, we are often told, "saved the Union." "Consensus school" historians like Daniel Boorstin see in Lincoln's life the strong strain of bourgeoisie agreement that has guided the exceptional character of the American project, even in the midst of its greatest, bloodiest division.[8]

Of late, it seems we are awash with Lincolns who are praised for their political skill and pragmatism. Richard Norton Smith, pundit-turned-presidential-historian, seeks to rehabilitate the image of the American politician through examples of Lincoln's pragmatism, illustrating how he "played up" his antislavery credentials for some audiences and his backwater racism for others. Indeed, Smith, who has made a career of creating presidential libraries for presidents who served before such libraries were a thing, rehabilitates what earlier scholars like Hofstadter had used as a critique of Lincoln, speaking rhapsodically (for approximately $10,000/speech) about Lincoln's life as a "permanent campaign."[9] Similarly, former FCC chairman, telecom executive, and prolific amateur historian Tom Wheeler sees Lincoln as a tech visionary and an important early adopter of telecommunication.[10]

Those praising Lincoln end up sounding contradictory and confusing. Lincoln is celebrated as a visionary, moralist, martyr, "Father Abraham," and protector of the republic and, at the same time, as a master politician, pragmatist, and hustling self-promoter. Ultimately, it is difficult to reconcile the staunch, defiant idealist, who closed his remarks at Liberty Hall in Philadelphia after his election, but before his inauguration, by claiming, "I have said nothing but what I am willing to live by, and if it be the pleasure of Almighty God, to die by,"[11] with the impish pragmatist who justified political flexibility by quipping that "bad promises are better broken than kept."[12]

Some recent Lincoln apologists like John Patrick Diggins see no paradox here, however. Lincoln was the model of a "Christian pragmatist," who had no problem resolving his moral absolutes with his political flexibility. Those who see this as a conflict he labels as "fashionable" "postmodernists" and relativists without an anchor. That's some rather snarky name-calling in defense of a man who famously eschewed such personal attacks, even in the most vituperative of times.[13]

Even if one is convinced that Lincoln masterfully melded political pragmatism with loftier motives, one must admit that some of the claims get rather loony. I don't just mean the obvious, silly apocryphal mythologizing that goes on about all great statesmen: all that rail-splitting and frontier backwoodsery, mostly fabricated after his death. Nor am I talking about the patriotic praise that Lincoln attracts. In a schoolboy printing of Lincoln's literary gems from 1894, editor C. W. French asserts in a succinct introductory essay: "He was emphatically a man of the people," who developed "a reputation for incorruptible honesty and wise judgment. Wherever he was known he was trusted and loved." As president, "in him every hope rested; and he never failed. His coolness, courage, and judgment never deserted him. For every emergency he was ready, and in the end he gained the victory and laid down his life for his country."[14] Who better for young scholars to study?

Such praise is earnest but a little thin, I think. What's more interesting is how French also uses Lincoln as an object lesson for students about the importance of education, effectively using the same awkward logic served up by degreeless NBA stars who regularly urge *other* (shorter) children to "stay in school."[15] French writes of Lincoln: "He was born in poverty and ignorance, and his early life was spent in the cabin of the pioneer. . . . But Lincoln was possessed of a burning thirst for knowledge, and the education which his circumstances denied him he obtained by his own unaided exertion."[16]

Just as French sought to make the self-educated Lincoln into a mascot for early-twentieth-century schools, others lionize Lincoln to serve their own modern agenda. Queer studies scholars and Log Cabin Republicans champion Lincoln's alleged homosexuality, the sketchy evidence mainly stemming from his frosty relationship with Mary Todd Lincoln, his fondness for sharing a bed on occasion with business partner and lifelong friend Joshua Speed, or his relationship with another male peer, Billy Greene, who praised the perfection of Lincoln's manly thighs.[17] Similarly, Lincoln, who suffered from black moods and periods of inactivity and despair, has been asked to stand in as a champion for those suffering from depression.[18] Still others debate whether or not the lanky Lincoln suffered from Marfan syndrome.[19] This "Lincoln is one of us" contrivance, whether connected to his sexual orientation, mood swings, or physical anomaly, seems to me the most curious and the most historically detached wing of the Great Man School of thought, and perhaps its most pernicious. If we can all read in Lincoln what we like, he truly becomes nothing other than an unmoored historical logo, linked vaguely to "quality" like the Nike swoosh or the script "Coca-Cola." In a review of two recent Lincoln biographies, Eric Foner invokes an old maxim from *Esquire* magazine: "there is nothing that can be marketed that cannot be marketed better using the likeness of Honest Abe Lincoln."[20] It's no surprise, I suppose, that Lincoln's birthday has long been a day to sell sheets and towels and to move last year's models off of car lots across the nation. Consider the moment in that seminal 2007 film *National Treasure 2: Book of Secrets* when both fictional treasure hunter and fictional president can pause, in the middle of a kidnapping of the latter by the former, to agree that Lincoln was their favorite president.[21] Lincoln has become a sort of American historical Esperanto.

A salesman at heart, our forty-fifth president clearly bought into the President's Day version of Lincoln—and the entire concept of his office—as a vague assertion of quality. Many have remarked that Donald Trump's vernacular is peppered with imprecise words that connoted quality in the broadest (and least precise) sense.[22] It is therefore unsurprising that he relies on Lincoln so often to afford him an air of importance. At a rally in Youngstown, Ohio, he asserted, "With the exception of the late, great Abraham Lincoln, I can be more presidential than any president that's ever held this office."[23] Lincoln is a benchmark of "presidentiality," itself an entirely undefined and undefinable quality. It is like the copy in perfume ads that seeks to evoke something without actually saying anything.

Yet, even as President Trump continued to wrap himself in the mantle of the "late, great Lincoln," Lincoln's fans who opposed the president saw Lincoln criticizing Trump from beyond the grave, at least according to *New Yorker* columnist Philip Gourevitch, who insisted that "Abraham Lincoln Warned Us About Donald Trump."[24] Gourevitch's criticism has merit, and his reading of Lincoln's worry that "alienation" from public institutions was a civic crisis is relevant to our present moment, but the invocation of Lincoln as a venerated rabbi of American political propriety is striking.[25]

Good Lincoln is everywhere. At least since 1909, he's been in almost every pocket, too. In 1909, to commemorate the centenary of Lincoln's birth, Theodore Roosevelt urged that Lincoln become the first U.S. president commemorated on a coin. Since then, notes *New York Times* columnist David Margolick, "probably no art object in human history has been reproduced more often."[26] In the intervening 111 years, Lincoln's ubiquity, both as a cultural touchstone and as a coin, has only expanded. Debates about doing away with the penny continue to grow as inflation has dipped its value below the cost of production, but the humble Lincoln penny survives, perhaps more as a national Saint Christopher medal, reassuring Americans that the republic he loved and defended has not, yet, perished from the earth.[27]

Ultimately, all those tiny reassurances add up, much like the mountains of copper (and, since 1982, zinc) used in minting billions of tiny memorials. In celebrating the centennial anniversary of the Lincoln penny, another *Times* author, Thomas Vinciguerra, described the coin's long run as a "triumph," but nothing compared to the legacy of the true Lincoln. He wistfully titled the piece, "Now If Only We Could Mint Lincoln Himself."[28]

Even if scholars are inclined to shy away from this unalloyed, heroic Lincoln, we must acknowledge his lasting import as a figure of integrity and leadership. We do need to give the heroic vision of Lincoln its due. There can be no disputing that his presidency covered the most tumultuous and transformative years the American republic has seen. As president, he navigated a fractured nation through those challenges with seldom-matched rhetorical skill. Despite minimal martial experience, he took the U.S. military into the modern age through a war that began like the Napoleonic Wars and ended, tactically and technologically, much closer to World War I. At the same time, he kept that army—and the national coalition behind it—in a fight to defend the rather diffuse and metaphysical goal of "union." Most importantly, though we can quibble about his precise role in it, his presidency oversaw the destruction of slavery, an enormous social and economic transformation, even if the completeness of that transformation remained—and remains—elusive. While we might chip at the edges or problematize those accomplishments, these are some pretty powerful reasons to get behind Team Lincoln.

Historians love their caveats and their complexities. At our best, we provide a powerful corrective to hagiographic and polemical uses of the past and its heroes. That often also makes us kind of a drag. As a discipline, we're long on "well, actually . . . ," always ready to spike the fun of a better, apocryphal narrative.

At the end of my U.S. survey class this term, I asked students which past leader they wish could be leading the nation in the midst of the current pandemic. The most popular response, unsurprisingly, was Lincoln. One student noted that Abe was already good at giving speeches to reassure us amidst mass American deaths, but, more earnestly, even she identified him as a powerful touchstone of unifying leadership, who found ways to rise above the turmoil of his moment. Thus, in the end, for the adherents to the Good Lincoln idea, the actual history matters far less than the reassuring notion that there have been great leaders.

BAD LINCOLN

The second approach to Lincoln, the position of the curmudgeon, apostate, and debunker, was the pose I took during the next phase in my ongoing struggle with Lincoln. My schoolboy experiences left me intellectually confused and socially humiliated. After that, I'd managed to duck Lincoln fairly successfully for years. My professors in both college and graduate school mostly shied away from the centrality of Lincoln, even in courses on the Civil War. After finishing graduate school, however, I took a teaching position in an epicenter of Lincoln mania: Galesburg, in west-central Illinois. Illinois, the self-described "land of Lincoln," seemed to be obsessed. And it made me irrationally angry. I could never even bring myself to change my car registration. I balked at the prospect of having Lincoln's profile on my license plates, preceding and following me wherever I went. Apart from Wrigley Field, the state's entire tourist agenda seems divided between worship of Lincoln and worship of Reagan. Galesburg is on *both* the "Lincoln Trail" *and* the "Reagan Trail." After a decade in New York City, this felt like hostile terrain. The Reagan connection is tangential, but Galesburg's Lincoln ties are deep.

Galesburg is a fascinating, beautiful historic city. It is the birthplace of Carl Sandburg, whose epic biography of Lincoln had overmatched me on a sixth-grade book report, but, as James Hurt notes, more than eighty years since the publication of the first volume, "Carl Sandburg's *Abraham Lincoln: The Prairie Years and The War Years* is, for better or worse, the best-selling, most widely read, and most influential book about Lincoln."[29] But the Sandburg connection was merely an amuse-bouche for the massive buffet of all-Lincoln-all-the-time to come. Knox College is unapologetically Lincoln Country, just as it was in the 1850s, and the dude is everywhere. Statues, friezes, portraits abound. Big donors to the school are in the "Lincoln-Douglas Society." Thanks to the excellent scholarship and tireless work of Douglas Wilson and Rod Davis, Knox has its own Lincoln Studies Center that oversees a dedicated Lincoln Studies imprint shared with Illinois University Press.[30] There's not just a professorial endowed chair, but also a "Lincoln chair," roped off and crying out for reupholstering. There are 1,250 students and seven historians, two dedicated solely to Lincoln. I was the "non-Lincoln" nineteenth-century U.S. historian.

My office at Knox was in Old Main, a beautiful 1857 brick-and-limestone tower and the only surviving site of a Lincoln-Douglas debate. Had I looked straight down out of my office window on October 7, 1858, I would have been staring at the tops of the heads of Abraham Lincoln and Stephen Douglas debating each other during their Senate campaigns.

I loved teaching at Knox, a school with a collegial faculty, engaged student body, and, to my way of thinking, excellent institutional priorities. I loved that big office. But the nonstop Lincoln stuff rubbed me the wrong way, and I started letting my anti-Lincoln flag fly. I didn't fall for some of the more out-there anti-Lincoln critiques, like the states' rights fetishists (there seems to be one per law school faculty) who relish challenging Lincoln's reading of secession as unconstitutional and marking down students who don't capitalize the *S* in *state*. And we finally seem to be seeing some public repudiation of the Confederate apologists who display the empty symbols of the Confederacy with equally vacant slogans justifying their stars-and-bars regalia as "heritage, not hate."[31] I had somewhat more empathy for scholars on the left who see Lincoln and his fellow early Republicans as heartless boosters for unbridled capitalism, but having seen how that thinking has turned brilliant Marxist scholars like Eugene Genovese into rhapsodizers of the slaveholding class as anticapitalist heroes, that was a short-lived flirtation.[32]

Not surprisingly, I spent a lot of time thinking about the Lincoln-Douglas debates during my year in Old Main. As I looked out that window, I found myself feeling for Douglas, who agreed to debate at Knox, an avowedly abolitionist college whose president, Rev. Jonathan Blanchard, claimed that the purpose of Knox was to create "martyrs" in the inevitable war against slavery.[33] Talk about a mission statement for a college. By some accounts, the two debated under a giant banner proclaiming "Knox College for Lincoln!" One can compare those conditions to the recent complaints at today's debates about the unfairness of moderators, podium heights, or who gets which question first.[34]

What does become clear from the Lincoln-Douglas debates is that Lincoln understood the value of playing the underdog. Even a casual student of the debates can conjure up the image of an awkward, homespun Lincoln against the slick, well-dressed "Little Giant" of the Democrats. Indeed, Lincoln tapped into something upon which the producers of *Matlock* would later capitalize: Americans love watching the country lawyer stick it to the corporate shill.

Yet Stephen Douglas was every bit the self-made man that Lincoln was. In 1833 he arrived in Illinois from Vermont as an unhealthy twenty-year-old without money, friends, or prospects. He was admitted to the bar the following year, entered politics as a Democrat (the traditional party for self-starter types in that era), became a state legislator, then secretary of state for Illinois, then a state supreme court judge, and then, at only thirty-two, a U.S. senator and a leading light in the national party, as well as the heir apparent to master negotiator Henry Clay. By contrast, Lincoln's résumé was thin. He had been a store clerk before practicing law. Then he served four undistinguished terms in the Illinois House and one in the U.S. Congress as a Whig before returning to private practice in 1849. Nevertheless, the Senate race displayed Lincoln's brilliant political judo of using Douglas's accomplishments against him, praising "Judge Douglas" so as to lower expectations for his own performance and simultaneously position himself as the candidate of "regular" folk. It was a maneuver still quite successful in American political life. How else could one explain how the Harvard- and Yale-educated scion of a wealthy oil and political family could put on a western-wear shirt, clear some brush, and run as an "everyman" in 2000? It is not that Lincoln's rough-hewn origins were false, but he was masterful in fusing the "regular guy" appeal of the Jacksonian Democrats with the moralist ideology of affluent, northeastern Whigs. Lincoln figured out how to be both "regular" *and* sanctimonious, still a winning combination in American politics.

The Lincoln-Douglas debates were simply not a fair fight. As a national figure, Douglas was saddled with his party's platform and his own impressive but politically fraught legislative record. For Douglas, the Senate campaign was merely a tune-up for his expected presidential bid in 1860. He had to think down the road. By contrast, Lincoln had almost no record to defend and represented a party only two years old with no members south of Kentucky. As the unknown, Lincoln merely had to critique Douglas's record and point out the contradictions in his previous words and deeds, rather than offer anything programmatic of his own. As any academic will admit after a few drinks, it's far, far easier to critique than to create.[35]

Also, ultimately the Illinois legislature returned Douglas to Washington, and Lincoln went back to Springfield to practice law. Lincoln naysayers like to argue that the loss of the senatorial bid in 1858 did more to make Lincoln president than anything else he did. To those disposed to dislike Lincoln, it serves as illustration that, for all the praise heaped upon him after the fact, Lincoln was surprisingly limited as a visionary leader. He received the Republican nomination in 1860 precisely because he had so unremarkable a résumé. When party leaders met in Chicago to choose the presidential candidate, it took three ballots to put Lincoln forward as a compromise candidate over the more qualified but polarizing choices of William Seward and Salmon P. Chase. They ran Lincoln as the most inoffensive candidate available. He was morally opposed to slavery but deeply ambivalent about acting against the institution except in the case of its continued expansion west.

On racial matters Lincoln was also no radical. He clung to the fantasy of ending slavery by compensating slaveholders and repatriating slaves to an unfamiliar Africa, long after other Republicans had given up such "colonization" schemes as quaint, immoral, unaffordable, and impractical.[36] Indeed, Charles B. Dew, a historian of unusual insight and honesty, notes in his provocative memoir *The Making of a Racist* that as an undergraduate he found Lincoln's expansiveness useful. He could "walk into [his] sophomore American History class and cite Abraham Lincoln as [his] authority for defending racial segregation in the South."[37]

Perhaps the most damning critique of Abraham Lincoln is that he stood for so little that he can be claimed by all. Sometimes even the same hands fashioned very different Lincolns, as when D. W. Griffith portrayed him ambivalently in his *Birth of a Nation* in 1919 only to provide the template for what became the standard film hero treatment eleven years later in *Abraham Lincoln*.[38] Because Lincoln kept his own counsel and wrote relatively little, his legacy is particularly malleable. Many of Lincoln's modern critics see him as a man of surprisingly limited political will, buffeted by the grand forces that surrounded him. In this interpretation, Lincoln is little more than a vessel for the historical actions that surrounded him. To repurpose Seward's alleged quote, perhaps Lincoln "belonged to his age" long before his death. Hofstadter saw Lincoln as "a follower and not a leader in public opinion," both before and during his presidency, often well behind both the radicals in Congress and his field commanders in accepting the realities that faced him.[39] David Herbert Donald notes the "passivity of his nature," taking quite literally Lincoln's modesty when he insisted: "I claim not to have controlled events, but confess plainly that events have controlled me."[40]

Indeed, many of the same political and rhetorical maneuvers that some see as the mark of a brilliant tactician are seen by the anti-Lincoln crowd as despicable. For example, in his first inaugural address, Lincoln makes clear his belief that, if war comes, it will be the action of the South: "In your hands, my dissatisfied fellow-countrymen, and not in mine, is the momentous issue of civil war. . . . You can have no conflict without being yourselves the aggressors."[41] To his fans, it is a deft move to put defense of the Union on firm ground throughout the North, undermine the legitimacy of the seceded states, and most importantly, reassure the states of the upper South still contemplating secession. For Lincoln haters, he is an American Pontius Pilate, washing his hands of official responsibility for the 750,000 dead that would follow.

Perhaps that goes too far. But I do think it is fair to wonder why the president who oversaw the only violent transfer of the presidency in American history (so far), who presided over a war of spectacular death and destruction, is necessarily the hero of that story. Just as it seems unjust to lay all of the mayhem and bloodshed of the American Civil War at Lincoln's feet, it seems too easy to claim that all the situations were unavoidable, and only mighty Lincoln's resolve could have "saved" the Union.[42] Although it is impossible to engage in counterfactuals in any kind of scholarly way, we are left with considerable "what ifs" about what would have happened had another man with a different character ascended to the presidency in 1861.

Other scholars see feet of clay in Lincoln's image as the leader who expunged the scourge of slavery from the national conscience. Lincoln, they rightly point out, was, at best, a reluctant emancipator. Despite the more radical origins of the Liberty Party, the Republicans appealed frankly to the racist wing of the Free Soil movement, made up of poor white Midwesterners fearful of having to compete economically with the "slave power" of the South or interact socially with black people. "I will say then that I am not, nor ever have been, in favor of bringing about in any way the social and political equality of the white and black races," explained Lincoln at the fourth debate with Douglas, reassuring a decidedly less radical audience in Charleston than in Galesburg, "I am not nor ever have been in favor of making voters or jurors of negroes, nor of qualifying them to hold office, nor to intermarry with white people; and I will say in addition to this that there is a physical difference between the white and black races which I believe will forever forbid the two races living together on terms of social and political equality."[43] Is this an abolitionist hero? Contemporary activists thought not. The abolitionist Wendell Phillips decried him as a "huckster" and as "first rate" at being a "second rate man."[44]

Lincoln's reputation as the Great Emancipator is the weakest element of his historical legacy, and the destruction of slavery offers perhaps the best test of his malleable historical legacy. Within the Emancipation Proclamation is the ultimate Rorschach test for interpreting Abraham Lincoln. Viewed one way, it is the single greatest seizure of private property in world history by an individual government actor. Nothing in Soviet collectivization can compare with the seizure and eventual freeing of nearly one-third of the nation's wealth, precipitated by a lone executive pen and justified as a wartime necessity. Through other eyes, it is the moment at which the United States began to live up to the promise of its birth. With emancipation, the nation moved incrementally but inexorably toward fulfilling the claim that "all men are created equal," first asserted amidst the intoxicating blend of tax rebellion and Enlightenment philosophy that birthed the Declaration of Independence. Lincoln echoed that declaration, consecrating the field at Gettysburg with his famously terse address. Although his explicit defense of emancipation had been decidedly constitutional, drawn from his powers as wartime commander in chief, his larger justification, obliquely referred to at Gettysburg, came from the older, more radical declaration. He called for a "new freedom," a rebirth in the blood of the martyrs of the battlefield, for a nation "conceived in Liberty and dedicated to the proposition that all men are created equal."[45] Thus, argue his fans, Gettysburg took the political action of the Emancipation Proclamation and gave it its moral benediction.

But there is a bolder, better interpretation available, first outlined by W. E. B. Du Bois, who stated that the Emancipation Proclamation didn't do anything. Lincoln was late to the game, merely validating what was, in Union-controlled areas, already a military reality and what, for Confederate terrain, was an impotent assertion.[46] So the Emancipation Proclamation was, depending on your interpretation, either a cataclysmic pivot not only in U.S. history but also in the march of liberty worldwide, or a pointless scribble, giving cover to what slaves and generals had already seen and exploited as the essential key to victory.

By contrast, slaves understood best and earliest just how malleable the legacy of Lincoln would be. Bolstered by the prewar rhetoric of southern fire-eaters who sought to sell secession to their white neighbors through images of an emancipating "Black Republican" and promises of a racial bloodbath, slaves seized on Lincoln as potential emancipator while he was still promising to protect the institution of slavery.[47] Lincoln did not lead; rather, he was dragged forward to face the inevitability of emancipation. Du Bois termed it a "general strike," whereby slaves freed themselves and forced Lincoln to confront first the logistical headache and later the military value of their mass escape from bondage. In this version of Exodus, the Israelites hijacked Moses and forced him, over his objections, to lead them to freedom.[48]

The slaves understood the power of the image of Lincoln as Great Emancipator even if he did not, and they used it to their own ends. They fashioned him into an engine of radical social, economic, and political change through their reappropriation of his preexisting image. In other words, the slaves did all the work, and some white dude still gets all the credit. That could not have seemed like new news to the freedmen and freedwomen, even if this process of self-emancipation remains occluded in the popular imagination by the shadow of the Great Emancipator.

Talk about "white savior" fantasies.[49] An important part of Lincoln's lasting appeal is as a moderate face for radical change. Ultimately, this widely accepted vision of Lincoln as an honorable force for imprecise "good" is what irks the Bad Lincoln gang. Eric Foner has suggested that it is the messianic zeal of the abolitionist rebel John Brown that should be credited with moving the United States bloodily toward freedom.

"Today, Lincoln is widely revered, while many Americans, including some historians, consider Brown mad. Yet it was Brown's strategy that brought slavery to an end."[50] In either case, Lincoln is a comforting avatar of American change, less terrifying than the fiery Brown, and more comforting to many Americans than a tale of Black self-liberation. More radical observers—then and now—remain frustrated by Lincoln's timidity.

ABSURD LINCOLN

"In a way, we have found it too easy to understand Lincoln," argues Foner, who, after an illustrious career in Civil War and Reconstruction history only took on Lincoln directly in his fifth decade as a historian. "We think we know him because in looking at Lincoln, we are really discovering ourselves."[51] Foner's insight is essential in trying to parse Lincoln the historical figure from Lincoln as remembered and mythologized. Read earnestly, it means that historians are always examining the past with today's tools to answer today's questions and to meet present needs. Such, ultimately, is part of the essential humanist value of the study of the past. In the hands of a deft scholar like Foner, it can inspire work that goes beyond the parochial antiquarianism of the historical profession to create a history of value and impact that reaches out well beyond academe. Yet, more dangerously, it can mean we've reversed the process of history. In this reading, we don't make meaning out of the past. Instead, we stuff our modern meanings into hollowed-out symbols of the past for our own ends, be they grand or absurd.

This brings me to the third interpretation of Lincoln: as a postmodern cultural football, bouncing around in strange but powerfully illuminating ways, a fascinating American grotesque played alternatively for pathos, patriotism, profit, or just laughs. It also brings me to a third personal brush with Abraham Lincoln. Several years ago, I interviewed for a job at a large state institution. As far as campus job visits go, this one was pretty standard, except that the person I would be replacing presented unusually big shoes to fill, both literally and metaphorically. Not only would I replace a respected scholar at the sunset of an august and productive career, but the person currently in the line was also a professional Lincoln impersonator.

I knew I was sunk. I'm not the man to replace a part-time Lincoln. Unlike the 150 members of the Association of Lincoln Presenters, I'm simply not "ready, willing and Abe L."[52] In desperation, I assured my interviewers that, although I'd make a poor showing in both physical and character traits as a Lincoln, I'd make a fantastic John Quincy Adams as a dour, unlovable New Englander. They weren't buying it. Still, I think there's mileage in that idea: if this historian thing doesn't work out, I'm available for your children's birthday parties.

There was certainly something absurd about unexpectedly finding myself interviewing to replace a Lincoln impersonator. But then, perhaps the best way to learn from Lincoln and among the most powerful is to relish his role as unmoored cultural icon. Why *is* it possible to supplement your income as a Lincoln impersonator, and not as John Quincy Adams?[53]

Slaves used the war to reinvent Lincoln as an emancipator. But that was just the opening act. Once he was dead and unable to complain, his image and legacy were wide open to be hijacked and deployed; a national martyr was created in whose death we commemorate the shared sacrifice of both sides of the war, a symbol of union, a patriotic inspiration, a stalwart hero, a cash-generating logo, a punchline. By the end of his own century, Lincoln had already become a semi-mythological figure, "a kind of second cousin to America's frontier heroes—Davy Crocket and Kit Carson."[54]

From the angels/ages confusion forward, Lincoln has attracted a bizarre and culturally telling following, disconnected from scholarly or political legacy. Among the smartest exponents of this mixture of lurid fascination and thoughtful examination is National Public Radio regular Sarah Vowell, whose *Assassination Vacation* centers on her long-standing Lincoln death fetish. Much of Vowell's Lincoln tourism tends toward the ghoulish: visiting floating pieces of Lincoln's brain at Walter Reed Medical Center comes to mind.[55] She's not alone in Lincoln death tourism, though. We, as a nation, enjoy some kind of catharsis from our secular reliquaries. And reliquaries they are. From the moment of his death, people began collecting relics. Mary Todd Lincoln asked for a lock of hair. Everyone else in the room helped themselves to one, too. They knew this death would be big, and everyone wanted a piece of the legacy. Those in the room went for literal pieces. Those outside the inner circle had to settle for all sorts of memorial cards, photographs, badges, and specially printed poetic remembrances, but they still sought their own touchstone to commemorate Lincoln's death. From those nineteenth-century memento mori to modern fridge magnets, Americans still feel the need for a little piece of Lincoln.[56]

To the eternal chagrin of John Wilkes Booth, who sought to brand Lincoln as a tyrant for eternity, his bullet instantly created the most impenetrably heroic figure in the national consciousness. It also let Lincoln off the hook for anything that followed. The secret to both great politics and great comedy is timing, and Lincoln's death could not have come at a better moment for his legacy. Winning a war often proves far easier than reordering the society after hostilities end. Asserting the Union's preservation in blood took four horrible years. Stitching the nation back together took eleven more years, until moral exhaustion, corruption, and the seductive call of racial solidarity trumped mutual economic interest and left the greatest radical promises of emancipation and reconstruction deferred. Despite the civil rights movement nearly seventy years after Reconstruction failed, most would argue that the grandest promises of Lincoln's rhetoric still remain at least partially unfulfilled. Yet, thanks to his death, Lincoln carries little of the baggage of what Foner calls the "unfinished revolution" of Reconstruction.[57] If his last public address was any indication, his plan was vastly more forgiving of the former traitors who rose against the enduring republic. But Lincoln died. He avoided the dirty work of Reconstruction, so we are free to see in him whatever answer we want to the complicated, compromised questions that followed.

Instead, Lincoln became the beta test for Elvis Presley Enterprises.[58] But, just because we know Graceland is silly does not mean we don't cry at Elvis's (or Lincoln's) grave. It may enrage earnest Lincolnites like Duggins, but Vowell and other Lincoln tourists define a Lincoln for our ambivalent, postmodern age. By now, Lincoln is so available to us as Americans that his image can sell Wendy's 99¢ burgers and launch the Aqua Teen Hunger Force into space. There is *always* work for tall guys dressed in stovepipe hats. Indeed, the current Lincoln is best defined in terms of other pop-culture icons. Russian-Kazakh director Timur Bekmambetov sees Lincoln as "the Batman of the nineteenth century."[59]

Americans retrofit their Lincolns for their own moments. One can look at Lincoln veneration through the ages: from the overwrought statuary of the nineteenth century, seeking to heal the nation in stone metaphors of shared sacrifice, to the weird positivist animatronic Lincoln cyborg in "Great Moments with Mr. Lincoln" created for the 1964 World's Fair and then permanently installed at Disneyland to educate and bewilder, to the bizarrely postmodern 2010 book and subsequent film *Abraham Lincoln, Vampire Hunter*.[60]

We know our heroes are flawed. And, although we mock our own earnestness when we revel in ironic historical tourism, we're still seeking something true, even while we wink at our own foolishness. Vowell rightly points out that "going to Ford's Theatre for the show is like going to Hooters for the food."[61] Perhaps, then, it is unsurprising that the Oak Ridge Cemetery in Springfield, Illinois, is the second most visited graveyard in the United States behind Arlington. (Elvis's is the most visited grave *site*.) And I don't think that folks trek to Springfield to pay homage to Lincoln's eternal neighbor, Roy "Mr. Accordion" Bertelli.[62]

I'm reminded of "Abraham, Martin and John," the weepy, socially conscious ballad recorded by Dion as a comeback in 1968, linking the deaths and mourning the lost promise of Lincoln, Martin Luther King Jr., and John and Robert Kennedy, noting that in each case "he freed a lot of people." It's a dreadful song, but its dopey, hopeful lyrics are instructive: "Didn't you love the things that they stood for? / Didn't they try to find some good for you and me? / And we'll be free."[63] In essence, that's the Lincoln legacy: a vague sense of having stood for some undefined good, pointing us to some future promised land. Lincoln is still the Moses the slaves made him.

At my second academic posting, I was paired with a senior political scientist to give a presentation called "What Can We Learn from Lincoln?" as part of a campus "Great Thinkers" series, some of which finds its way into this essay.[64] In the middle of my presentation, a woman from the community whispered loudly to her fellow audience members, "He's ruining America!" She spent the remainder of my talk with arms folded, slowly shaking her head in disapproval.

I'm still not popular with the Lincoln crowds, but the episode taught me a good deal about the powerful mythologizing that still lingers around the man. It also reminded me of a lesson from my first Lincoln run-in that I'd forgotten: the Lincoln most encounter may be largely myth, but to many, it is a powerfully necessary myth, and a direct assault is unlikely to persuade anyone to take a more nuanced look. Far more intellectually rigorous deconstructions than mine have met with similar popular hostility.

Sandburg may have played "free and easy with his sources," but his was clearly the Lincoln the public sought.[65] The poet's Lincoln, not the historian's, still dominates. From Sandburg's sweeping prose to Ken Burns's romance of reunion in his wildly influential *Civil War* documentary, the popular move is to make people feel rather than know Lincoln. Still, however fantastical and factually flawed Sandburg's portrait may be, it is hard not to see the path from *The Prairie Years* to *Abraham Lincoln: Vampire Hunter* as a journey of cultural decline.

Currently, I teach at the University of Redlands in Redlands, California, which is also home to the Watchorn Lincoln Memorial Shrine. The shrine boasts "the largest collection of Lincolniana west of the Mississippi open to the public," which, despite its tangle of qualifiers, is a very fine archive (although it does seem oddly situated in a Victorian southern California citrus capital).[66] Yet I'm in no way surprised to find Lincoln still looming over both my work and my residence in complex, fraught ways. Indeed, the shrine's founder, a postbellum immigrant to the United States, saw in Abraham Lincoln the best essence of his adopted land and worthy of enshrinement in a state Lincoln himself never visited.

In the end, perhaps there are some useful intersections between popular and scholarly explorations of Lincoln. Back in the 1950s, in one of his brilliant phone call sketches, comedian Bob Newhart argued that the times required a Lincoln, and had he not been there, the advertising wizards of Madison Avenue would have needed to create one for us, complete with focus group–vetted stovepipe hats and market-tested speeches handwritten on the backs of envelopes.[67] Given the critique of Lincoln as shallow or self-mythologizing, Newhart's schtick seems trenchant as well as funny. And yet, in this bit of midcentury stand-up comedy there is a good deal of hope. Knowingly or not, Hofstadter's tart critique of self-mythologizing found its way into Newhart's gag.

For every earnest attempt to grapple with the "real" Lincoln, there are dozens of folks cheerfully meme-ifying Lincoln by digitizing cool sunglasses onto his dour visage. How can an earnest scholar be heard over the noise of this ubiquitous, powerful, yet nebulous popular Lincoln? How do we cut through the thicket of images thrown off by a playful popular culture with little interest in the words of hand-wringing historians? Even in my own experiences, those pop-culture Lincolns loom large. Especially at a moment when the academy as a whole and historians in particular are vilified as dangerous radicals seeking to destroy what is most precious in American history, I can certainly understand the despair I see among some academics. Historian Carl R. Weinberg asks his fellow teachers and scholars somewhat desperately, "Does Lincoln Still Matter?"[68] Rather, I think his question should be inverted: do we scholars still matter to the public's Lincoln? Why has Du Bois's observation, that Lincoln's centrality to the story of emancipation is overstated, barely cracked the national consciousness eighty-five years after his seminal work?

Outside academic circles, however, we must contend with a kaleidoscope of competing, conflicting Lincolns. If we are to do meaningful public work, we must find ways to acknowledge and demonstrate his historical importance and his personal complexity amidst both the boosterism and the absurdity. Foner describes Lincoln as "perennially relevant; he is always our contemporary,"[69] and this presentism, this "living" Lincoln, holds immense cultural power while simultaneously making the historical Lincoln hard to reach through that pervasive miasma of Lincolniana. We can use his words and his life to explore not only his own time, but also those times that followed. We can be earnest cynics, and we can even take smart, thoughtful pleasure in the quixotic journey of Lincoln *since* his death, as he still walks through our political and popular culture. Whatever scholars do, like the pennies that continue to bear his visage, Lincoln will remain ubiquitous, totemic, and reassuring, even as the actual value and meanings remain complex and conflicted. And I suspect he'll continue to haunt me personally in unexpected ways, as a quixotic national angel who continues to soar across the ages in ever-changing, sometimes useful, sometimes silly, but always interesting, forms.

NOTES

I wish to thank my University of Redlands colleague Kathy Feeley for her advice and input. My former colleagues at Gonzaga University, Eric Cunningham and Michael Leiserson, gave invaluable insight on an earlier lecture that in part inspired this essay. I also want to thank my graduate adviser, Eric Foner, who remains an inspiration for making careful history accessible to a wide audience.

1. To the best of my recollection, the production was *Goodnight Mr. Lincoln*, written by and starring Edward Bryce, which was sporadically performed in and around Connecticut and the New York area beginning in 1979. See, e.g., "Connecticut/This Week," *New York Times*, February 11, 1979; *Westport* (CT) *News*, February 6, 1981.
2. Richard Hofstadter, *The American Political Tradition* (New York: Alfred Knopf, 1948), 93–136.
3. David Donald, "Getting Right with Lincoln," *Atlantic*, 1956; Thessaly La Force, "Lincoln Love," *New Yorker*, January 16, 2009.
4. Eric Foner, "This Guilty Land," *London Review of Books* 42, no. 24 (December 17, 2020), https://www.lrb.co.uk/the-paper/v42/n24/eric-foner/this-guilty-land.
5. Fred Kaplan, "Abraham Lincoln: Breaking Down the Myth of a Perfect President," *Literary Hub*, June 11, 2018, https://lithub.com/abraham-lincoln-breaking-down-the-myth-of-a-perfect-president/.
6. Adam Gopnik, "Angels and Ages: Lincoln's Language and Its Legacy," *New Yorker*, May 28, 2007; see also Adam Gopnik, *Angels and Ages: A Short Book about Darwin, Lincoln, and Modern Life* (New York: Knopf, 2009).
7. James Russell Lowell, "Ode Recited at the Harvard Commemoration, July 21, 1865," in *The Poetical Works of James Russell Lowell in Four Volumes* (Boston: Houghton Mifflin, 1890), 4:22.
8. Gopnik, "Angels and Ages."

9. Smith has been at the helm of the Eisenhower, Ford, and Reagan presidential libraries and was instrumental in the creation of both the Lincoln and Hoover libraries; see http://www.speakers.com/Speaker/Richard-Norton-Smith-speaker-biography.
10. Tom Wheeler, *Mr. Lincoln's T-Mails: How Abraham Lincoln Used the Telegraph to Win the Civil War* (New York: Harper, 2006).
11. Abraham Lincoln, "Address in Independence Hall, Philadelphia, February 22, 1861," in *Selections from the Writings and Addresses of Abraham Lincoln* (New York: Charles E. Merrill, 1910), 41.
12. Abraham Lincoln, "Last Public Address, April 14, 1865," in *The Collected Works of Abraham Lincoln*, ed. Roy P. Basler (New Brunswick, NJ: Rutgers University Press, 1953), 8:402.
13. John Patrick Diggins, *On Hallowed Ground: Abraham Lincoln and the Foundations of American History* (New Haven, CT: Yale University Press, 2000).
14. C. W. French, ed., *Words of Lincoln* (New York: Maynard, Merrill, 1989), 7–8.
15. The NBA launched its "Stay in School Jam" as part of its All-Star weekend festivities in 1991. By 2005, the program was folded into the larger "NBA Cares" initiative, although individual teams such as the Boston Celtics and the Los Angeles Clippers continue programming under the "Stay in School" banner. See David Stern, "A Brief History of NBA All-Star Weekend Weirdness, as Told by YouTube," *Grantland*, February 15, 2013; *NBA All-Star Stay in School Jam*, directed by John Gonzalez (NBA Entertainment, 1992); http://www.nba.com/celtics/community/stay-in-school; http://www.nba.com/clippers/community/education_programs.
16. French, *Words of Lincoln*, 7.
17. The most extensive exploration of this theory can be found in C. A. Tripp's *The Intimate World of Abraham Lincoln* (New York: Basic Books, 2006). A somewhat more measured exploration appears in Charles B. Strozier, *Your Friend Forever, A. Lincoln: The Enduring Friendship of Abraham Lincoln and Joshua Speed* (New York: Columbia University Press, 2016). See also Martin P. Johnson, "Did Abraham Lincoln Sleep with His Bodyguard? Another Look at the Evidence," *Journal of the Abraham Lincoln Association* 27, no. 2 (Summer 2006), 42–55; Dinita Smith, "Finding Homosexual Threads in Lincoln's Legend," *New York Times*, December 16, 2004; and Andrew Sullivan, "Abe and the Boys," *Advocate*, March 1, 2005, 72.
18. Joshua Wolfe Shenk, *Lincoln's Melancholy: How Depression Challenged a President and Fueled His Greatness* (Boston: Houghton Mifflin, 2005); Joshua Wolfe Shenk, "Lincoln's Great Depression," *Atlantic*, October 2005.
19. Gabor S. Boritt and Adam Boritt, "Lincoln and the Marfan Syndrome: The Medical Diagnosis of a Historical Figure," *Civil War History* 29, no. 3 (September 1983): 212–29; see also H. Schwartz, "Abraham Lincoln and Cardiac Decompression: A Preliminary Report," *Western Journal of Medicine* 128, no. 2 (February 1978): 174–77.
20. Foner, "This Guilty Land."
21. *National Treasure 2: Book of Secrets*, directed by John Turteltaub, produced by Jerry Bruckheimer (Walt Disney Pictures, 2007).

22. Steven Poole, "'Winning, Winning, Winning': The Genius of The Donald's Trumpspeak," *Guardian*, March 4, 2016; George Lakoff, "Understanding Trump's Use of Language," *Huffington Post*, August 24, 2016, http://www.huffingtonpost.com/george-lakoff/understanding-trumps-use-_b_11675280.html; Joshua David Stern, "The Loud, Empty Word That Defines President-Elect Trump," *Daily Beast*, January 1, 2017, http://www.thedailybeast.com/the-loud-empty-word-that-defines-president-elect-trump.
23. *Fox News*, July 25, 2017, https://www.facebook.com/FoxNews/videos/10155721782051336/.
24. Philip Gourevitch, "Abraham Lincoln Warned Us About Donald Trump," *New Yorker*, March 15, 2016.
25. Gourevitch is not the only person to find in Lincoln's words warnings that we need constant vigilance to defend the country's fragile political institutions against demagoguery and the frenzied mob. With the very same title as Gourevitch's piece, John C. Waugh points to Lincoln's speech to the Springfield, Illinois, Young Men's Lyceum in 1832 as predicting the state of modern American politics. See John C. Waugh, "Abraham Lincoln Warned Us About Donald Trump," *History News Network*, September 23, 2018, https://historynewsnetwork.org/article/169901.
26. David Margolick, "Penny Foolish," *New York Times*, February 11, 2007.
27. On the production costs of pennies, see Katherine Ellen Foley, "The U.S. Mint Lost $69 Million Making Pennies Last Year," *Government Executive*, July 11, 2018, https://www.govexec.com/management/2018/07/us-mint-lost-69-million-making-pennies-last-year/149621/.
28. Thomas Vinciguerra, "Now If Only We Could Mint Lincoln Himself," *New York Times*, February 7, 2009.
29. James Hurt, "Sandburg's Lincoln Within History," *Journal of the Abraham Lincoln Association* 20, no. 1 (Winter 1999): 55.
30. https://www.knox.edu/about-knox/lincoln-studies-center.
31. For a recent popular volume in this vein, see Thomas DiLorenzo, *Lincoln Unmasked: What You're Not Supposed to Know About Dishonest Abe* (New York: Crown Forum, 2006); for a more nuanced depiction of the long shadow of anti-Lincoln chic both outside and within the academy, see Tony Horwitz, *Confederates in the Attic: Dispatches from the Unfinished Civil War* (New York: Vintage, 1999), especially 145–56.
32. Eugene Genovese, *The World the Slaveholders Made: Two Essays in Interpretation* (1969; repr., Hanover, NH: Wesleyan University Press, 1988).
33. Hermann Richard Muelder, *Missionaries and Muckrakers: The First Hundred Years of Knox College* (Champaign: University of Illinois Press, 1984), 19.
34. Rodney O. Davis and Douglas Wilson, eds., *The Lincoln-Douglas Debates: The Lincoln Studies Center Edition* (Champaign: University of Illinois Press, 2008), 174.
35. Perhaps even more interesting is how the Lincoln-Douglas debates have faded in the national consciousness even as the increasingly content-less Lincoln continues to rise. Once the stuff of grammar school memorization drills and a central demonstration of the greatness of American rhetoric, the debates are increasingly relegated to the cultural gulag of late-night C-SPAN reruns. Even the 2008 sesquicentennial only provided a small bump.

36. Eric Foner, *The Fiery Trial: Abraham Lincoln and American Slavery* (New York: Norton, 2010), 258–61; Michael J. Douma, "The Lincoln Administration's Negotiations to Colonize African Americans in Dutch Suriname," *Civil War History* 61, no. 2 (June 2015): 111–37.
37. Charles B. Dew, *The Making of a Racist: A Southerner Reflects on Family, History, and the Slave Trade* (Charlottesville: University of Virginia Press, 2016), 62.
38. Tony Pipolo, "Hero or Demagogue? Images of Lincoln in American Film," *Cinéste* 35, no. 1 (Winter 2009): 15.
39. Hofstadter, *American Political Tradition*, 133.
40. David Herbert Donald, *Lincoln* (New York: Simon and Schuster, 1996), 14.
41. Abraham Lincoln, "First Inaugural Address, March 4, 1861," in Basler, *Collected Works*, 4:271.
42. Interestingly, legend often has it that Lincoln laid blame for the war elsewhere, blaming a woman for all that bloodshed. In an oft-repeated but likely apocryphal quip, Lincoln is said to have greeted Harriet Beecher Stowe in 1862 by saying, "So you're the little woman who wrote the book that made this great war!" Although scholars have repeatedly challenged (if not wholly debunked) this claim, it lives on as an oddly gendered piece of Lincoln's (and Stowe's) lore. See Daniel R. Vollaro, "Lincoln, Stowe, and the 'Little Woman/Great War' Story: The Making, and Breaking, of a Great American Anecdote," *Journal of the Abraham Lincoln Association* 30, no. 1 (Winter 2009): 18–34.
43. Fourth Joint Debate, at Charleston, September 18, 1858, in *Political Debates Between Hon. Abraham Lincoln and Hon. Stephen A. Douglas, in the Celebrated Campaign of 1858 in Illinois: Including the Preceding Speeches of Each at Chicago, Springfield, Etc., Also the Two Great Speeches of Mr. Lincoln in Ohio, in 1859, as Carefully Prepared by the Reporter of Each Party and Published at the Times of Their Delivery* (Columbus, OH: Foster, Follett, 1860), 136.
44. Wendell Philips, quoted in Donald, "Getting Right with Lincoln."
45. Abraham Lincoln, "Address Delivered at the Dedication of the Cemetery at Gettysburg," November 19, 1863, in Basler, *Collected Works*, 7:22.
46. W. E. B. Du Bois, *Black Reconstruction* (1935; repr., New York: Touchstone, 1995), 79–83.
47. Charles B. Dew, *Apostles of Disunion* (Charlottesville: University of Virginia Press, 2001), 4–81.
48. Du Bois, *Black Reconstruction*, 55–126.
49. See Teju Cole, "The White-Savior Industrial Complex," *Atlantic*, March 21, 2012.
50. Foner, "This Guilty Land."
51. Foner, *Fiery Trial*, xv; on Foner's earlier reluctance to take on Lincoln directly, see *Fiery Trial*, 337.
52. http://www.lincolnpresenters.net/.
53. Although I have still seen no competition as a John Quincy Adams impersonator, I do note that the twitter account that excerpts his diary, @JQAdams_MHS, run by the Massachusetts Historical Society, has over 26,000 followers, so maybe this market *can* be tapped.
54. Barry Schwartz, *Abraham Lincoln and the Forge of National Memory* (Chicago: University of Chicago Press, 2000), 256.

55. Sarah Vowell, *Assassination Vacation* (New York: Simon and Schuster, 2005), 49–50.
56. *Memento Mori* (portrait of Lincoln within a black border containing 13 stars), 1865, Alfred Whital Stern Collection of Lincolniana, Library of Congress, photograph, https://www.loc.gov/item/scsm000466/.
57. Eric Foner, *Reconstruction: America's Unfinished Revolution* (New York: HarperCollins, 1988).
58. On the wild legal world of profiting off dead celebrities, see Peter Colin Jr., "Elvis and Prince: Personality Rights Guidance for Dead Celebrities and the Lawyers and Legislatures Who Protect Them," *National Law Review* 6, no. 284 (October 10, 2016).
59. Timur Bekmambetov, quoted in Scott Meslow, "An Icon Divided: Abraham Lincoln's Dual Pop-Culture Legacy," *Atlantic*, June 22, 2012.
60. Seth Grahame-Smith, *Abraham Lincoln, Vampire Hunter* (New York: Grand Central Publishing, 2010); *Abraham Lincoln: Vampire Hunter*, directed by Timur Bekmambetov, produced by Tim Burton (20th Century Fox, 2012).
61. Vowell, *Assassination Vacation*, 21.
62. They should, though. Bertelli, who was sold his plot by accident and managed to keep it despite Oak Ridge Cemetery's litigious attempts to undo the sale, would, for years before his death, sit atop his own headstone cheerfully playing the accordion to bemused Lincoln pilgrims. Actually, he is not buried next to Lincoln; his military service permitted him to be interred in a military cemetery at Camp Butler, but he apparently did bury some of his beloved squeezeboxes in the aboveground crypt just up the path from Lincoln's memorial. Jerome Pohlem, *Oddball Illinois* (Chicago: Chicago Review Press, 2000), 211; Edward J. Russo and Curtis R. Mann, *Oak Ridge Cemetery* (Mount Pleasant, SC: Arcadia, 2009), 211.
63. Dion, "Abraham, Martin and John," by Dick Hollar, Laurie Records LR 3646, 1968.
64. Matthew Raffety and Michael Leiserson, "Linked to Great Thinkers: What Can We Learn from Lincoln?" Gonzaga University, March 27, 2008; see also Meg Houlihan, "Lincoln's Legacy the Subject of Upcoming Lecture," *Gonzaga Bulletin*, March 17, 2008.
65. Hurt, "Sandburg's Lincoln Within History," 57.
66. http://www.lincolnshrine.org.
67. Bob Newhart, "Abe Lincoln vs. Madison Avenue," *The Button-Down Mind of Bob Newhart*, Track 1, Warner Brothers, 1960.
68. Carl R. Weinberg, "Does Lincoln Still Matter?" *OAH Magazine of History* 23, no. 1 (January 2009): 64.
69. Foner, *Fiery Trial*, xv.

6

IN SEARCH OF THE COSTS OF SEGREGATION

ELIZABETH A. HERBIN-TRIANT

In the 1954 opinion of the Supreme Court in *Brown v. Board of Education*, Chief Justice Earl Warren laid out the argument that would come to shape the way Americans thought about segregation. "To separate [black children] from others of similar age and qualifications solely because of their race," Warren wrote, "generates a feeling of inferiority as to their status in the community that may affect their hearts and minds in a way unlikely ever to be undone."[1] *Brown* has, of course, proven to be important in many ways—primarily as a first step toward undoing our segregated public education system, a process yet to be completed. It has also shaped how Americans have thought about the problem of segregation. The problem, according to *Brown*, was that it caused psychological harm.[2]

Americans accepted this idea, at least up to a certain point. Daniel Patrick Moynihan, a sociologist working as assistant secretary of labor who was influenced by *Brown*, advanced the "damage thesis" in his report *The Negro Family: The Case for National Action* (1965). The psychological damage caused by three centuries of oppression, Moynihan claimed, was responsible for problems within the black community that led to "aberrant, inadequate, or antisocial behavior that . . . serves to perpetuate the cycle of poverty and deprivation." Middle-class African Americans who might have been capable of escaping such patterns of behavior had trouble doing so, according to Moynihan, because they were "constantly exposed to the pathology of the disturbed group" due to residential segregation.[3]

Segregation did hurt the souls of black people, of course, and it continues to do so—though, as numerous critics of Moynihan have pointed out, this did not mean that African Americans were any more damaged than other people (after all, segregation hurt white people, too).[4] Fortitude, tenacity, and resilience partially protected African Americans. But the public's narrow focus on how segregation harmed the psyches of Americans of African descent is a problem because it distracts from another pernicious effect of segregation. Segregation also made the activities undertaken by African Americans—from renting property to gaining an education—more expensive for them, and it excluded them from opportunities to make economic advances.[5]

In the International Civil Rights Center and Museum in Greensboro, North Carolina, sits a perfect example in microcosm of this economic effect, a Coca-Cola dispenser that was used in segregated waiting rooms. One side of the machine dispensed soda to buyers in the white waiting room for 5 cents, while the other side sold African Americans the same soda for 10 cents in a separate waiting room.[6] Other examples showing costs associated with segregation were reported in *The Crisis*, the journal of the NAACP, in a March 1915 column:

> In Atlanta, the white Alkahest Lyceum Course sold balcony tickets to colored teachers and then gave them seats in the gallery despite their protests. . . .
>
> The city of Richmond has finally allowed a colored church to buy a former white church, but has ordered it to change its entrance so that its worshippers shall not enter from a "white" street. . . .
>
> It is claimed that in Baltimore segregation is a boon to real estate sharks who are raising the rentals at least 20 percent in the restricted Negro districts.[7]

What were the costs imposed here? The teachers in Atlanta purchased more expensive balcony tickets but were seated in a section with less valuable seats. Presumably, they did not regain the difference in value between the balcony and gallery seats. Black teachers, considered part of the middle class yet never well compensated and also paid less than white teachers, resented donating portions of their income to institutions like the Alkahest Lyceum.[8] Richmond, which, like Baltimore, had a residential segregation ordinance in place that limited where African Americans could purchase property, required that a black church take on the expense of moving its entrance—an expense that could be substantial if there was no entrance already fronting a different street. Baltimore's residential segregation ordinance limited African Americans to majority-black blocks. Confined to certain neighborhoods, African Americans looking to purchase or rent homes had to pay whatever prices were charged within that area—and the prices charged were often much higher than that of comparable property in white neighborhoods.[9] They were kept from enjoying benefits of the free market such as lower prices due to competition.

Ta-Nehisi Coates has described segregation as "plunder"—as the redistribution of African American wealth to white people and the institutions that operated to benefit white people. The examples noted in *The Crisis* certainly fit that description. Coates's perception of Jim Crow, slavery, and an unjust incarceration system as systems of plunder is an important part of his argument in favor of reparations.[10] Indeed, it is the reparations literature more than the historical scholarship on segregation that has paid attention to the financial costs of segregation. Sociologist Joe R. Feagin, for example, also focusing on reparations, argues that the effects of the plundering of African Americans have been passed from one generation to the next, resulting in a wealth gap between white and black Americans. In his view, the plundering of African Americans has advantaged white Americans: "Today, the relative prosperity, long life expectancies, and high standard of living of white Americans are significantly rooted in centuries of exploitation and impoverishment of African Americans and other Americans of color."[11]

The advantages enjoyed by white Americans have been codified in law, allowing white people access to a set of opportunities and legal protections as well as the right to exclude nonwhites from these benefits.[12]

White privilege reproduces itself outside the confines of the law, too, through what Daria Roithmayr calls the "lock-in model," as individuals make "everyday decisions" (to, for example, pay for their children's college education, or refer a friend for a job). According to this theory, "competitive advantage can begin to automatically reproduce itself over time until the advantage eventually becomes insurmountable."[13] Ira Katznelson describes the privileges that attend whiteness as an "affirmative action" for whites.[14]

Historians have been aware of segregation as a system with economic consequences for decades, and scholars in other fields have also grappled with this idea.[15] Yet they tend to ignore Jim Crow as an economic system (by which I mean a system that influences what work people do, how well they are compensated for their labor, and what standard of living they are able to afford)—with some exceptions, including those historians looking at residential segregation, who certainly address topics like the higher rents paid for worse housing in segregated neighborhoods.[16] Important work has been done on the costs of slavery to the enslaved people who were torn away from their families by sales, were subjected to increasingly harsh violence as cotton growers sought to extract more work to meet expanding demand, and left slavery with "nothing but freedom" and little prospect of gaining wealth.[17] Slavery functioned by stealing the labor of enslaved people and denying them ownership of resources, so it makes sense that scholars would understand it as an economic system. But Jim Crow did these things, too.

Historians have investigated the when, why, and how of Jim Crow—including the psychological boost and social advantages given to white workers as African Americans were relegated to separate spaces (described as the "wages of whiteness") and the corresponding psychological drag on black children and adults, the different experiences of black men and women under segregation, the ways that southerners both white and black navigated a segregated world by "performing" Jim Crow, the operation of segregation in anonymous cities as compared to more intimate rural communities in the South, and the often beneficial effects of segregation on African American businesses and churches.[18]

They tend to treat Jim Crow almost exclusively as a legal, political, and cultural system—shaping where African Americans went, whether they voted, and how they acted in public. One historian, for example, points to the most devastating "collective cost" of segregation as an anemic culture in which Americans were unable "to imagine an inclusive America."[19]

Let us pause to consider another important aspect of Jim Crow—to think of it as an economic system that imposed financial burdens on African Americans.[20] I will not attempt to tally these costs, but will rather point to some of the shadows where these costs lie, focusing on the segregation of public accommodations, neighborhoods, and schools.[21] Rather than being isolated examples, these are elements of a broad system of economic confiscation and exclusion—a system that helped to create America's racial wealth gap. My hope is that historians will investigate more fully how Jim Crow enriched some people at the expense of others, and in doing so will broaden the discussion of segregation beyond its psychological and social impact.

There is a growing literature on "racial capitalism," which describes racism as an essential component of capitalism, with capitalist enterprises thriving thanks to the subjection of nonwhite people to economic exploitation.[22] As Walter Johnson points out, for example, textile production flourished in the antebellum period only because enslaved African Americans produced cheap cotton.[23] At the same time that racism made nonwhite people subject to violence and exploitation, white people gained advantages from their whiteness and felt entitled to state protection of these benefits; as W. E. B. Du Bois put it, they believed that "whiteness is the ownership of the earth forever and ever."[24] Indeed, whiteness is so valuable—under slavery, their color gave whites the right to own black people and the fruits of their labor, and also to possess the land of Native Americans—that it has functioned as a type of "property" protected by law, according to Cheryl I. Harris. As Harris explains, "it was solely through being white that property could be acquired and secured under law."[25] What I propose fits within this literature: exploring the economic costs associated with being African American in the context of Jim Crow.[26] To do this, we need to rethink Jim Crow as a system that granted whites a type of property—a right to "public" resources like libraries and universities, as well as housing loans, better housing stock, and better-funded schools—that it denied to African Americans.[27]

Southern states enacted the first Jim Crow laws during Reconstruction, often segregating public schools and prohibiting interracial marriage, and the bulk of them just after the turn of the twentieth century.[28] Gilbert Stephenson, a contemporary observer and attorney, saw a pattern in Jim Crow laws. The first set of laws (such as the Black Codes), passed shortly after the Civil War, sought to control the labor of black people by "regulating the relations of the master and his colored apprentice, of the employer and his colored laborer" and "restrict[ing] the movement of negroes." Stephenson considered these first laws different in nature from later laws, which worked to "prevent any sort of social association between the races."[29]

The segregation of public space served a number of purposes beyond ensuring that "social association" did not take place. As historians understand it, it worked to "solidify racial difference," to mark black and white people as different, and one as inferior to the other, after the institution of slavery had ended.[30] Glenda Gilmore describes the segregation of public space as essential in reining in upwardly mobile blacks and keeping them in "their place"—a place defined by low social status, low income, inability to vote, and low expectations. "As a living testament to capability, successful African Americans' lives provided a perpetual affront to whites," Gilmore argues. "The black lawyer, doctor, preacher, or teacher represented someone out of his or her place. The danger lay not in their numbers, but in the aspirations they inspired in their fellow African Americans and the proof they gave to the white lie of inherent African inferiority."[31]

Upwardly mobile African Americans were a new "problem" in the postbellum South. Grace Elizabeth Hale presents segregation as a way of creating order in a modern America that was working through the changes wrought by the Civil War and its aftermath. Stephen Berrey points to the discomfort brought about as a generation of African

Americans that had never been enslaved entered adulthood, "occup[ying] new spaces" as well as "familiar spaces in new ways." Troubled by the new experience of "[finding] themselves in public spaces where African Americans insisted on playing the part of social equals," whites looked to segregation, which provided roles for each race to play in a type of "performance." This was a performance with high stakes, as the consequences for failing to perform or flubbing one's performance could include harassment, the destruction of property, or lynching.[32]

There was more to it than just marking one group as superior to the other. According to Paul Escott, segregation was also meant to help bring about disfranchisement, which was one of the larger aims of Democrats in the South. Wishing to rein in black voters and their white allies in the Republican and Populist Parties, the Democratic leadership envisioned segregation as a way of preventing lower-class whites from aligning themselves with black voters. "The purpose of an 1899 Jim Crow law covering trains and steamboats" in North Carolina, Escott argues, "was in major degree to stigmatize the Negro race and thereby stigmatize all cooperation with Negroes. . . . An expanding system of segregation . . . placed blacks in an official pariah caste." It also boosted the self-esteem of poor whites, Escott points out, though this was more "by-product" than intention.[33]

Creating a hierarchy with one group permanently on the bottom also proved beneficial for employers. After the end of slavery, white southerners had attempted to replace slavery with other methods of controlling the labor of black people. They forced African Americans to sign labor contracts through Black Codes and lynched thousands of black people, which created a climate of fear that made sharecroppers and tenants less likely to fight against the terms of their labor, for example.[34] White southerners also turned to segregation, which kept black people poor and lacking in opportunities so that they would have to accept low-paying agricultural and industrial jobs. Stuck in jobs that were relegated to people on the bottom tier, with no prospects of advancement, African Americans were made a class of low-paid workers. When Robert Penn Warren asked one black man, "What are the white man's reasons for segregation?" he responded, "so the white man can have cheap labor, can make the money."[35] An article in *The Crisis* explained this phenomenon.

> [African Americans] may be placed in such positions as the white men in power choose for them, and may be paid such a wage as the same powerful white men deem suitable for a Negro. This has happened so often in the South as to be entirely familiar to every southern colored laborer. The Southern Railway, for instance, has two scales of wages—one for its white and one for its colored workers; the latter, when doing the same work, receive only two-thirds of the amount received by the white employees. Colored waiters are a segregated group and receive a smaller wage than white.[36]

Segregated public spaces excluded black people from institutions and amenities that they had helped to fund through their tax dollars. As contemporary observer Stetson Kennedy pointed out, "Virtually all of the public swimming areas in the segregated territory have been reserved for whites only, including those which have been purchased and operated with tax money"—money coming from white and black taxpayers.[37] Even more significantly, as Ta-Nehisi Coates notes, black would-be college students who were denied education at public universities were also robbed of the education their families paid for through taxes.[38] To give himself an education using his local public library, Richard Wright had to borrow a library card from a white man and then pretend that the books he checked out were requested by this white man.[39] In all of these examples, money was taken from African Americans and funneled into "public" resources reserved for the use of white people.[40]

After segregating public spaces, segregationists proposed ordinances to separate the black and white inhabitants of cities. They argued that segregating public space and segregating private property were similar, that if they could do one, then they should also be able to do the other. As one supporter of residential segregation laws put it, "Negro children are not allowed to attend school with whites; Negroes do not sit in the same cars, loaf in the same depots and feed at the same hotels as the white folks. Why, then, should landlords be allowed to impose them on white [residents]?"[41] A number of southern cities, including Baltimore, Winston-Salem, and Atlanta, put in place residential segregation ordinances between 1910 and 1917. These ordinances generally forbade African Americans from moving onto majority-white blocks and white people from moving onto majority-black blocks. People who already owned property on a block that was not of their racial designation were allowed to reside on that property. The rationale given for these laws was that they would prevent "race conflict" (most often seen when white people responded with violence to African Americans moving into their neighborhoods, and it is worth noting that the segregation laws in a sense rewarded these people for their violence). The laws would also help white owners maintain their property values (which declined when white owners dumped their properties on the market as African Americans moved in).[42]

After their city enacted an ordinance, the black community in Louisville, Kentucky, formed a branch of the NAACP and prepared for a legal battle. This battle began with an elaborate test case in which a white man, Charles H. Buchanan, sued a black man, William Warley, for breach of contract. Warley was editor of the *Louisville News*, a newspaper that demanded justice for African Americans, and an active member of the local NAACP; he had agreed to purchase property from Buchanan but had then backed out. A provision in the contract stated that Warley was not obligated to purchase the property if he could not reside there, and the segregation ordinance prevented Warley from living on the property, which was located on a majority-white block. Meanwhile, however, because the property was near other property owned by African Americans, white buyers had no interest in it. As a result, Buchanan could not sell his property to black or white buyers, and his counsel argued that he was thus deprived of his property. Buchanan's lawyers viewed the city's ordinance as a violation of the Fourteenth Amendment, focusing on the violation of Buchanan's property rights without due process of law. The case went up to the Supreme Court, which agreed with the case made by Buchanan's team and declared residential segregation laws unconstitutional in 1917.[43] The plundering of African Americans by segregation could be ignored, but when the same thing happened to whites—as had happened to Charles Buchanan—the law had gone too far.

At the same time that ordinances were segregating cities, planners were designing segregated suburbs, often utilizing restrictive covenants that prohibited property owners from selling their property to nonwhites. Focusing on the Roland Park Company in Baltimore, Paige Glotzer argues in *How the Suburbs Were Segregated* that planners designed segregated suburbs to "attract residents and augment sales."[44] The money made through selling segregated real estate enriched whites not just in the United States but also in Britain, home to many of the Roland Park Company's investors.

It was not just municipal governments and companies like Roland Park that supported residential segregation. The federal government also played a key role in creating segregated neighborhoods. Starting during the New Deal, the Home Owners' Loan Corporation and the Federal Housing Administration appraised the credit-worthiness of neighborhoods by labeling black and mixed-race neighborhoods as risky, whether the African Americans living there were poor or well-to-do. This process, called redlining, meant that black homebuyers had difficulty qualifying for government-backed loans. They had to turn to predatory private loans.[45]

However residential segregation came about, it extracted a price. African American homebuyers saw segregation draw money from their pockets at different steps in the process of buying property, from agreeing to a price (often higher in African American neighborhoods, as there was more demand than housing stock) to acquiring a loan (at higher interest rates) to receiving municipal services (or not) at their new homes.

Thanks to segregation ordinances, restrictive covenants, the unwillingness of realtors to show them properties in white neighborhoods, or other measures, African Americans found themselves living in all-black neighborhoods. It was not a question of where they could afford to live, but where they were allowed to live. Booker T. Washington, trying to explain why black people wished to move out of these neighborhoods, focused on the lack of basic services and the fact that vice was allowed to flourish in black neighborhoods:

> The negro objects to being segregated because it usually means that he will receive inferior accommodations in return for the taxes he pays. If the negro is segregated, it will probably mean that the sewerage in his part of the city will be inferior; that the streets and sidewalks will be neglected, that the street lighting will be poor; that his section of the city will not be kept in order by the police and other authorities, and that the "undesirables" of other races [such as prostitutes] will be placed near him, thereby making it difficult for him to rear his family in decency. It should always be kept in mind that while the negro may not be directly a large taxpayer, he does pay large taxes indirectly. In the last analysis, all will agree that the man who pays house rent pays large taxes, for the price paid for the rent includes payment of the taxes on the property.[46]

The last point, about the taxes paid by African Americans, draws attention again to African Americans' not getting their money's worth out of their tax dollars. Tax dollars were taken from them directly (as property owners, through taxes) or indirectly (as renters, through rent) for municipal services, but little was given them in return.

Black buyers, even while they received fewer city services, also found themselves paying above the white market rate for properties as "blockbusting" took place. Realtors purchased properties from a few white people and then sold them at inflated prices to blacks eager to move into better housing stock. As these black buyers moved in, white homeowners fled, selling their property to realtors at low prices. These properties were then resold to blacks at high prices. Blockbusting was quite lucrative for realtors.[47] Renters, too, lost money in paying higher rents for properties in segregated neighborhoods. African Americans, restricted to neighborhoods of limited size that were often bursting at the seams, found that realtors took advantage of their lack of other options by hiking up prices. Blacks paid more for housing stock that would have rented for lower prices in white neighborhoods.

As one Baltimore newspaper reported, "Colored people find themselves restricted to a small section of the city. Rents have advanced 25 per cent on them, while desirable houses a few squares away rent for less." Of course, buyers and renters who paid more money for their homes then had less money available to spend on their other expenses (including, for buyers, the principal on their property). Black people paid more in a number of cities that found themselves attracting migrants—such as Winston-Salem and New York City—as industrial jobs and the promise of better education for their children lured African Americans from the rural South to cities.[48]

Limited to "ghettoes" because of practices like redlining, by the 1970s African Americans became targets of what Keeanga-Yamahtta Taylor terms "predatory inclusion." According to Taylor, "far from being a static site of dilapidation and ruin, the urban core was becoming an attractive place of unparalleled opportunity, a new frontier of economic investment and extraction for the real estate and banking industries." These industries sought out poor black women for high-interest loans, knowing that these borrowers were likely to "fail to keep up their home payments and slip into foreclosure." It was their isolation in segregated neighborhoods and the poverty associated with living in the ghetto that made these borrowers targets for unscrupulous capitalists.[49]

The economic consequences of segregation are visible, too, in education. White southerners did not favor universal public schooling for African Americans, as they thought it spoiled good field hands. This meant that black southerners had to scrape together what money they could to educate their children. In many places in the South, there were no schools for black children; by 1900, only 36 percent of black children ages five to fourteen attended school. The education of black children conflicted with the desire of white landowners to use cheap labor to plant and harvest their crops; children were the cheapest workers available, and the crops would not wait for the school term to finish up.[50]

By the 1910s, aware that the desire to educate their children was one factor propelling black workers to migrate to the North, white leaders in the South had become somewhat more open to black education. The Julius Rosenwald Fund sent money from the North to help pay for the construction of schools for black children in the rural South (African Americans also contributed cash, labor, and tax dollars), and by the 1930s, a system of education was in place for African Americans. Outside funding was essential in getting schools for black children, as southern white leaders would not use the funds contributed by black taxpayers for black schools. After disfranchisement, less and less money was put toward educating black students, as African Americans could not advocate for themselves politically. In the South between 1900 and 1910 (the years during which disfranchisement was rolled out), less money was spent on black education per student, school terms for black students were shortened, and salaries paid to black teachers were cut. Less money was spent on the education of African Americans than blacks paid in tax dollars; the money that black taxpayers paid into the system was siphoned off for white schools. This trend meant that African Americans experienced "double taxation," according to James D. Anderson. "Southern public school authorities diverted school taxes largely to the development of white public education," and blacks responded by "making private contributions to finance public schools." In order to qualify for any government contribution, they handed ownership of these schools over to the state.[51]

By February of 1916, ninety-two schools for black students in the South had been built using Rosenwald funds and money from other sources. Of the $103,783 spent on these schools, Rosenwald contributed $33,821, public tax funds of $16,550 were used, local whites chipped in $6,209, and African Americans contributed $47,203.[52] These numbers should give us pause. African Americans, forced to educate their children separately from the children of their white neighbors, donated cash, land, and labor for the construction of their local schools. As Anderson puts it, "rural black southerners . . . paid from their limited resources a tremendous private cost for their 'public' education." He quotes a Rosenwald school agent who argued that funds for the schools came not so much from the Rosenwald Fund as from "people who represented a poor working class, men who worked at furnaces, women who washed and ironed for white people, and children who chopped cotton in the heat of the day for money to go in their snuff boxes [donated to the construction projects]."[53]

In her poem "Women," Alice Walker describes the determination of African Americans—women in particular—to educate their children: "How they battered down/Doors/And ironed/Starched white/Shirts/How they led/Armies/Headragged generals/Across mined/Fields/Booby-trapped/Ditches/To discover books/Desks/A place for us/How they knew what/We/*Must* know/Without knowing a page/Of it/Themselves."[54] These women—these "generals"—waged war against Jim Crow to help the next generation access education, using the money earned through difficult jobs like hand-laundering clothing to pay for the construction of schools.

According to Adam Fairclough, black schools, even while they were short on resources, were successful in some ways (such as helping to strengthen black communities) and often inspired pride in students rather than, as many assume, causing feelings of inferiority.[55] But segregated schooling did exact a cost, and it continues to do so. African American students often attend underfunded schools in inner cities, where they receive educations inferior to those offered in nearby suburbs and where they are not prepared to get into or do well in college. By attending these schools, black students, we can assume, miss out on the opportunity to cultivate what Pierre Bourdieu calls the "cultural capital" and "social capital" that would allow them to more successfully network with elites once they enter the workforce (Bourdieu does not address racial segregation in his discussion of the transmission of elite status). Cultural capital includes things like accent, tastes, and modes of behavior—qualities that make someone seem to fit within a particular group or class, while social capital describes a person's social network. It is at the moment of entering the workforce that these other types of capital most directly connect to "economic capital" (Bourdieu describes elites as hiding the extent to which these other forms of capital are "convertible" to economic capital, as they want privilege to seem tied to merit). According to sociologist Lauren Rivera, the people responsible for hiring at high-status companies tend to prioritize cultural fit when considering job candidates. Job candidates who lack the cultural signifiers of "fit" are less likely to be hired for elite jobs. Nancy DiTomaso connects social capital to employment, offering the insight that "much of the 'action' in reproducing racial inequality comes in the form of advantages, that is, in the positive things that whites do for each other," rather than in the form of discrimination. How much status and income have been lost to capable African Americans who might have achieved more had they been given a decent education and access to the culture of whites?[56]

Brown v. Board shows the psychological damage that segregation can do to children. But what are the economic consequences (including through damage to health) of a "feeling of inferiority," or of what Nell Irvin Painter calls "soul murder"?[57] In *The Fire Next Time*, James Baldwin mentions the low expectations that white society held for African Americans; he tells his young nephew, "You were not expected to aspire to excellence: you were expected to make peace with mediocrity." The effect of low expectations, of course, is that often one is unable to see oneself in positions beyond the lowest tier. Jim Crow, in putting blacks on the lowest level of society and expecting that they stay there, dampened their aspirations.[58] While it may be impossible to measure the cost of low aspirations—the lost esteem and pay due to the doctors and lawyers and professors who might have been—there is indeed a cost.

Historians have acknowledged that residential segregation has hindered African Americans from building up wealth—that African Americans' property has been devalued and their economic opportunities limited by segregation.[59] But the economic toll of Jim Crow is much broader than this. The types of segregation that limit social opportunities (as in theaters or churches) or intellectual opportunities (as in schools or libraries) have economic consequences, and the toll on psychological and physical health also creates economic costs. So why does the economic aspect of Jim Crow not get the attention it deserves?

Part of the problem is that there are incorrect or inadequate assumptions at play: that Jim Crow was driven by racism alone, by a distaste for African Americans and fear of intimacy with them. Racism is not sufficient in explaining this program. The larger story includes elites who maligned and segregated African Americans to justify disfranchising them and underpaying them in the jobs set aside for them, as well as poor and middling whites who enjoyed elevated standing in their communities compared to African Americans and, with this, access to better jobs.[60] Surely, too, the sources are difficult for historians to access.

For example, while enslavers left account books showing how much labor they stole each day from the people they owned, it is difficult to quantify the wages lost due to a system of segregation that labeled certain jobs "black-only" and others "white-only."[61] The larger problem is that the most significant costs of segregation are related to activities that never happened because segregation prevented them from happening—such as, for example, African Americans taking advantage of better schools and networking opportunities to advance in society. Ascertaining the economic toll of Jim Crow is a daunting task, but an essential one for those of us who wish to understand the extent of inequality in America and the myriad ways that white supremacy has plundered African Americans over the generations.

NOTES

For helpful feedback on this essay, I thank Devin Fergus, Kenneth Mack, Tony Szczesiul, and the Massachusetts Historical Society's seminar in Modern American History and Culture. Portions of this essay were previously published in Elizabeth A. Herbin-Triant, *Threatening Property: Race, Class, and Campaigns to Legislate Jim Crow Neighborhoods* (New York: Columbia University Press, 2019).

1. *Brown v. Board of Education of Topeka*, 347 U.S. 483 (1954), 494.
2. While the *Brown* decision focused on the psychological damage caused by segregation, Gavin Wright points out that the case itself was brought forward for economic reasons: African Americans viewed education as an engine of economic mobility, and they wanted their children to enjoy full access to this engine. Gavin Wright, *Sharing the Prize: The Economics of the Civil Rights Revolution in the American South* (Cambridge, MA: Harvard University Press, 2013), 11.

   There are a number of excellent studies of the *Brown* case, including Richard Kluger, *Simple Justice: The History of* Brown v. Board of Education *and Black America's Struggle for Equality* (New York: Knopf, 2004); James T. Patterson, Brown v. Board of Education: *A Civil Rights Milestone and Its Troubled Legacy* (New York: Oxford University Press, 2001); and Mark V. Tushnet, *Making Civil Rights Law: Thurgood Marshall and the Supreme Court, 1936–1961* (New York: Oxford University Press, 1994).

   Brown was not the first to stress the psychological damage done by Jim Crow. Carter G. Woodson, for example, focused not on segregation per se but on what white and black schools taught their students about African Americans; he wrote, "The same educational process which inspires and stimulates the oppressor with the thought that he is everything and has accomplished everything worth while, depresses and crushes at the same time the spark of genius in the Negro by making him feel that his race does not amount to much and never will measure up to the standards of other peoples." Woodson, *The Mis-Education of the Negro* (Mineola, NY: Dover Publications, 2005), ix–x.

3. *The Negro Family: The Case for National Action* (Washington, DC: Office of Policy Planning and Research, U.S. Department of Labor, 1965). See https://www.theatlantic.com/politics/archive/2015/09/the-moynihan-report-an-annotated-edition/404632/#Chapter%20IV, accessed January 22, 2018. See also Daryl Scott, *Contempt and Pity: Social Policy and the Image of the Damaged Black Psyche, 1880–1996* (Chapel Hill: University of North Carolina Press, 1997), especially chapter 7; and James T. Patterson, *Freedom Is Not Enough: The Moynihan Report and America's Struggle over Black Family Life, from LBJ to Obama* (New York: Basic Books, 2010).
4. On the criticism of the Moynihan Report, see Daniel Geary, "Introduction," in *Beyond Civil Rights: The Moynihan Report and Its Legacy* (Philadelphia: University of Pennsylvania Press, 2015). Segregation also damaged white people, as was pointed out by Kenneth Clark, one of the psychologists upon whose research *Brown* relied. Clark lamented the fact that the Supreme Court in the *Brown* decision did not discuss "the equally dehumanizing educational and human damage inflicted upon white children." Kenneth B. Clark, "The Brown Decision: Racism, Education, and Human Values," *Journal of Negro Education* 57, no. 2 (Spring 1988): 131.
5. Cheryl I. Harris points out that the harm created by segregation went beyond psychological damage—that "legalized race segregation structured material inequalities into all socioeconomic relations and institutions including publicly funded schools." She considers it a mistake, then, that *Brown* did not "expose the problem of substantive inequality in material terms produced by white domination and race segregation." She does not flesh out these "material" inequalities. Harris, "Whiteness as Property," *Harvard Law Review* 106, no. 8 (June 1993): 1709–91, 1752.
6. According to museum staff, Coca-Cola intended for white and black buyers to pay the same amount for their soft drinks, but people refitted the machines to charge more for African Americans; sometimes they also removed the refrigeration apparatus on the side that served black customers. Staff also stated that Coca-Cola has asked to buy the machine on display to remove it from public view.
7. "The Ghetto," *The Crisis* 9, no. 5 (March 1915): 220.
8. On teacher pay, see Adam Fairclough, *A Class of Their Own: Black Teachers in the Segregated South* (Cambridge, MA: Harvard University Press, 2007), 4.
9. On Baltimore's residential segregation ordinance, see Gretchen Boger, "The Meaning of Neighborhood in the Modern City: Baltimore's Residential Segregation Ordinances, 1910–1913," *Journal of Urban History* 35 (January 2009): 236–58; Garrett Power, "Apartheid Baltimore Style: The Residential Segregation Ordinances of 1910–1913," *Maryland Law Review* 42, no. 2 (1983): 289–328; and Roger L. Rice, "Residential Segregation by Law, 1910–1917," *Journal of Southern History* 34 (May 1968): 179–99.
10. See Ta-Nehisi Coates, keynote address at the Radcliffe conference "Universities and Slavery: Bound by History," March 3, 2017. See also Coates, "The Case for Reparations," *Atlantic*, June 2014, https://www.theatlantic.com/magazine/archive/2014/06/the-case-for-reparations

/361631/, accessed March 6, 2017; section V, "The Quiet Plunder," highlights the United States's theft from African Americans starting in slavery and continuing into the twentieth century:

> The federal government is premised on equal fealty from all its citizens, who in return are to receive equal treatment. But as late as the mid-20th century, this bargain was not granted to black people, who repeatedly paid a higher price for citizenship and received less in return. Plunder had been the essential feature of slavery, of the society described by Calhoun. But practically a full century after the end of the Civil War and the abolition of slavery, the plunder—quiet, systemic, submerged—continued even amidst the aims and achievements of New Deal liberals.

11. Joe R. Feagin, "Documenting the Costs of Slavery, Segregation, and Contemporary Racism: Why Reparations Are in Order for African Americans," *Harvard BlackLetter Law Journal* 20 (2004): 49–81.
12. See, for example, Harris, "Whiteness as Property." According to Harris, "in ways so embedded that it is rarely apparent, the set of assumptions, privileges, and benefits that accompany the status of being white have become a valuable asset that whites sought to protect" (1713).
13. Daria Roithmayr, *Reproducing Racism: How Everyday Choices Lock in White Advantage* (New York: New York University Press, 2014), 4–5.
14. See Ira Katznelson, *When Affirmative Action Was White: An Untold History of Racial Inequality in Twentieth-Century America* (New York: Norton, 2005).
15. See George Tindall, "The Cost of Segregation," in *The Age of Segregation: Race Relations in the South, 1890–1945*, ed. Robert Haws (Jackson: University Press of Mississippi, 1978), 117–32; and Manning Marable, *How Capitalism Underdeveloped Black America: Problems in Race, Political Economy, and Society* (Chicago: Haymarket Books, 2015). See also the literature on reparations, including William A. Darity, Jr. and A. Kirsten Mullen, *From Here to Equality: Reparations for Black Americans in the Twenty-First Century* (Chapel Hill: University of North Carolina Press, 2020); Randall Robinson, *The Debt: What America Owes to Blacks* (New York: Penguin, 2000); and Boris Bittker, *The Case for Black Reparations* (Boston: Beacon Press, 2003). David H. Swinton, "Racial Inequality and Reparations," in *The Wealth of Races: The Present Value of Benefits from Past Injustices*, ed. Richard F. America (New York: Praeger, 1990), attempts to tally the costs of labor discrimination between 1929 and 1969; cited in Feagin, "Documenting the Costs," 54.
16. See, especially, N. D. B. Connolly, *A World More Concrete: Real Estate and the Remaking of Jim Crow South Florida* (Chicago: University of Chicago, 2014). Connolly demonstrates how money extracted from impoverished black renters in segregated housing in greater Miami enriched not just whites, but also middle-class black landlords.
17. Two important studies that (1) investigate what slaves thought of how their society valued their bodies and that (2) explain how slave owners used harsh systems of labor control to ensure that they made a tidy profit are, respectively, Daina Ramey Berry, *The Price for Their Pound of Flesh: The Value of the Enslaved, from Womb to Grave, in*

the Building of a Nation (Boston: Beacon Press, 2017), and Edward E. Baptist, *The Half Has Never Been Told: Slavery and the Making of American Capitalism* (New York: Basic Books, 2014). See also Eric Foner, *Nothing but Freedom: Emancipation and Its Legacy* (Baton Rouge: Louisiana State University Press, 1983).

18. For a few examples, see David R. Roediger, *The Wages of Whiteness: Race and the Making of the American Working Class* (London: Verso, 1991); LaKisha Michelle Simmons, *Crescent City Girls: The Lives of Young Black Women in Segregated New Orleans* (Chapel Hill: University of North Carolina Press, 2015); Stephen A. Berrey, *The Jim Crow Routine: Everyday Performances of Race, Civil Rights, and Segregation in Mississippi* (Chapel Hill: University of North Carolina Press, 2015); Grace Elizabeth Hale, *Making Whiteness: The Culture of Segregation in the South, 1890–1940* (New York: Vintage Books, 1998); Mark Schultz, *The Rural Face of White Supremacy* (Urbana: University of Illinois Press, 2005); and Robert Kenzer, *Enterprising Southerners: Black Economic Success in North Carolina, 1865–1915* (Charlottesville: University Press of Virginia, 1997).
19. Hale, *Making Whiteness*, 10.
20. While segregation also imposed costs on white southerners and state, county, and municipal governments through double overhead and other mechanisms, I do not address those costs here.
21. I do not have space in this essay to address all aspects of segregation. Some topics I have omitted are segregation in transportation and public higher education, and environmental racism.
22. While there has been a resurgence of academic interest in racial capitalism, this idea was laid out decades ago by W. E. B. Du Bois and others. See, for example, W. E. B. Du Bois, *Black Reconstruction in America: Toward a History of the Part Which Black Folk Played in the Attempt to Reconstruct Democracy in America, 1860–1880* (New York: Routledge, 2017); and Cedric J. Robinson, *Black Marxism: The Making of the Black Radical Tradition* (Chapel Hill: University of North Carolina Press, 2000).

    Nancy Leong has a different definition of racial capitalism: "the process of deriving economic and social value from the racial identity of another person." Leong argues that while "nonwhiteness" has not historically been considered valuable, recently the "preoccupation with diversity" has led to nonwhiteness being "commodified" by people and institutions that reap economic gains by adopting the appearance of diversity (in this situation, nonwhiteness is valuable not so much to nonwhite individuals, but to white people or institutions). Nancy Leong, "Racial Capitalism," *Harvard Law Review* 126, no. 8 (June 2013): 2153–56.
23. Walter Johnson, "To Remake the World: Slavery, Racial Capitalism, and Justice," *Boston Review*, February 20, 2018, https://bostonreview.net/forum/walter-johnson-to-remake-the-world.
24. William Edward Burghardt Du Bois, *Darkwater: Voices from Within the Veil* (New York: Harcourt, Brace and Howe, 1920), 30.
25. Harris, "Whiteness as Property," 1724. Harris argues that the "core characteristic" of whiteness as property is "the legal legitimation of expectations of power and control that enshrine the status quo as a neutral baseline, while masking the maintenance of white privilege and domination" (1715). See also George Lipsitz, *The Possessive Investment in*

Whiteness: How White People Profit from Identity Politics (Philadelphia: Temple University Press, 2006).

26. Of course, exploring the value of whiteness during Jim Crow is also important.
27. As Harris points out, property is "a right, not a thing." "Whiteness as Property," 1725.
28. C. Vann Woodward, *The Strange Career of Jim Crow*, 3rd ed. (New York: Oxford University Press, 1974), 97–98.
29. Gilbert Stephenson, "Racial Distinctions in Southern Law," *American Political Science Review* 1 (November 1906): 60–61.
30. Berrey, *Jim Crow Routine*, 21.
31. Glenda Elizabeth Gilmore, *Gender and Jim Crow: Women and the Politics of White Supremacy in North Carolina, 1896–1920* (Chapel Hill: University of North Carolina Press, 1996), 21.
32. Hale, *Making Whiteness*, 6–7, 124–25; Berrey, *Jim Crow Routine*, 20–21, 3.
33. Paul D. Escott, *Many Excellent People: Power and Privilege in North Carolina, 1850–1900* (Chapel Hill: University of North Carolina Press, 1985), 260.
34. See Eric Foner, *Reconstruction: America's Unfinished Revolution, 1863–1877* (New York: Harper and Row, 1988); Stewart E. Tolnay and E. M. Beck, *A Festival of Violence: An Analysis of Southern Lynchings, 1882–1930* (Urbana: University of Illinois Press, 1995).
35. Robert Penn Warren, *Segregation: The Inner Conflict in the South* (New York: Vintage Books, 1956), 30–32.
36. Mary White Ovington, "Segregation," *The Crisis* 9, no. 3 (January 1915), 142–43.
37. Stetson Kennedy, "Jim Crow Guide to the U.S.A.: The Laws, Customs and Etiquette Governing the Conduct of Nonwhites and Other Minorities as Second-Class Citizens" (1959), in *The Age of Jim Crow: A Norton Casebook in History*, ed. Jane Dailey (New York: Norton, 2009), 316.
38. Coates, keynote address at "Universities and Slavery: Bound by History."
39. Richard Wright, *Black Boy*, in *Richard Wright Reader*, ed. Ellen Wright and Michel Fabre (New York: Harper and Row, 1978), 13–17.
40. The poor often pay a heavy tax burden—through regressive taxes like sales taxes—yet see little gain from their tax contributions. In their introduction to *Taxing the Poor: Doing Damage to the Truly Disadvantaged* (Berkeley: University of California Press, 2011), Katherine S. Newman and Rourke L. O'Brien discuss an impoverished single mother in Alabama who can afford only cheap food options, which are generally unhealthy. Alabama taxes food but has low property taxes, shifting much of the tax burden on those, like this single mother, who can least afford it.
41. Quoted in W. E. B. Du Bois, "The Last Word in Caste," *NAACP Fourth Annual Report, 1913* (New York City, 1914), p. 74, Moorfield Storey Papers, 1876–1929, Library of Congress, Box 9, folder "Printed Matter, 1913."
42. See Elizabeth A. Herbin-Triant, *Threatening Property: Race, Class, and Campaigns to Legislate Jim Crow Neighborhoods* (New York: Columbia University Press, 2019); and Elizabeth A. Herbin-Triant, "Race and Class Friction in North Carolina Neighborhoods: How Campaigns for Residential Segregation Law Divided Middling and Elite Whites in Winston-Salem and North Carolina's Countryside, 1912–1915," *Journal of Southern History* 83, no. 3 (August 2017): 531–72.

43. *Buchanan v. Warley*, 245 U.S. 60 (1917).
44. Paige Glotzer, *How the Suburbs Were Segregated: Developers and the Business of Exclusionary Housing, 1890–1960* (New York: Columbia University Press, 2020), 2.
45. Thomas W. Hanchett, *Sorting Out the New South City: Race, Class, and Urban Development in Charlotte, 1875–1975* (Chapel Hill: University of North Carolina Press, 1998), 229–32; Coates, "Case for Reparations"; see also Richard Rothstein, *The Color of Law: A Forgotten History of How Our Government Segregated America* (New York: Liveright, 2017).
46. Booker T. Washington, "My View of Segregation Laws," *New Republic* 5 (December 1915): 113–14. Reprinted in Louis R. Harlan and Raymond W. Smock, eds., *The Papers of Booker T. Washington, 1914–1915* (Urbana: University of Illinois Press, 1984), 13:358.
47. Amanda I. Seligman, *Block by Block: Neighborhoods and Public Policy on Chicago's West Side* (Chicago: University of Chicago Press, 2005), 151–52.
48. "Boycott Them," *Afro-American* (Baltimore), July 28, 1917, 4; see Kevin McGruder, *Race and Real Estate: Conflict and Cooperation in Harlem, 1890–1920* (New York: Columbia University Press, 2015), 9.
49. Keeanga-Yamahtta Taylor, *Race for Profit: How Banks and the Real Estate Industry Undermined Black Homeownership* (Chapel Hill: University of North Carolina Press, 2019), 4–5.
50. James D. Anderson, *The Education of Blacks in the South, 1860–1935* (Chapel Hill: University of North Carolina Press, 1988), 149–50. On black education in the urban South, see Hilary Green, *Educational Reconstruction: African American Schools in the Urban South, 1865–1890* (New York: Fordham University Press, 2016).
51. Anderson, *Education of Blacks*, 152–56. On how the identity of "taxpayer" was deployed to exclude African Americans from access to rights such as equal education, see Camille Walsh, *Racial Taxation: Schools, Segregation and Taxpayer Citizenship*, 1869–1973 (Chapel Hill: University of North Carolina Press, 2018).
52. Anderson, *Education of Blacks*, 159.
53. Anderson, *Education of Blacks*, 161–62; see also Fairclough, *A Class of Their Own*, 10–11. On the various ways that African Americans brought about their own education, see also Heather Andrea Williams, *Self-Taught: African American Education in Slavery and Freedom* (Chapel Hill: University of North Carolina Press, 2005).
54. Alice Walker, "Women," in *The Norton Anthology of African American Literature*, ed. Henry Louis Gates Jr. and Nellie Y. McKay (New York: Norton, 1997), 2377–78.
55. Fairclough, *A Class of Their Own*, 6, 13.
56. See, for example, Eric A. Hanushek, John F. Kain, and Steven G. Rivkin, "New Evidence about *Brown v. Board of Education*: The Complex Effects of School Racial Composition on Achievement," *Journal of Labor Economics* 27, no. 3 (July 2009): 349–83; Carl Bankston and Stephen J. Caldas, "Majority African American Schools and Social Injustice: The Influence of De Facto Segregation on Academic Achievement," *Social Forces* 75, no. 2 (December 1996): 535–55; Russell W. Rumberger and J. Douglas Willms, "The Impact of Racial and Ethnic Segregation on the Achievement Gap in California High Schools," *Educational Evaluation and Policy Analysis* 14, no. 4 (1992): 377–96; Pierre Bourdieu,

"The Forms of Capital" (1986), accessed March 12, 2018, at https://www.marxists.org/reference/subject/philosophy/works/fr/bourdieu-forms-capital.htm; Lauren A. Rivera, *Pedigree: How Elite Students Get Elite Jobs* (Princeton, NJ: Princeton University Press, 2015); and Nancy DiTomaso, *The American Non-Dilemma: Racial Inequality Without Racism* (New York: Russell Sage Foundation, 2013), xxiii.

57. Nell Irvin Painter, "Soul Murder and Slavery: Toward a Fully Loaded Cost Accounting," in *U.S. History as Women's History: New Feminist Essays*, ed. Linda K. Kerber, Alice Kessler-Harris, and Kathryn Kish Sklar (Chapel Hill: University of North Carolina Press, 1995), 125–46. Painter's essay discusses slavery, but her idea of "soul murder" as "depression, lowered self-esteem, and anger" applies more broadly (127).

There is a recent literature that shows the health effects of racism—effects such as increased hypertension. This literature notes that perceived racism causes stress, which leads to an array of health problems, but that racism can harm people's health even when it is not felt; "institutional racism . . . may reduce access to goods, services, and opportunities for African Americans in ways that have important health consequences." For example, doctors are less likely to recommend certain lifesaving medical tests for African Americans. The health problems associated with racism extract a toll, obviously, as they can be costly to treat, lead to missed workdays and lost income, and bring about an earlier death. Rodney Clark et al., "Racism as a Stressor for African Americans: A Biopsychosocial Model," *American Psychologist* 54, no. 10 (October 1999): 805–16. See also David R. Williams et al., "Racial Differences in Physical and Mental Health: Socio-economic Status, Stress and Discrimination," *Journal of Health Psychology* 2, no. 3 (July 1997): 335–51; Joe R. Feagin and Karyn McKinney, *The Many Costs of Racism* (Lanham, MD: Rowman and Littlefield, 2003); and Nancy Krieger and Stephen Sidney, "Racial Discrimination and Blood Pressure: The CARDIA Study of Young Black and White Adults," *American Journal of Public Health* 86, no. 10 (October 1996): 1370–78.

58. James Baldwin, *The Fire Next Time*, reprinted in James Baldwin, *The Price of the Ticket: Collected Nonfiction, 1948–1985* (New York: St. Martin's, 1985), 335.

59. See, for example, Rothstein, *Color of Law*, xi.

60. On the class dimensions of white-supremacist thinking, see Herbin-Triant, *Threatening Property*.

61. As an example of jobs set aside for black and white southerners, consider the industrial jobs available in North Carolina in the early twentieth century. Whites were hired to work at textile factories, where they made sure the machines were working properly. African Americans were hired to work in tobacco factories, which were not mechanized; the rationale was that black people were unsuited to working with machinery. Roger Biles, "Tobacco Towns: Urban Growth and Economic Development in Eastern North Carolina," in *North Carolina Tobacco: A History*, ed. Billy Yeargin (Charleston, SC: History Press, 2008), 109–10; Robert Rodgers Korstad, *Civil Rights Unionism* (Chapel Hill: University of North Carolina Press, 2003), 43–44; Jacquelyn Dowd Hall et al., *Like a Family: The Making of a Southern Cotton Mill World* (New York: Norton, 1987), 67.

PART III

HISTORY MATTERS

7

WHY HISTORICAL FILM MATTERS

KELLIE CARTER JACKSON

In the summer of 2017, creators David Benioff and D. B. Weiss announced they were concluding the final season of their popular television drama: *Game of Thrones*. They were also preparing for their next project: *Confederate*. Set to go into production after the final season of *Game of Thrones*, *Confederate* was slated to be a period piece, of sorts. Taking place in an alternate timeline, it would chronicle events leading to a third American Civil War. The premise was that the southern states that seceded from the Union were successful in forming their own confederacy. In the world Benioff and Weiss created, slavery was still legal and had evolved into "a modern institution." They promised that the alternate universe would feature characters on both sides of the Mason-Dixon "demilitarized zone," including abolitionists, slave catchers, journalists, politicians, and executives from the planter class.[1]

The public backlash to the announcement was swift and fierce for a number of reasons. In many ways, the Confederacy might have lost the political battles but won the ideological war. In 2017, the Southern Poverty Law Center and the Anti-Defamation League noted increases in hate crimes and hate groups across the country. Cities big and small, southern and northern, are still in intense debates over the removal of Confederate statues and memorials, many of which were erected decades after the Civil War to commemorate white-supremacist ideology. White power groups believed they had both friends and allies in President Donald Trump and many in his White House staff, such as former adviser Steve Bannon. On August 12, 2017, tensions reached a climax in Charlottesville, Virginia, during a White Nationalist rally supporting a statue of Robert E. Lee in the town square. After the police broke up both the rally and the counterdemonstration, Heather Hyer was struck by James Alex Fields Jr., a white supremacist who plowed his car through a crowd of people. In the ensuing controversy, President Trump took over two days to respond to the violence and then proclaimed, "I think there's blame on both sides. . . . You had some very bad people in that group. But you also had people that were very fine people on both sides." Critics and reporters accused the president of putting the "alt left and white supremacists on the same moral plane."[2] Thus a high-profile television drama to be featured on HBO gave many Americans pause. Detractors complained that a show like *Confederate* would only fuel the fantasies of white-supremacist groups.

WHY HISTORICAL FILMS MATTER

In the *Atlantic*, author and critic Ta-Nehisi Coates wrote, "At this very hour, black people all across the South are still fighting the battle which they joined during Reconstruction—securing equal access to the ballot—and resisting a president whose resemblance to Andrew Johnson is uncanny." He claimed, "*Confederate* is the kind of provocative thought experiment that you can be engaged in when someone else's lived reality really is fantasy to you, when your grandmother is not in danger of losing her vote, when the terrorist attack on Charleston evokes honest sympathy, but inspires no direct fear."[3] For Coates and many others, the idea of a show like *Confederate*, premised on a southern victory, rings hollow. The question "What if the South won?" can be answered not by fantasizing about counterfactuals, but by reading the daily news from just about any American news outlet. Perhaps not legally, but politically, economically, socially, and certainly ideologically, the war waged over 150 years ago is still being contested.

The Civil War was complicated. For a series like *Confederate*, historians will also wonder how writers will achieve the nuance required to tell this history. For instance, Maryland, Delaware, Kentucky, and Missouri were all southern states that did not secede from the Union. At one point, New York City attempted to secede with the South. And more Mississippians fought for the Union than for the Confederacy. These are often some of the most invisible facts that are forgotten when retelling this historical moment. Too much of the Civil War has been diluted down into simple binaries, freeing readers and audiences of the complicated past that actually existed. Furthermore, the lack of consensual sex that was rampant throughout *Game of Thrones* was disturbing. During slavery, not only was the sexual assault on black women lawful, but black women were seen as unable to be raped at all. "Rape" was a category reserved for women who were considered respectable and worthy of respect.

It is not hard to imagine black pain and suffering or black subservience on the silver screen. It can be argued that film, especially Hollywood, has done more harm than any other outlet by obstructing a truthful appreciation of slavery, the Civil War, and America's capitalist origins.[4] From 1915, when D. W. Griffith's *Birth of a Nation* featured nearly four hours of the silent and heroic men of the Klu Klux Klan, to the romantic epic of Margaret Mitchell's *Gone with the Wind* in 1939, virtually every slave film has found itself in conversation with the tenets put forth by these narratives. One might argue that billions of dollars have been made peddling ahistorical slavery-based films and their "alternative facts." Thus when Coates writes that "one need not wait to observe that any foray by HBO into the Civil War must be met with a spirit of pointed inquiry and a withholding of all benefit of the doubt,"[5] it is clear that Americans are being offered more ahistorical slavery-based films—the exact opposite of what we desperately need. In many ways, black bodies are the comfort food of Hollywood, which indulges in stereotypical troupes of mammies, maids, and wisecracking black male sidekicks.

More films have debuted regarding slavery in the past several years than in the past several decades. During the age of Obama, films such as *Lincoln, Django Unchained, 12 Years a Slave, Belle, Free State of Jones, Birth of a Nation*, and a *Roots* remake, along with WGN's television series, *Underground*, all debuted. The intersection between slavery and film has become the basis of conversations and even courses on the history of race, power, and visual culture. The controversy surrounding HBO's forthcoming *Confederate* has prompted questions surrounding the motivations and desires behind envisioning black pain, loss, and degradation. More often than not, historical films have focused on black suffering. In the retelling of sports heroes, musical legends, civil rights leaders, or NASA mathematicians, it has become nearly impossible to tell the African American story without prefacing, signposting, or centralizing violence, exploitation, and racial oppression.

This essay confronts Hollywood's perennial desire to imagine and market black suffering. Historical films based on slavery have made black pain a lead character. Violence is the protagonist. Black pain has often become a spectacle where *who looks* and *how people look* are both intimate and controversial. Cinematic representations of American slavery have not only defined mainstream ideas about the institution of slavery, but they have in many ways eclipsed historians' painstaking research. Entertainment trumps information and thus robs black humanity, even in an attempt to preserve it. Historical films about slavery matter. The perceptions of history have an impact on every aspect of our lives: from statues, to rallies, to voting, to policy, to interpersonal relationships.

Without question, African American history and violence are inseparable, and I would never encourage people to forget how exploitation and oppression have shaped the experiences and outcomes of black Americans. However, rather than continuously visualizing black pain, can we also ask: What does it look like to see white supremacy fail on film? Other than the "revenge porn" of whipping the white man or fantastically blowing up the plantation as seen in Quentin Tarnatino's *Django Unchained*, what does real justice look like? Furthermore, can this justice be achieved visually without the presence of a white savior? Can historians point filmmakers to the richly diverse ways that African

Americans combatted and overcame (either individually or collectively) suppression of their inalienable rights to enjoy their humanity? Equally important as illustrating the violence of slavery is contemplating and encapsulating images of black survival and black success. These deeper questions compel us to think about what constitutes justice in both the historical and imaginary realms.

VISUALIZING VIOLENCE: HOLLYWOOD'S OBSESSION WITH BLACK PAIN

Few films that feature slavery fail to include the infamous whipping scene. Audiences have come to expect it. With each act of defiance, we wait for it. In 1977, audiences across America witnessed the infamous whipping scene for the first time in the comfort of their homes while watching Alex Haley's television miniseries *Roots*. More than 130 million Americans—nearly half of the country's population—watched at least one episode of the eight-part miniseries.[6] In episode two, Kunta Kinte, played by Levar Burton, is strung up high for attempting to run away. As the character Fiddler pleads his case to master John Waller, the whip has already begun to crack on Kunta's back. Everyone is gathered from in and around the barn to witness the whipping of "the African." For nearly three minutes, viewers and the cast watch as Ames asks repeatedly through the cracking of the whip for Kunta to state his new given name, Toby. In the 2016 remake of *Roots*, the whipping scene of Kunta, played by Malachi Kirby, is over four minutes long and infinitely more graphic, revealing blood spatters, open flesh wounds, and Kunta coughing up blood. Both overseers insist that everyone present must watch. The whipping scene becomes one of the most definitive and memorable aspects of the eight-part series. In *Roots*, seemingly every attempt to assert black humanity or black self-determination is met with violence. Author Delia Mellis claimed, "When Kunta finally gives in and calls himself 'Toby,' Ames is vindicated: he has, with the whip, made the man a slave."[7] The whip is not just a conduit to force the servitude of the enslaved; it's a character, a character that makes its unforgettable debuts with each film that comes after *Roots*.

Even in an attempt to illustrate black manhood and courage, Edward Zwick's 1989 film *Glory* sought fit to include a whipping scene during a moment that would never have happened historically. *Glory* tells the story of the all-black Fifty-Fourth Massachusetts Regiment that fought bravely during the Civil War. One of the most dramatic scenes in the film, and no doubt the scene that clinched the Academy Award for Denzel Washington, was the flogging of his rebellious character, Trip. In the film, Trip leaves his military camp in search of shoes. Accused of desertion, Trip is whipped forty stripes in front of the entire regiment with the approval of his commanding officer, Robert Gould Shaw, whose parents are staunch abolitionists. Historian Joseph C. Glatthaar called the scene "wholly inaccurate" and a gross distortion of the facts.[8] In 1861, two years before black men were able to enlist in the army and navy, Congress outlawed whipping in the military.[9] Furthermore, Trip would have been accused of being absent without leave, as opposed to desertion, in which case a legal hearing would have taken place. While it may be powerfully dramatic to watch a solitary tear slide down Washington's face, it is important to ask this question: In a world where whipping soldiers, even black soldiers, was illegal, why was this scene necessary?

Perhaps the screenwriter, Kevin Jarre, or the director, Zwick, wanted to remind his audiences of the horrors of slavery. But why not show black soldiers entering the South and interrupting a whipping or have the enslaved whip their masters in front of the entire plantation? No, empowerment in *Glory* only comes through the graces and good judgment of white authority. Audiences will not question the whipping because they have been conditioned to expect it, even where it does not exist. What is troubling is that some may argue that the whipping of Trip made the film stronger. Just as in *Roots*, the whipping of Trip is one of the most memorable scenes. Violence in any and all forms gives slave films a sense of legitimacy. However, something is lost when audiences cannot recognize black bravery without floggings. The real men who fought in the Fifty-Fourth Massachusetts Regiment were free men who never experienced or witnessed slavery. They were, after all, from

Massachusetts. The bravery in *Glory* is not being flogged without crying out, but risking one's life, one's freedom, to ensure the freedom of others. Zwick did not show us that the fight for freedom was just as important to free black men as it was to the enslaved.[10]

The bravery of African Americans and the brutality of slavery need no exaggeration or embellishments. But once again, in 2012, Quentin Tarantino's *Django Unchained* went beyond showing the daily violence of enslaved life. The film manufactures a Mandingo fight-to-the-death scene that would not have taken place in slavery. A slave owner's "best man" is too valuable to be gambled way in mythical gladiator-style fighting. One year later, in Steven McQueen's realistic *12 Years a Slave*, viewers watched, stared, and gazed at a four-minute scene of Solomon (played by Chiwetel Ejiofor) grasping for his life with the tips of his toes while hanging by his neck from a tree, and the scene culminates in the tortuous and violent whipping of Patsey, played by Lupita Ny'ongo. Even in the television series *Underground*, season two illustrates a long and graphic scene in which the lead character, Rosalee, played by Jurnee Smollett-Bell, is attacked and beaten by several men while far along in her pregnancy. We know that violence during slavery was unrelenting, but the film has somehow made the enslaved experience a cliché, or worse, pleasurable.

In the early twentieth century, white audiences and readers gained "enormous pleasure" from the sadistic whippings scenes depicted in Harriet Beecher Stowe's *Uncle Tom's Cabin*. Author Erica Ball claims that "some late nineteenth century European psychiatrists reported that some of their patients 'found sexual pleasure' in 'the scenes of beating in Stowe's novel meant to dramatize the horrors of slavery.' "[11] Even in a contemporary context, these sentiments are not new or unique. Author Zadie Smith wrote that when Jordan Peele directed the film *Get Out*, he captured "a concrete metaphor for the ultimate unspoken fear: that to be oppressed is not so much to be hated as obscenely loved."[12] Black suffering and violence have become a sport for public consumption. This idea is also captured in Aimé Césaire's work. He cautions, "Beware, my body and my soul, beware above all of crossing your arms and assuming the sterile attitude of the spectator, for life is not a spectacle, a sea of griefs is not a proscenium, and a man who wails is not a dancing bear."[13] In film, black pain and suffering run the risk of being paraded as a tool for entertainment or deemed as superficial. More important, repeated or recycled tropes of violence strip the humanity of the enslaved. The whipped man and raped woman become a dancing bear.

Scholars, activists, and artists have been representing the violence of slavery within visual culture since the seventeenth and eighteenth centuries. By the nineteenth century, abolitionists had an arsenal of images and imagery to dramatize the brutality of slavery: daguerreotypes of enslaved men with keloid scarred backs, enslaved women withering under the lash, or engravings of "tightly packed" human cargo among slave ships.[14] In 1857, abolitionist Theodore Parker described the brutality of chattel slavery: "The Slave is not, theoretically, considered as a Person; he is only a Thing, as so much as an axe or a spade; accordingly he is wholly subject to his master, and has no Rights—which are an attribute of Persons only, not of Things. All that he enjoys therefore is but a privilege. *He may be damaged but not wronged* [emphasis mine]." Parker goes on to add, "The relation of master and slave begins in violence; it must be sustained by violence—the systematic violence of general laws, or the irregular violence of individual caprice. There is no other mode of conquering and subjugating a man."[15] Often in Hollywood, we are watching African Americans as damaged, but not wronged. Without historical context, we lose the economic, political, and social dynamics that created antiblackness and required violence to fuel America as a world power and whiteness as a privileged class.

Films have perfected this horrific imagery. These scenes do not engender empathy as much as they reinforce who is in power. They obscure the humanity of the enslaved. In the same way, Americans have been inundated with videos of black men and women physically and often fatally abused by police, such as the endless media loop of Eric Garner trapped in a chokehold or footage of Walter Scott running unarmed from the police and arching his back as bullets repeatedly enter his body. If, according to critic James Baldwin, the future of America will be about white people discovering their need "to have a nigger in the first place," then the future of film, particularly historical film, will depend on the industry discovering why it needs to see black suffering without historical context. Black suffering has lost public concern, and as a result, a movement was born to remind the world that Black Lives Matter.

IMAGINING JUSTICE

For Hollywood, there are many true and heroic stories yet to be told in African American history where little imagination or exaggeration is required to make for a thrilling film. Along the veins of *Confederate*, what if filmmakers and Americans imagined a world much like Dr. Martin Luther King Jr.'s dream? What if, in 1857, Dred Scott won his Supreme Court case and black men and women were granted rights that white men were "bound to respect"? What if we envisioned a Reconstruction where political reform was met with economic reform and revolutionized a newly freed black class? What if Homer Plessy won his Supreme Court case against Judge Ferguson's ruling regarding "separate but equal"? Or what if, when Chief Justice Warren declared, "with all deliberate speed," a plan and task force were put in place to ensure that segregation would die in 1954? The problem for many Americans is that it is often difficult to imagine something that does not exist. Even in the postapocalyptic science fiction world of *The Hunger Games*, audiences had a hard time accepting the beloved and innocent character of Rue as black, even though she was described as such in the book.[16] We can imagine justice not by avoiding violence or racism, but by showing how victory can be obtained and expressed when violence and racism are conquered. This practice may prove to be difficult for white readers and audiences to conceptualize because often black success is connected to the idea that it comes at the expense of white supremacy or, at the very least, white privilege. The fallacy that there is barely enough success to go around is a powerful one in a capitalist society.

Interestingly, justice may well be imagined in the form of another television drama. Not long after the *Confederate* controversy, Amazon announced that it would be debuting its own series called *Black America*.

While not created in response to *Confederate*, this new series will also be an alternate historical drama, but this time about newly freed slaves who have been given the states of Louisiana, Mississippi, and Alabama as a form of reparation after the Civil War to start a sovereign nation, known as "New Colonia." Created by Will Packer and Aaron McGruder, *Black America* will explore the turbulent history and future of this nation with its neighbor the United States. The creators used the controversy surrounding *Confederate* to announce and explain the premise of *Black America*:

> The past 150 years have been witness to military incursions, assassinations, regime change, coups, etc. Today, after two decades of peace with the U.S. and unprecedented growth, an ascendant New Colonia joins the ranks of major industrialized nations on the world stage as America slides into rapid decline. Inexorably tied together, the fate of two nations, indivisible, hangs in the balance.[17]

Make no mistake, New Colonia is not Haiti, but perhaps what Haiti should have become. *Black America* is a revolution that will literally be televised. "It was something that was personally intriguing for me as a black American," Packer admitted. "You would be hard pressed to find many black Americans who have not thought about the concept of reparation, what would happen if reparations were actually given." He also acknowledged that, as a content creator, he thought now was a tremendous opportunity to "delve into the story, to do it right."[18] In the hope of "doing it right," Packer and his team consulted with a host of historians to ensure that the series had both accuracy and authenticity in its retelling of the past and its thinking about the future of "New Colonia."

This is how history and film can work together in creating spaces both literally and figuratively to offer paths for progress. For much of history and in many films, the dominant way to illustrate slavery has been through two modes that are equally problematic. One mode is to visualize slavery and its violence to the point where the pain inflicted on black bodies borders on the pornographic. Another path ignores the violence of slavery altogether in order to foster a nostalgia for a romantic past of enslaved life that never existed.

In history and in film, we need to be able to tell complete truths. We can reveal stories that illustrate the trials, trauma, and triumphs of enslaved people but that also encourage readers and audiences to think about how many more triumphs could be had if we simply forfeited the power, privilege, and position that allow so many to be marginalized into subordinate and exploitative roles. While audiences raved over the film *Hidden Figures*, which featured the efforts of several African American women whose incalculable contributions to the space program forever changed the way NASA operated, it only made me think, "How much sooner could we have gotten to space or the moon had we not let color and gender block what we believed was possible?" Film tied to popular historical narratives has an extraordinary influence on American attitudes toward slavery and racism and informs our political and social agendas. Moreover, historical films that capture slavery or civil rights have a duty to present narratives in which the greatest destruction is not caused by the violence of racism, but by white cowardice in the face of white supremacy.

Much of Eric Foner's work has been about giving voices to the most vulnerable in society, allowing them to have agency within the historical narrative and in public spaces. History and film combined can have a potent impact on mainstream Americans. When it came to historical films on slavery, it was always Eric Foner's opinion that I valued most. Foner was always candid in his opinions, particularly about films that earned critical acclaim, such as Steven Spielberg's *Lincoln*. When *Lincoln* debuted to enthusiastic reviews in 2012, Foner was among the few historians who were not impressed with the narrative presented to audiences. Foner's 2010 book, *The Fiery Trial: Lincoln and American Slavery*, shows us a Lincoln who is complicated regarding his views of slavery and African Americans.[19] Spielberg's Lincoln shows us a man who is deeply dedicated to the idea of freeing the enslaved, but the reality was that Lincoln needed to be constantly prodded and persuaded toward emancipation and equality. Foner argues that initially Lincoln refused to support the

Thirteenth Amendment when it was proposed in 1864 by the Women's National Loyal League, led by Susan B. Anthony and Elizabeth Cady Stanton. And scholars have been writing for decades about the hundreds of thousands of enslaved men and women who freed themselves throughout the war. In addition, the Emancipation Proclamation freed roughly 3 million of the 4 million enslaved. Foner maintains, "The film grossly exaggerates the possibility that by January 1865 the war might have ended with slavery still intact. . . . Louisiana, Maryland, Missouri, Tennessee and West Virginia, exempted in whole or part from the proclamation, had decreed abolition on their own." Foner rightly contends that "slavery died on the ground, not just in the White House and the House of Representatives."[20]

By the time the Thirteenth Amendment was ratified, slavery was already dead. The Thirteenth Amendment was similar to a coroner's report that announced the official time of death. According to Foner and other leading historians, the enslaved largely freed themselves, and attempts to formally abolish slavery through a constitutional amendment were led by women. But Spielberg emphasizes white male voices and places black Americans on the periphery of their own efforts.[21] In Spielberg's *Lincoln*, there are no whipping scenes or rape scenes. But with over $275 million grossed at the box office and twelve nominations from the Academy Awards, perhaps the real violence is the simplification of black agency, in exchange for a comfortable, palatable, and profitable story.

History matters. Film matters. Together, these disciplines can both inform and empower and even entertain. Readers and audiences deserve a story in which the words "based on a true story" are true. The idea and prosepcts of *Confederate* were eventually and officially canceled, but the problem of storytelling remains. Yet, if we are willing to do the reading, historians have been writing for decades about the present "past." We know that any TV drama will be at best a disappointment and, at worst, a lie. The movement Black Lives Matter arose not to speak to a South that lost, but to illustrate to the world that police shootings, mass incarceration, school segregation, housing discrimination, and other oppressive and exploitative practices that promote antiblackness are what America looks like when the brutality of slavery and racism wins.

NOTES

1. Elizabeth Wagmeister, "'Game of Thrones' Creators Land New Series at HBO," *Variety*, July 19, 2017, http://variety.com/2017/tv/news/hbo-confederate-tv-show-game-of-thrones-creators-david-benioff-db-weiss-1202500538/.
2. Jessica Taylor and Dana Farrington, "Another Reversal: Trump Now Says Counterprotesters Also to Blame for Charlottesville," *National Public Radio (NPR)*, August 15, 2017, https://www.npr.org/2017/08/15/543743845/another-reversal-trump-now-says-counter protesters-also-to-blame-for-charlottesvi.
3. Ta-Nehisi Coates, "The Lost Cause Rides Again," *Atlantic*, August 4, 2017.
4. Coates, "The Lost Cause Rides Again."
5. Coates, "The Lost Cause Rides Again."
6. Erica L. Ball and Kellie Carter Jackson, eds., *Reconsidering Roots: Race, Politics, and Memory* (Athens: University of Georgia Press, 2017), 2.
7. Delia Mellis, "Roots of Violence: Race, Power, and Manhood in *Roots*," in Ball and Jackson, *Reconsidering Roots*, 85.
8. David Nicholson, "What Price Glory?" *Washington Post*, January 21, 1990.
9. Martin Blatt, "Glory: Hollywood History, Popular Culture, and the Fifty-Fourth Massachusetts Regiment," in *Hope and Glory: Essays on the Legacy of the 54th Massachusetts Regiment*, ed. Martin H. Blatt, Thomas J. Brown, and Donald Yacavone (Amherst: University of Massachusetts Press, 2001), 223. See also David Nicholson, "What Price Glory?" *Washington Post*, January 21, 1990.
10. Moreover, when the regiment's soldiers forfeit their salaries until they receive the same wages as their white counterparts, audiences are also left to believe that these "former slaves" were never entitled to receiving payment. Once again, their sacrifices on screen are cheapened.
11. Erica Ball, "The Politics of Pain: Representing the Violence of Slavery in American Popular Culture," in *Violence in American Popular Culture*, ed. David Schmid (Santa Barbara, CA: Praeger, 2015), 31; see also Linda Williams, *Playing the Race Card: Melodrama of Black and White from Uncle Tom to O. J. Simpson* (Princeton, NJ: Princeton University Press, 2001), 86; and Marcus Wood, *Blind Memory: Visual Representations of Slavery in England and America, 1780–1865* (New York: Routledge, 2000), 185. Wood notes that Richard von Krafft-Ebbing and Sigmund Freud both reportedly had patients that shared the fantasy of slaves being whipped and were aroused by it.
12. Zaydie Smith, "Getting In and Out: Who Owns Black Pain?" *Harper's Magazine*, July 2017, 86.
13. Aimé Césaire, *Notebook of a Return to the Native Land* (Middletown, CT: Wesleyan University Press, 2001).
14. Ball, "The Politics of Pain," 28.
15. Theodore Parker, *A Letter to the People of the United States Touching the Matter of Slavery* (Boston: J. Munroe and Company, 1848).
16. Christopher Rosen, "'Hunger Games' Racist Tweets: Fans Upset Because of Rue's Race," *Huffington Post*, March 26, 2012; Fahima Haque, "Watching 'The Hunger Games'

Through a Racial Lens," *Washington Post*, March 28, 2012; Bim Adewunmi, "Why Wasn't The Hunger Games Cast as I Imagined in My Racist Reading?!" *Guardian*, March 28, 2012.

17. Nellie Andreeva, "'Black America': Amazon Alt-History Drama from Will Packer & Aaron McGruder Envisions Post-Reparations America," *Deadline*, August 1, 2017, http://deadline.com/2017/08/black-america-amazon-alt-history-drama-will-packer-aaron-mcgruder-envisions-post-reparations-america-1202139504/.
18. Andreeva, "'Black America.'"
19. Foner's *The Fiery Trial: Lincoln and American Slavery* won the Pulitzer Prize, the Bancroft Prize, and the Lincoln Prize in 2011.
20. Eric Foner, "Letter to the Editor: Lincoln's Use of Politics for Noble Ends," *New York Times*, November 26, 2012.
21. Foner, "Letter to the Editor"; see also Jon Wiener, "The Trouble with Steven Spielberg's 'Lincoln,'" *Nation*, November 27, 2012, https://www.thenation.com/article/trouble-steven-spielbergs-lincoln/. Foner also illustrates that, prior to the Thirteenth Amendment, Lincoln believed that slavery should have been abolished on a state-by-state basis, but Radical Republicans pressured him to change his mind.

8

A MOB MUSEUM MATTERS

MICHAEL GREEN

On the evening of October 4, 1982, an explosion blew up the car belonging to Frank "Lefty" Rosenthal, who once had operated four Las Vegas hotel-casinos for organized crime syndicates based in Chicago, Kansas City, and Milwaukee. When he put his key into his Cadillac's ignition and turned it, he still had not completely gotten into the car, just in case of . . . well, he declined to say exactly why. But that action may have saved his life: the blast set the car ablaze and threw him several feet. He was lucky to escape with minor injuries, although the car bomb allegedly was intended only as a message not to testify against his old associates. But in the 1995 film *Casino*, which depicts Rosenthal and other mob figures like his longtime friend Anthony Spilotro, he was already in the car, with seemingly no reason to suspect the mob had violent plans for him. The movie also suggests that Rosenthal was a brilliant and an innovative casino operator, but a similarly lauded operator, Steve Wynn, complained to the film's director, Martin Scorsese, "Lefty Rosenthal was so dumb that he couldn't spell 'it' if you spotted him the 't.' "[1]

The night of the explosion, I was a teenager, working at a small Las Vegas newspaper. The *Valley Times* had become known for its in-depth, unsparing coverage of organized crime, at the behest of its publisher, Bob Brown, one of Nevada's most respected journalists. The irony of its reputation was that Brown helped Rosenthal skim money by kicking back most of the revenue from the advertisements his casinos bought in the paper. The largest casino in question, the Stardust, employed a blackjack dealer whom Rosenthal personally fired because the previous mob regime had hired him. That was my father, who recalled Rosenthal lining up dealers and randomly terminating them, and sometimes gumming up casino operations.[2]

By the time of the blast, mob control of Las Vegas casinos was winding down, thanks mainly to crackdowns by federal and state officials. Not that corporations had completely taken over, or that Las Vegas was the mega-resort center it has since become. But ever since the mob's decline and fall, various writers, literally from Las Vegas to Texarkana, have frequently asked, "Was life really better when the Mob ruled Las Vegas?" The question, like the responses to it, requires context: Did the mob actually rule Las Vegas? If so, when, which mob, and for whom was it better? The answers often depend on the memories of those giving them: women tend to respond differently than men, African Americans differently than Caucasians, and gourmands differently than less finicky eaters, just as *Casino*'s depictions resonate with some viewers as accurate, with others as capturing the aura of the time but not the reality, and with still others as ridiculous.[3]

These issues and distinctions, long part of Las Vegas lore and discussion, became even more evident with the announcement of plans to open the Mob Museum in downtown Las Vegas. As the mayor who came up with the idea before leaving office a year before, Oscar Goodman was especially proud of the museum's opening on February 14, 2012 (naturally, on the anniversary of the St. Valentine's Day Massacre in Chicago; the museum included the wall where the gangsters were lined up and shot). He was also proud of its success, which eventually included accreditation by the American Association of Museums and more than 2 million visitors in seven years. Before becoming mayor, Goodman had been a lawyer who often represented organized crime figures; I spent part of my youth in Las Vegas watching him defend people accused of skimming money from casinos or of committing violent crimes. In that job, Goodman denied that the mob existed. But as mayor, in public, and in meetings with museum board members and researchers—of whom

I was one—he insisted that, above all, the museum must tell the "truth," or at least get as close to it as possible.

As Goodman and those of us working on the museum understood, truth has varied meanings that memory helps to shape, especially for those who remember at least some of the events and people depicted in this museum—or, for that matter, any other museum, or any work of history. Furthermore, as Woody Allen once wrote, "the Mafia spends very little for office supplies"—criminals have generally deemed it unwise to write down what they are doing. This increased the difficulty of creating the museum. But we succeeded, and it succeeded, in finding enough source material to describe and analyze how organized crime and law enforcement shaped and were shaped by Las Vegas—and the nation and the world. Understanding either the museum or Las Vegas requires an understanding of both the museum and Las Vegas—how they developed, why they matter, and what they say about the people who built them and are still building them.[4]

Although Las Vegas is still being built, it also has a reputation for unbuilding itself—for imploding important parts of its past, replacing older hotel-casinos with new pleasure palaces. That has been true for Strip hotels but not the rest of the community, where efforts to save historic buildings and neighborhoods have led, as historic preservation inevitably does, to both successes and failures. Thus the Mob Museum's mere existence stands Las Vegas's reputation on its head, because it is in a building that the city saved from destruction. Opened in 1933, the area's first federal building housed every federal office and official at the time. Numerous trials and hearings involving organized crime took place there in ensuing decades. But by 1999, the construction of newer federal buildings and the decline of the downtown area had left only a couple of offices in the old courthouse. Goodman, recalling that he tried his first case in Las Vegas there, set out to save it. In 2002, the city bought the structure from the federal government for $1, but the deal came with a proviso: it had to be used for cultural purposes.[5]

But what is culture, anyway, and what did the community want in that building? Las Vegas had no major art museum—and still does not—but Goodman reasoned that they needed something to drive tourists and locals into the area. "I'm a great believer in the arts, painting, culture," said Goodman, whose mother was an artist. "But I knew a watercolor museum or a porcelain museum wasn't going to do it."[6] City officials conducted a survey that showed that locals wanted something "vintage" and tourists preferred a museum about the mob. If the mob was not vintage Las Vegas, what was?[7]

Unsurprisingly, the idea of a museum about organized crime proved controversial. Part of the problem was Las Vegas's past: organized crime was indeed associated with vintage Las Vegas. Soon after significant settlement began in Las Vegas early in the twentieth century, one downtown street, Block 16, morphed into a red-light district with saloons (including during Prohibition), gambling (which was not yet legal), and prostitution (which was not supposed to be happening). Block 16 included those who were both enterprising and engaged in thuggery, and some form of organized crime existed almost at once. Then, in 1931, as the federal government began construction of a dam on the Colorado River southeast of town, Nevada legislators reduced the residency requirement for divorce from three months to six weeks and made gambling legal. One of the nightclub operators already in the area before gambling was legal brought along a pocket watch from his friend Al Capone, and California racketeers opened a club soon after legalization.[8]

But the first significant mob operators in Las Vegas appear to have been tied into a national network associated with the likes of Charles "Lucky" Luciano and Meyer Lansky. The idea that Benjamin "Bugsy" Siegel was first, or for that matter invented Las Vegas, is evident only to those who watched the film *Bugsy*, but he and some of his partners unquestionably were involved in casino operations in the 1940s. After Siegel's death, and especially after Senator Estes Kefauver's hearings on organized crime prompted reform movements in cities across the country, other mobsters descended on Las Vegas and built or ran hotel-casinos. They came from Cleveland (Desert Inn), New York (Sands), Chicago (Riviera and Stardust), St. Louis (Dunes), and Miami (Tropicana), and they created the original Strip that more recent operators imploded to make room for new mega-resorts. As the twenty-first century arrived, Las Vegas tended to see itself as beyond that past.[9]

Worse, from the standpoint of some civic boosters, emphasizing the mob's involvement in the past might convince some that there was a role for it in the present. As *USA Today* noted, "After years of trying to forget Bugsy, Moe, Lefty, Tony the Ant and other mobsters who made their mark here, this city of casinos has decided to play them like a hand of aces." The Las Vegas Strip had morphed into a destination for families and foodies in addition to gamblers, and it seemed far different from the place where gangsters once reigned. Another problem was Goodman's past: as a successful defense attorney, he had denied the mob's existence. He also announced, "As long as I'm mayor, we're going to keep on smiling at ourselves at how the mob founded us." While former law enforcement officials complained that the museum would "romanticize" the mob, Joe Yablonsky, who tangled with Goodman when he ran the FBI office in Nevada, said of the museum, "In my estimation, his purpose would be to glorify them. The only reason that he gets away with this is that he's in Vegas. If he was in some normal American city, he'd never make it." Yablonsky added, "If it were told truthfully, it would be OK, how we ridded the place of them and what they were really like." In 2008, one account with the headline "Defiant mayor hopes to rejuvenate his ailing city by celebrating the Mafia's role in its creation" described it the planned museum as "celebrating the Mafia's links with the gambling capital of the world," although it "dismays others weary of the city's historical association" with the mob.[10]

But Goodman and the city took two crucial steps to prove the critics wrong and disprove some of his earlier pronouncements. One came when Goodman spoke at a retirement party for Ellen Knowlton, one of Yablonsky's successors as FBI agent-in-charge. He told her, "I have a job for you," meaning the chair of the nonprofit that would oversee the museum. The *Los Angeles Times* reported, "Knowlton refused to sign on, organizers said, until she was assured that the city museum would not be a celebration of wacky mobsters but a somber take on the long law enforcement campaign to end mob rule of casinos." Knowlton had credibility, and she provided access that enabled the museum to work out partnerships with the FBI for programming and to obtain material for exhibits. She later wrote, "The Mob Museum in no way glamorizes or glorifies organized crime. . . . As part of our city's unique history, the impact of organized crime on Las Vegas should not be lost or forgotten." As one reporter later put it, she was "brought on to legitimize the downtown attraction." For many in the community, and especially in law enforcement, she did just that: an FBI spokesman said of the museum, "This is a way to connect with the public and show the results of our work."[11]

The other step was hiring curators to develop the museum. Dennis and Kathy Barrie had been the key figures behind the Rock and Roll Hall of Fame in Cleveland, Ohio, and the International Spy Museum in Washington, DC. Their work brought instant respectability to the Las Vegas project—and they knew how to build a museum from the ground up that would combine both historical accuracy and entertainment. They promised a controversial museum that addressed controversial topics: what the mob did and did not do, and what law enforcement did and did not do about it. "Why do a spy museum? Why do a rock museum? These are all part of our culture. Certainly organized crime is, and has been, a part of our culture," Dennis Barrie said. He also understood that a museum could be controversial: as director of the Cincinnati Contemporary Arts Center, he had put on an exhibition by artist Robert Mapplethorpe and as a result had been indicted for pandering obscenity and for a minor's presence in photos considered obscene. He was speedily acquitted, and Goodman—who was known for declaring that various people should be "whacked" (including, at one point, me)—joked that he had little respect for Barrie until learning of his legal escapades. Goodman reached a new conclusion: "He's an artist, and he's fearless."[12]

But once the city went forward with its plans, appointed a board of directors, and hired administrators and researchers, everybody had to confront another problem: Who and what would the museum include? Did crime have to be associated with mobsters to be organized? The Ku Klux Klan had marched in Las Vegas during the 1920s and certainly was an organized criminal group, but would it fit the definition of organized crime for the museum? Obviously, by organized crime, the museum meant the mob in its various guises and activities.[13]

Another concern involved ethnic stereotyping—historically, and whether the museum would perpetuate it. When Nevada created its

"Black Book" to bar mobsters from casinos, the first eleven entrants were all of Italian heritage. The term *mafia*, often used interchangeably with *organized crime*, suggested an Italian basis for all things gangsterish, but organized crime crossed ethnic, religious, and gender lines. The concern was legitimate, and popular culture had imbedded the idea, with Edward G. Robinson, born Emanuel Goldberg, playing Rico Bandello in *Little Caesar*, with *The Godfather* films, and with Leonardo DiCaprio as an Irish gang leader in *Gangs of New York*. Several scholars of Italian-American history expressed feelings about the museum ranging from concern to displeasure. Goodman spoke before the local Italian-American Club, whose members excoriated him until he announced that they heard him wrong: he had proposed a "mop museum" on the history of cleaning.[14]

Las Vegas itself presented difficulties. One was how new the city was and is. Some of its founders, or their descendants, are still alive, prominent, and powerful; how to address their families and other sensitive matters? Another involved different perspectives. During a discussion involving the curators and community members, one longtime Las Vegan recalled how "the mob ran the town." Another replied, "No, it didn't." Both were right, to an extent: the doubter first became prominent during the 1950s, when mobsters invested in local development but avoided public attention or undue involvement in local politics or crime; the other had been active in the 1970s and early 1980s, when Tony Spilotro oversaw a burglary ring and Frank Rosenthal was a television host and newspaper columnist—the kinds of attention-getting activities that their predecessors had shunned. Further, as one reporter noted, the museum "has to satisfy—or at least not enrage—those who see the mob's 1950's to 1970's heyday as a golden age for Las Vegas," with casinos small enough for the managers to know even minor customers by name and comps—free meals—or cheap food and entertainment the rule rather than the exception. But, as Knowlton said, "When organized crime people are controlling a segment of the economy, honest, decent people are shut out. Anytime you have a business that is getting skimmed, it can't reach its full potential." Not to mention that in the late 1970s, a detective with the local police department's organized crime task force resigned to join Spilotro's burglary ring, which would seem to have been enough to explode the myth of the mob keeping the streets clean.[15]

Another question was how to market the museum. During the planning stages, the city proclaimed that it would open "the [Redacted] Museum," with "Mob" blacked out. When the renovations on the old federal building began, a local newspaper noted that the museum's

> announcement could make your head spin from the contradictions. There were elected officials and a former U.S. senator dressed as mobsters in suits and fedoras. . . . Which just shows the tricky nature of the task of the Las Vegas Museum of Organized Crime and Law Enforcement: showcasing the role of mobsters in local history while trying not to glorify the organized crime.

Two years before the opening, the curators unveiled some of the exhibits with the hope that they would build anticipation of the museum's opening. Dennis Barrie also promised, "There'll be controversy in this museum. If there's not, we're not doing our job."[16]

Nationally and locally, some critics pounced on whether the museum would address a controversy involving Senator Harry Reid and complained when it did not. When he chaired the Nevada Gaming Commission and tangled with various mob figures, one of them, a show producer named Joe Agosto, claimed in wiretapped discussions with other Kansas City operatives that he had "a cleanface" in his pocket. Agosto suggested that he received favorable treatment from Reid. Not only did Reid deny the allegations, but federal and state officials defended him against the attacks. Kathy Barrie told one interviewer, "Reid was never charged with a crime. We don't go after people just because one person mentions it on a wiretap," asking, "Was Joe Agosto the most reliable?" The answer, she argued, was no: in fact, Agosto had been a front man for Kansas City and even assumed the name he used from someone who had died years before. The disclosure of the wiretaps prompted what the police considered a credible enough death threat to assign Reid protection. Ultimately, the museum website included a video interview in which Reid discussed the issue.[17]

Another problem was what story to tell. Research for the exhibits made clear that many in law enforcement heroically battled the mob, but some had succumbed to any number of temptations, from accepting bribes to joining the mob; for example, the museum ended up addressing charges that the FBI often ignored Boston mobster Whitey Bulger's activities because he provided the agency with information about another crime family. Thus Knowlton reminded the museum staff not to forget that law enforcement had misbehaved, just as gangsters had. Similarly, organized crime figures included businesspeople who would have fit in at any corporation as well as cold-blooded killers devoted to their families. As one of the researchers, I could discuss my grandfather, a New York policeman whom I grew up listening to as he recounted some dubious escapades, or discuss how I lived around the corner from the former home of Spilotro, whom neighbors remembered as a typical father and homeowner.[18]

Balancing these multiple dichotomies proved challenging. Related to these were questions that museum professionals regularly address: What are the artifacts? How many photographs and videos are available and necessary? How much text should accompany this material? How interactive should the museum be? And, in addressing all of these questions, those involved had to be conscious of logistics. Visitors would have to move through the museum slowly enough to see the exhibits but fast enough to avoid logjams. In addition, the 41,000-square-foot building itself remained under federal control. When the curators asked for permission to move a wall to improve an exhibit and the traffic through it, the National Park Service, which controls the building itself, said no.

But the 17,000 square feet of exhibit space still covered ample ground. Visitors entered the museum lobby on the first floor and walked past the old post office boxes before taking an elevator to the third floor, where, for a fee, they could obtain a mug shot of themselves in a lineup before moving on to a film about the mob, then an exhibit area on early Las Vegas, a section on Prohibition, and the wall from the St. Valentine's Day Massacre in 1929. They wended their way past photos, artifacts, and interpretations related to mob involvement in a variety of enterprises, popular culture, and a video reenactment of a mob induction ceremony, before heading to the second floor.

The second floor featured the key justification for the museum, the courtroom where Kefauver held a hearing on organized crime in Las Vegas. A video presentation explained Kefauver's role, as did the exhibit area leading into it. After a small section on Goodman—including both excerpts from a documentary on him and material from a roast of him—patrons went through sections on Las Vegas in the 1950s and 1960s, on information about cheating and skimming, and on the involvement of Howard Hughes and corporations. Then the exhibits focused on the national and international implications of organized crime, with a documentary about John Kennedy's assassination. Another area focused on how the mob disposed of witnesses and turncoat members.

The first floor focused on more recent developments in organized crime. Thanks to the FBI, visitors could listen to wiretaps and learn about prosecutors and investigators. They encountered rotating exhibits, a section on mob families, a wall of "100 Made Men" from organized crime, and displays related to John Gotti and to popular culture, including *The Sopranos*, culminating in a short film about how Hollywood depicted mobsters.

The political, professional, economic, and historical issues were not always settled, but the museum opened on February 14, 2012. The celebration drew protesters unhappy with the costs, but it also attracted community and national attention. The festivities included the presence of numerous former law enforcement officials: I walked into a party surrounded by mobsters-turned-informants Henry Hill of *Goodfellas* fame and Frank Cullotta, a one-time hitman for the Chicago outfit. By that October, the museum had welcomed 100,000 visitors, had prompted headlines like "Mob Museum shines a light on the good guys, too," and had become integral to downtown redevelopment efforts.[19]

The museum tried to define its mission narrowly and its subject matter broadly. Before opening, it changed from the Las Vegas Museum of Organized Crime and Law Enforcement to the National Museum. Executive director Jonathan Ullman noted, "You really cannot tell this story without addressing larger national content. We cover Prohibition, immigration, and the evolution of the criminal justice system." Thus it emphasized issues related to organized crime and law enforcement, including hosting community forums involving local police. It featured speakers and programs on topics ranging from the mob's role in Cuba to Kefauver's hearings, including several with his daughter. It presented exhibitions on "El Chapo," a drug kingpin in Mexico, and the scandal about World Cup Soccer's governing body, including a *New York Daily News* headline, "Fifa Nostra." Its speakers ranged from Robert Blakey, the main author of the Racketeer Influenced and Corrupt Organizations Act—key legislation in bringing down the mob—to authors Dan E. Moldea, Selwyn Raab, and Gus Russo, whose investigative reporting and writing had brought their work international acclaim and the mob unwanted attention.[20]

Just before the museum opened, a national Taxpayers Protection Alliance senior fellow published an op-ed declaring, "The museum will function as a shrine to two of the most shameful blemishes on America: organized crime and government waste." Two years later, he published another objection to the public funding and added that Goodman had sought "to build a museum that celebrates the mob lifestyle" and that it "glorified criminal behavior." While the museum certainly included information that humanized murderers—family photos and articles of clothing—no one who actually had gone through the museum with open eyes and an open mind could reach that conclusion—another example of how memory and image could outweigh reality. (I do not think I say this because I am a researcher and member of the board of directors.) Although he lamented the loss of the old days when, as he put it, "They knew your name. They treated you like a king," Goodman disclaimed a desire to romanticize the mob: "The bottom line is—and nobody knows it better than I do—law enforcement won. The mob is not here, and that's one of the reasons I became the mayor. I didn't have any clients left." But his biographer, Las Vegas journalist and historian John L. Smith, said, "Its creation threatens to send a false and dangerous message that organized crime is a relic of our notorious past and not an undercurrent in present Southern Nevada society." Organized crime may no longer control casinos, but news accounts of street crime, drug dealing, and topless dance clubs suggested that it was alive and well outside of the gaming industry.[21]

As the museum celebrated its first anniversary in 2013, it reported fewer visitors than were projected, but it finished in the black and has continued to do so since. In 2017, for the museum's fifth anniversary, Goodman toasted its success, bragging about the approximately 350,000 visitors the previous year and its $20 million economic impact on downtown. Yet neither the museum's staff nor the directors sat on their laurels. Ullman listed the challenges: "How do we make the experience more dynamic? How do we give people a reason to sign up and become a member and come multiple times and not simply see the same exhibits over and over again?" Varied programming helped, as did accreditation in 2017 from the American Academy of Museums and TripAdvisor including it in its list of the top twenty-five museums in the United States. But so did rotating exhibits, including one of classic Las Vegas photos and another in partnership with the University of Nevada, Las Vegas, History Department on Prohibition-era women's fashion.[22]

In 2018, the museum unveiled a $9 million renovation designed to make its space far more dynamic. Those responsible for the museum—the directors and the staff—long had grasped the need to address not just the more distant past, but also modern issues. The first-floor exhibits on recent organized crime were jettisoned, combined, or reconfigured to make room for a crime lab, which included forensic evidence from the St. Valentine's Day Massacre and modern technology that permitted visitors to study the use of DNA and involve themselves in autopsies of historic figures. The museum installed a "Use of Force" exhibit in which videos and interactives helped visitors understand how, when, and why the police resort to force and whether they should do so. Its installation after numerous controversies across the United States about that very issue—and the role of race and bias—opened the possibility for the museum to be seen as attacking law enforcement or defending it. Throughout the planning of the new interactive exhibit, all involved remained conscious of that problem and sought to provide a balanced version that would help the public understand a multifaceted issue.

The museum also sought to provide a balance in the other part of its renovation: "The Underground." The basement had housed the museum's staff, which had outgrown the space, requiring staff to rent offices nearby. Museum directors and officials decided to combine entertainment, profits, and history by developing the bottom floor as a speakeasy with a distillery, a bar, and private rooms, as well as exhibits and artifacts from the Prohibition era and rooms for panel discussions and lectures. The Mob Museum remains a nonprofit, but "The Underground" promised a potential new revenue stream while also enhancing the museum's coverage of the era in which organized crime first achieved great prominence in the United States.[23]

The museum also became part of a cultural corridor that combined downtown redevelopment with a sense of history. The Fifth Street School, a New Deal project in which thousands of Las Vegans went to elementary school, housed an art gallery, city and university offices, and public programs. The Neon Museum featured the classic signs from bygone hotels and other businesses, both at its "boneyard" and at intersections around town. The Old Mormon Fort State Park, including the state's oldest building, concentrated on the area's nineteenth-century history, which included a mission and ranches. Nearby, a few months after the Mob Museum debuted, the Smith Center for the Performing Arts, whose main building was redolent of the Art Deco architecture of Hoover Dam, opened just west of the original downtown.[24]

The controversy surrounding the Mob Museum's subject matter dissipated as visitors saw that it did anything but celebrate organized crime and its practitioners. The museum offered the opportunity to consider Las Vegas's history in a national and an international context. Those who felt nostalgic for the mob past could find information and interpretations that pleased them, but they would have trouble avoiding the less savory aspects of that past.

As a historian and lifelong Las Vegan, I have welcomed that emphasis on a multi-layered approach and the opportunity to be part of it. The experience also has made me a better historian because I have realized more clearly how much individual and collective memory shape how the public interprets the past. What I grew up believing and what actually happened were sometimes the same, but I also learned a great deal about my hometown and had to rethink what I knew about it. I understood much better what it entails to be a public historian, as well as a historian who engages with the public: people who knew and respected me and my work, or so I thought, told me that the museum would pay homage to the mob, which struck me as an insult, not only to me, but also to the officials who were part of the core group at the museum. These officials included not only veterans of law enforcement but also Goodman, who, as an officer of the court representing his clients, provided a zealous defense but hewed to the letter of the law. (While he has long since decided that I should not be "whacked," and we consider each other friends, that is not why I say this.)

I also realized that I played a small role in a much less important battle in the "history wars" that have gone on for more than a quarter of a century. In the 1990s, the left, right, and middle, as well as historians with no political skin in the game, engaged in controversial debates over school standards and exhibits like the Smithsonian's depiction of the *Enola Gay* and the dropping of the first atomic bomb. More recently, they have similarly disputed the statues that pay tribute to Confederate heroes and veterans but really are artifacts of opposition to African American civil rights during the Jim Crow era and then during the civil rights movement of the 1950s and 1960s. Colleges and universities have analyzed their institutional connections to slavery, and this analysis has become part of a broader discussion of reparations for the descendants of slaves.[25]

This is not to say that the Mob Museum ranks with any of these in terms of public controversy. It reminds us that the many ways in which American history is both admirable and reprehensible extend beyond the obvious subjects into such areas as organized crime and law enforcement—which, in turn, are connected to topics like immigration and exploitation that inform our history and demand our attention. For Las Vegas, the Mob Museum marks a coming to terms with its past and demonstrates the benefits of a community knowing that past, confronting it, understanding it, moving on, and trying to do better. For me, it has meant coming to terms with my own past and how it has shaped the present and future of the place I live—and my present, and perhaps my future.

NOTES

1. I would like to thank David Tanenhaus, professor of history and the James E. Rogers professor of law at University of Nevada, Las Vegas, and Geoff Schumacher, senior vice-president in charge of exhibits and programs for the Mob Museum, for their comments on a draft of this essay. I should note that, since I played a role in the museum, I am sometimes describing or analyzing events or discussions that I witnessed or played a part in and do not footnote them.

   Quotation from Harry Reid and Mark Warren, *The Good Fight: Hard Lessons from Searchlight to Washington* (New York: Putnam's, 2008), 265–66. *Las Vegas Review-Journal*, October 5, 1982; *Las Vegas Sun*, October 5, 1982; *Valley Times*, October 5, 1982; Nicholas Pileggi, *Casino: Love and Honor in Las Vegas* (New York: Simon and Schuster, 1995); *Casino*, directed by Martin Scorsese, https://www.imdb.com/title/tt0112641/.
2. I have written about some of these experiences in "Growing Up amid History," in *Back to Where You Once Belonged: Las Vegas Writers Weigh the Power of the Past*, ed. Scott Dickensheets and Geoff Schumacher (Las Vegas, NV: Huntington Press, 2017), 47–66; and "*The Valley Times*: A Personal History," in *Change in the American West*, ed. Stephen Tchudi (Reno: Nevada Humanities/University of Nevada Press, 1996), 213–32. Some of my father's experiences, and those of other workers, appear in H. Lee Barnes, *Dummy Up and Deal: Inside the Culture of Casino Dealing* (Reno: University of Nevada Press, 2002).
3. *Las Vegas Sun*, February 20, 2012; *Texarkana Gazette*, March 20, 2013; https://www.lasvegasadvisor.com/faq-general-safer-under-the-mob/. On the changes in Las Vegas, see also Geoff Schumacher, *Sun, Sin and Suburbia: The History of Modern Las Vegas*, rev. ed. (Reno: University of Nevada Press, 2015); and Larry Gragg, *Bright Light City: Las Vegas in Popular Culture* (Lawrence: University Press of Kansas, 2013).
4. Woody Allen, "A Look at Organized Crime," *New Yorker*, August 15, 1970, 24–25.
5. https://themobmuseum.org/case-files/the-building/.
6. https://themobmuseum.org/case-files/the-building/; *Las Vegas Review-Journal*, October 2, 2011; *Philadelphia Inquirer*, February 14, 2012; *New York Times*, January 9, 2009, and April 25, 2010.
7. *Las Vegas Review-Journal*, April 15, 2006; *Augusta Chronicle*, September 6, 2006; *Tribune Business News*, June 18, 2009.
8. Joan Burkhart Whitely, *Young Las Vegas, 1905–1931: Before the Future Found Us* (Las Vegas, NV: Stephens Press, 2010); Eugene P. Moehring, *Resort City in the Sunbelt: Las Vegas, 1930–2000* (Reno: University of Nevada Press, 2000), especially chapter 1; Eugene P. Moehring and Michael S. Green, *Las Vegas: A Centennial History* (Reno: University of Nevada Press, 2005), especially 9–79; *Las Vegas Review-Journal*, May 28, 2012; *Las Vegas Sun*, April 26, 2004; https://themobmuseum.org/blog/the-first-mobster-in-las-vegas-part-1/; https://themobmuseum.org/blog/the-first-mobster-in-las-vegas-part-2/; https://themobmuseum.org/blog/the-first-mobster-in-las-vegas-part-3/.
9. See, generally, Ed Reid and Ovid DeMaris, *The Green Felt Jungle* (New York: Trident Press, 1963); Sally Denton and Roger Morris, *The Money and the Power: The Making of*

Las Vegas and Its Hold on America, 1947–2000 (New York: Alfred A. Knopf, 2001); and John L. Smith, *Sharks in the Desert: The Founding Fathers and Current Kings of Las Vegas* (Fort Lee, NJ: Barricade Books, 2005).

10. *USA Today*, December 16, 2008; *Chronicle* (Augusta), September 6, 2006; *New York Times*, January 9, 2009; *Guardian*, November 23, 2008.
11. *Los Angeles Times*, May 15, 2011; *Las Vegas Review-Journal*, March 2, 2011; *Tulsa World*, December 11, 2007; *Post-Gazette* (Pittsburgh), February 19, 2012; *New York Times*, January 9, 2009.
12. *USA Today*, December 16, 2008; Alex Palmer, "When Art Fought the Law and the Art Won," *Smithsonian.com*, October 2, 2015, https://www.smithsonianmag.com/history/when-art-fought-law-and-art-won-180956810/; Erick Trickey, "Pop Goes the Museum," *clevelandmagazine.com*, February 20, 2012, https://clevelandmagazine.com/entertainment/museums-galleries/articles/pop-goes-the-museum; *Las Vegas Review-Journal*, April 16, 2010.
13. Lisa McGirr, *The War on Alcohol: Prohibition and the Rise of the American State* (New York: Norton, 2016); Linda Gordon, *The Second Coming of the KKK: The Ku Klux Klan of the 1920s and the American Political Tradition* (New York: Norton, 2017).
14. *New York Times*, January 9, 2009; Goodman, conversation with author; Ronald A. Farrell and Carole Case, *The Black Book and the Mob: The Untold Story of the Control of Nevada's Casinos* (Madison: University of Wisconsin Press, 1995).
15. *Orlando Sentinel*, February 27, 2012; *Las Vegas Review-Journal*, October 4, 2008, and February 14, 2012. See also Leslie Niño Fidance, "The Mob *Never* Ran Vegas," *Gaming Law Review and Economics* 13, no. 1 (February 2009): 27–40.
16. *Las Vegas Review-Journal*, October 2, 2008; August 5, 2009; March 26, 2010.
17. *Chicago Tribune*, February 22, 2012; *Las Vegas Review-Journal*, February 13 and 26, 2012, and January 20, 2014; https://themobmuseum.org/case-files/digital-experiences/. See also "The Mob on the Run," documentary, KLAS-TV, 1987, https://www.youtube.com/watch?v=BWtgb3lsYiw&t=143s; Reid and Warren, *The Good Fight*, 246–49, 257–63; and *Las Vegas Review-Journal*, March 27, 2010; February 16, 2012; December 8, 2016.
18. On Bulger, see, for example, *Boston Globe*, May 9, 2016. The issues discussed here came up in various conversations involving the curators, researchers, and museum directors.
19. *Tribune Business News*, August 4, 2009; *PR Newswire*, February 14, 2012; *Tribune Business News*, October 2, 2012; *Chicago Tribune*, March 4, 2012.
20. *Las Vegas Review-Journal*, October 11, 2011, and August 7, 2014; *New York Daily News*, September 2, 2015; *La Prensa San Diego*, March 18, 2016; *Las Vegas Sun*, November 15, 2012; *McClatchy-Tribune Business News*, November 15, 2012. For examples of the authors' work, see Selwyn Raab, *Five Families: The Rise, Decline, and Resurgence of America's Most Powerful Mafia Empires* (New York: Thomas Dunne/St. Martin's, 2016); Gus Russo, *Supermob: How Sidney Korshak and His Criminal Associates Became America's Hidden Power Brokers* (New York: Bloomsbury, 2007); Dan E. Moldea, *Interference: How Organized Crime Influences Professional Football* (New York: William Morrow, 1989), and www.moldea.com.

21. *Las Vegas Review-Journal*, February 12, 2012; Washington *Times*, June 23, 2014; *Tribune Business News*, August 6, 2009; *Las Vegas Review-Journal*, August 9, 2009, and February 22 and 26, 2012.
22. *Las Vegas Review-Journal*, February 14, 2013; The Mob Museum had to close during part of the 2020 pandemic, and had limited capacity at other times, affecting its profits and attendance. February 10, 2017; September 23, 2017.
23. *Las Vegas Weekly*, April 20, 2018.
24. *Las Vegas Review-Journal*, May 24, 2008.
25. A website that addresses some of the issues related to the statues and links to various analyses is https://www.historians.org/news-and-advocacy/everything-has-a-history/america-inside-out-welcome-page. See also https://www.csmonitor.com/USA/Society/2019/0822/The-future-of-America-s-past-Should-we-explain-Confederate-statues; Eric Foner, "Confederate Statues and 'Our' History," *New York Times*, August 20, 2017; and Janeen Bryant et al., "Are Museums the Rightful Home for Confederate Monuments?" *Center for the Future of Museums Blog*, April 3, 2018, https://www.aam-us.org/2018/04/03/are-museums-the-rightful-home-for-confederate-monuments/. On reparations, see https://www.nytimes.com/2019/05/23/business/economy/reparations-slavery.html; and https://www.wsj.com/articles/the-long-history-of-american-slavery-reparations-11568991623. Numerous universities have delved into their past; for a starting point, see Craig Steven Wilder, *Ebony and Ivy: Race, Slavery, and the Troubled History of America's Universities* (New York: Bloomsbury, 2013).

9

ON LIVING HISTORY AND STORIES UNFINISHED

TIMOTHY PATRICK McCARTHY

Who owns history? Everyone and no one—which is why the study of the past is a constantly evolving, never-ending journey of discovery.

—ERIC FONER, *WHO OWNS HISTORY?*

Knowledgeable civic actors can draw important lessons from history, which does incrementally increase civic capacity. Historical amnesia blocks the construction of potentially successful social movements. As the gap between the past, present, and future diminishes, individuals can acquire a greater sense of becoming the "makers" of their own history. Thus, for the oppressed, the act of reconstructing history is inextricably linked to the political practice, or praxis, of transforming the present and the future.

—MANNING MARABLE, *LIVING BLACK HISTORY*

From the start, my teaching was infused with my own history. I would try to be fair to other points of view, but I wanted more than "objectivity"; I wanted my students to leave my classes not just better informed, but more prepared to relinquish the safety of silence, more prepared to speak up, to act against injustice wherever they saw it. This, of course, was a recipe for trouble.

—HOWARD ZINN, *YOU CAN'T BE NEUTRAL ON A MOVING TRAIN*

PART ONE: AN ORIGIN STORY

I can't quite remember when I first fell in *love* with history. It was certainly before I became "credentialed" as a historian, but also before I became fully conscious of my competing—and often conflicting—responsibilities as a scholar and writer, teacher and troublemaker. I suppose one origin of such things dates back to when I first learned to *listen* to other people's stories. I grew up in an unorthodox family as the adopted only son and grandson of public school teachers and factory workers. We weren't fancy people, not by any means, but rather blue-collar folks, devoutly Catholic and derived from immigrant stock. We shared our home freely with other family members, foreign exchange students, and foster children, as well as neighbors and friends from all walks of life. Our dinner table was like a local convening of a rainbow coalition, which is why the concept of "chosen family" was so familiar to me from a very early age, even before I ever knew I was "different." As an only child, I experienced all of this as a kind of *beloved community*, where many kinds of people lived together, worked together, and broke bread together. It was a world where everyone seemed to have what they needed—food to eat and a place to sleep, room to gather and grow—where no one had *more* than their fair share. It was also a world where everyone treated others with respect, and where no one hated anyone or tried to hurt anyone. When I think about the various ways my life could have gone, and even some of the ways my life *did* go, all of this still feels like some kind of *jackpot*.

As a boy, I often spent my weekends with my grandparents, whose families had come to the United States in the late nineteenth and early twentieth centuries from Italy and Ukraine (on my mother's side) and Ireland and Hungary (on my father's side). My dad's folks had moved upstate from New York City to Albany the same year—1971—that I was born and adopted. They had a modest suburban home with an old-fashioned wooden swing in their backyard. My grandmother was a retired teacher who was the first woman in our family to go to college. She had such a lasting impact as an educator that her community renamed a street after her in 1971, the year she retired after four decades of teaching.

I knew none of this growing up, except that she always treated me, her only grandchild, as one of her students. We spent many long afternoons together on that swing, sitting directly across from each other and drinking Lipton iced tea, while she showered me with questions about school. Two, in particular, stick with me. "What did you learn this week that you want to share with me?" she would ask, eyes locked into mine. And then: "What did you learn this week that you still have questions about?" These intimate exchanges opened up endless frontiers of possibility—most critically, to share my learning, to ask questions about what I was being taught, and to do both in the presence of a teacher who was still committed to learning and teaching herself. Looking back, that swing may be the most important school I ever attended.

My grandmother was also an avid letter writer. She spent time each morning and evening writing letters to her many siblings and friends who lived in other places. I loved to watch the repertoire of her facial expressions—knowing smiles and punctuating chuckle bursts, searching eyes and accompanying pursed lips—as she carefully moved pen across paper, line after line, with a kind of mastered precision. Every once in a while, I would interrupt her flow to ask whom she was writing to, at which point she would launch into stories of peoples and places, many of which I did not yet know. My grandfather would sometimes chime in, his legendary Irish humor and impulse for exaggeration on lavish, often lubricated display. The combination—her and him, their very different styles and many decades of shared practice—always felt like a free, exclusive double feature. But my grandmother never read me her letters, the ones she wrote or the ones she received. These were not meant to be shared—at least not with me, not yet. I remember crying in the attic of my grandparents' home in late May 1986, just a few weeks shy of the fifteenth anniversary of when my grandmother and I first came into each other's lives. My father and I were sifting through boxes upon boxes of letters—from all those peoples and places, the other side of all that correspondence—wondering what to do with them now that the pancreatic cancer had finally stolen her from us. Hers was the first death of my life, those boxes of letters my first archive. I still had so many questions, so much I wanted to learn and share. But my first teacher was gone.

Textbooks have always frustrated me. I suppose it all goes back to one middle school social studies assignment in which we were forced to memorize in order—chapter by chapter, with every victory and defeat—all the U.S. presidents and vice presidents, from George Washington and John Adams to Ronald Reagan and George Herbert Walker Bush. Even then, this seemed like a titanic waste of time, all the more so because I couldn't keep track of the time line during the decades leading up to the Civil War, which I would later discover was something of a wasteland of American political leadership and party division, to say nothing of its moral mendacity insofar as slavery and other betrayals of freedom were concerned. Four history degrees later, I still have trouble keeping track of Millard Fillmore, Zachary Taylor's vice president who never had a vice president of his own. (I Googled that.) I've always been struck by how many of us are turned off to history at an early age because of how we were taught history in schools. And the textbooks—what's left out of them as much as what's left in them—are more than partly to blame. As my late teacher Manning Marable has written:

> The history that is generally codified in classroom textbooks and sets the boundaries of civic discourse emphasizes the character of the American experience as "exceptional" and "unique," but also "universal," in the sense that our history's underlying core democratic values can be transported and adopted by other peoples in distant lands, thereby enhancing the quality of their lives. To become "American" is to accept the legitimacy of this master narrative.[1]

Like so many Americans, I was routinely taught such falsehoods in school, and thus received a treacherous mis-education. Three things stand out. First, we are taught that America's "greatness" is without precedent, impossible to reproduce except by force. Second, we are taught that presidents and vice presidents—along with all the captains of conquest and capitalism—are the "greatest" Americans, the ones who make the nation "great." And third, by implication and extrapolation, we are taught that we should either *want* to become them or that we can *never* become them, *especially* if we are not *like* them. (For what it's worth,

I never wanted to become like *any* of *them*.) It took me some time to discover that this "master narrative" of American exceptionalism is a dangerous mythology deeply rooted in deliberate historical exclusion and arrogant national supremacy—among other things.

Fortunately, the fact that my grandmother persistently encouraged me to ask questions inspired me to take hold of my learning from the very beginning. As it turns out, this was not always welcomed by my other teachers. "Timmy talks too much" was an early refrain on my report cards, just as visits to the principal's office became a consistent feature of my life at school in those early years. But every once in a while, I got lucky. One conspicuous illustration, insofar as American history is concerned, occurred in seventh grade, when I was assigned my first research project by a social studies teacher, Mr. McCormack, who was mercifully more interested in our creative and critical thinking than in our mundane capacity for rote memorization. Living in upstate New York, I had developed an interest in Iroquois history, in part because my large public middle school was divided into three "houses"—Tawasentha, Mohawk, and Hiawatha—whose names I did not initially recognize but about which I became increasingly curious.[2] My father, who taught high school social studies for decades, encouraged my curiosity, taking me on weekends to the state library and museums in Albany, where I learned the origin and meaning of these words, as well as the history of the Iroquois Confederacy, its complex relationship with Dutch settlers in colonial New York and the so-called 'founding fathers' of the American Revolution, and the Iroquois crop rotation calendar with its seasonal and cyclical conceptions of both land and time. My mother, a longtime third-grade teacher, helped me create the more artistic components of my project—the overhead projections, the multicolored storyboards, the diorama of the Iroquois longhouse—and Mr. McCormack gave me time in class to present my work. (I assume this is because we had gone well beyond the requirements of the assignment.) While my peers had submitted papers, I had produced a *performance*, my own little staged rebellion against what—and who—was missing from our American history textbook (for what it's worth, it was also my first "A+"). The following year, when I was elected to be the school's first student body president, I organized a flag design competition, the winner of which was an image of differently colored hands clasped together within the outline of the interconnected houses of our school. As naïve as the design probably was—an image of multicultural connection and collaboration with no sign of conflict—the flag still flies. Part of me is still proud of that fact.

In retrospect, the questions I kept asking—not only about *what* I was learning, but also about what I was *not* learning, and *why*—were equal parts curiosity and rebellion. I have always been drawn to rebels, the people who refuse to accept what is given to or required of them. This certainly has something to do with my own history, the way I came into and was raised in the world as a child, as well as who taught me and how. But it also has something to do with the moment in American history during which I came of age. I was born just after "the sixties," in the midst of the criminal war in Vietnam and the disgraced presidency of Richard Nixon. I started middle school the year Ronald Reagan was elected president and graduated high school just after his two terms ended. Raised on MTV and hip-hop, my adolescent years were dominated by the dueling fears of dying from AIDS and nuclear holocaust, as well as the integrated classrooms and interracial friendships that were only made possible by earlier rebellions.[3] The month we graduated from high school, tanks rolled through Tiananmen Square in Beijing. My first year of college, the Wall in Berlin was torn down. My second year of college, the United States waged its first war on Iraq and Nelson Mandela finally walked free from Robben Island prison in South Africa. My third year of college, the Soviet Union dissolved in Moscow and race riots exploded after the Rodney King beating in Los Angeles. My last year of college, the election of Bill Clinton ended the twelve long years of the Reagan-Bush era. Those were turbulent times, world-historical by any measure, and they swept me up. My parents and I now laugh about the fact, still telling, that during my first year of college I participated in anti-apartheid demonstrations and AIDS actions before registering for classes or getting a work-study job.

As tempting as it is sometimes to view history through the lens of inevitability—or worse, *destiny*—it is often moments of serendipity that foster and forge our contexts and capacities for change. My unlikely acceptance to Harvard was one of these moments. My undergraduate years happened to coincide with the spectacular reemergence—subsequently called a "renaissance"—of the Department of African American Studies, following the hiring of prominent Black professors like Henry Louis Gates Jr., Kwame Anthony Appiah, Julian Bond, and many others. Inspired by the student solidarity movement demanding that American colleges and universities "divest" from apartheid South Africa, I began taking courses in nineteenth- and twentieth-century African American history, literature, and politics. I will never forget my first day of "African American Literature from the Slave Trade to 1900," taught by a young literary scholar named Phillip Brian Harper (who, it turns out, was my first Black *and* queer teacher). The class met on the third floor of Sever Hall, and I was late. I ran across the Yard, into the building, up three flights of stairs, and down the hall to the classroom. As I pushed open the door, panting and more than a little embarrassed, I heard Professor Harper say, "and the white man . . . ," at which point people turned to look at me and then burst into laughter. I was the only white man, one of only a handful of white people, in the room. I smiled apologetically and slinked into the last seat of the back row. Regardless of whether that moment was just a bad first impression or yet another trifling confirmation about "the white man"—it may have been both—I fell in love with that class. I read every page of every book, soaked in every minute of every lecture, and listened intently to my peers as they debated matters of importance and urgency. But I didn't talk. About three weeks into the course, before the first paper assignment, I went to the office hours of my graduate teaching fellow, a brilliant Black woman, who asked me why I wasn't contributing to the section discussions. "Because I don't know enough yet," I replied. I will never forget her response—or her generosity: "That's not what I expected you to say. I thought you were going to tell me you were *afraid* to talk, and I want *all* my students to speak in class. So take your time, listen and learn, but work to find your voice." Slowly but surely, that's exactly what I did.

The summer following that class, another moment of serendipity manifested itself. I had also just taken "Civil War and Reconstruction" with David Herbert Donald, an older white southern professor who was a leading scholar of Abraham Lincoln. It was his last class before retirement, and he mentioned in one of his lectures that he was working on a biography of the sixteenth president.[4] Encouraged by one of my advisers, I decided to pursue a summer research assistantship rather than return home to paint houses and play basketball as I had always done. I made an appointment with Professor Donald, during which I offered to work for him for free, a fact then unbeknownst to my parents, who would have killed me if they had known I had done something so absurd. (We were not an "unpaid internship" kind of family.) Professor Donald asked me what I was interested in, and I responded: "I want to know what Black people thought about Abraham Lincoln." He smiled sweetly and said: "Well, you're in luck—so do I!" As luck would indeed have it, that year the Black Abolitionist Papers had just become available on seventeen reels of microfilm and he was looking for someone to go through them.[5] He hired me the next week and helped me secure a research fellowship (my first), after which I spent the entire summer and much of the subsequent year in the basement of Harvard's Lamont Library, where I slowly made my way through this treasure trove of documents. The rest, one could say, is history.

I had developed a serious interest in Abraham Lincoln during a high school "mock trial" exercise, when I had to take the stand *as Lincoln* (and the Black abolitionist Frederick Douglass, too) to offer my defense against impeachment charges during the U.S. Civil War. That was cool enough, but it was something else entirely to *study Lincoln* in depth for the first time through the critical eyes of his Black contemporaries—to get *their* perspective on his unlikely candidacy and political ascendancy, the charged debates over the enlistment and equal pay of Black troops, the various emancipation proclamations, and his untimely assassination and complex legacy. During my first real immersion in an archive—the letters in my grandmother's attic notwithstanding—I learned about Lincoln's deep discomfort with the abolitionists, his persistent pragmatism and stubborn moderation, his long-standing support for the colonization of free African Americans in Liberia, and his ongoing public struggles over slavery and secession. This was a different portrait of the man than

I had previously been taught. On the pages of these newspapers—*Weekly Anglo-African, North Star, National Era, Douglass' Monthly, Christian Recorder*, and others—Lincoln emerged as less of a hero who "freed the slaves" and more of a human being who was flawed, frustrating, and full of contradictions. It was here that I first came to understand what Frederick Douglass meant, in April 1876, when he proclaimed: "He was preeminently the white man's President, entirely devoted to the welfare of the white man. . . . Abraham Lincoln was not, in the fullest sense of the word, either our man or our model. In his interests, in his associations, in his habits of thought, and in his prejudices, he was a white man. . . . We are at best only his stepchildren; children by adoption, children by forces of circumstances and necessity." Douglass also said: "His great mission was to accomplish two things: first, to save his country from dismemberment and ruin; and, second, to free his country from the great crime of slavery. . . . Viewed from the genuine abolition ground, Mr. Lincoln seemed tardy, cold, dull, and indifferent; but measuring him by the sentiment of his country, a sentiment he was bound as a statesman to consult, he was swift, zealous, radical, and determined."[6] It is never an easy thing to have your childhood heroes—those textbook titans—knocked from the pedestal by the people. But this is precisely what happened with Abraham Lincoln and me. And it taught me the most valuable lesson (again, quoting Douglass): "power concedes nothing without demand." I never learned *that* in my history textbooks.

This awakening in college—intellectual, political, personal—eventually led me to write my senior thesis on five works of what I call "freedom's fiction": Frederick Douglass's *The Heroic Slave* (1853), William Wells Brown's *Clotel* (1853), Frank Webb's *The Garies and Their Friends* (1857), Harriet Wilson's *Our Nig* (1859), and Martin Delany's *Blake* (1862).[7] These were the first Black-authored novels in the history of the United States, all published during the decade leading up to the Civil War. I had studied the popular genre of the "slave narrative," nearly one hundred of which were published during the antebellum period by formerly enslaved people who either wrote or told their stories to an eager and growing reading public. But these novels were different. They told an even bigger story of the complex and contested terrain of slavery and freedom in the United States: slave rebellions and fugitive escapes, racial terror and lynching, inequality and indentured servitude in the North, the violent relationships between white and Black women, cultural anxieties over "race-mixing" and interracial alliances, and the fraught politics of race, sex, and class since America's founding. Imbued with abolitionist themes and written by authors who were also activists, these novels rocked my world when I first read them my junior year. They were unapologetically *political*, what I would later come to call "protest literature."[8] Along with the Black Abolitionist Papers and slave narratives, these texts demonstrated how enslaved, fugitive, and free Black people made creative use of print culture—their autobiographical facts and imaginative fictions, as well as papers, pamphlets, poetry, and petitions—not only to "write themselves into existence" and "tell a free story," but also to demand radical change and imagine a different world in the decades leading up to the "Second American Revolution."[9] This was definitely not the kind of education I *ever* imagined getting at Harvard. But as a white man in America, I am grateful *every* day that I did.

The moral of this origin story is threefold. The first lesson is the value of *slowing down*, of taking the time to listen to other people's stories, to learn from them, to read and reflect before we do anything else. As I've learned over and over again from my family and teachers and peers, sometimes this can be done in community—at dinner tables, on swing sets, and in classrooms. But sometimes this can only be accomplished alone, in the more solitary spaces of libraries and archives, where primary sources become portals to distant places where we can have other kinds of conversations with other kinds of people—namely, those who came before us. I like to think of history this way: as an ongoing conversation across the grave with our ancestors. The second lesson is the value of *serendipity*, of realizing that our lives are shaped by the historical circumstances that swirl around us and sweep us up, the surprises that sometimes manifest themselves without notice. When I think back to the family that chose me and raised me, the teachers who lit a fire in me, the schools where I fell in love with learning, and the world in which I came of age, I can't help but appreciate just how much our own living histories shape our relationships—to the past, of course, but also to the present and future. And the third lesson is the value of the *shifting gaze*. In all of this, I learned to see things differently, not simply to accept a view of history and the world distorted by myths of exceptionalism and textbooks of exclusion, but instead to hear and heed the voices that tell a different story and allow us to do the same. In these early conversations across the table, swing, classroom, and grave, that is precisely what happened. This is how I fell in love with history. What I couldn't know is that all this would lead to a very different kind of life.

PART TWO: AN EVOLUTION STORY

It was the summer before starting my Ph.D. program in history at Columbia that I first read Howard Zinn's *A People's History of the United States*, his powerful work of revisionist history, first published in 1980. The book did indeed "knock [me] on my ass," as Matt Damon's title character exclaims in the famous bar scene in the 1997 Oscar-winning film *Good Will Hunting*. I was startled by the conclusion of the first chapter, which thoroughly upended the textbook myths too many of us were taught to believe about Christopher Columbus's "discovery" of the "New World." After retelling this story from the shifted gaze of the indigenous Arawak people, Zinn writes:

> If history is to be creative, to anticipate a possible future without denying the past, it should, I believe, emphasize new possibilities by disclosing those hidden episodes of the past when, even if in brief flashes, people showed their ability to resist, to join together, occasionally to win. I am supposing, or perhaps only hoping, that our future may be found in the past's fugitive moments of compassion rather than in its solid centuries of warfare. That, being as blunt as I can, is my approach to the history of the United States. The reader may as well know that before going on.[10]

At its most fundamental definition, *radical* means "getting to the root of things," and that is clearly one of the many things Zinn set out to accomplish. *A People's History* turned the "master narrative" on its head, narrating the story of America from the point of view of "the people" who are usually written out of history rather than the powerful and well positioned who usually dominate and determine it. As Eric Foner wrote in his *New York Times* review: "The book bears the same relation to traditional texts as a photographic negative does to the print: the areas of darkness and light have been reversed."[11] Upon first reading it, I remember thinking that I had finally found a textbook I liked. And I was hardly the only one. *A People's History* remains, some forty years on, the best-selling work of American history *in* American history.[12]

Zinn's groundbreaking work was, in many ways, the first "synthesis" of what became known as the "new social history," an emerging body of scholarship, inspired by the radical movements of the 1960s and 1970s, that emphasized history from the "bottom up." This new research dramatically altered and expanded our understanding of how African Americans and women, socialists and students, immigrants and indigenous peoples, communists and civil rights activists, and laborers and LGBTQ people were "makers" not only of their own histories, but of the nation's as well. This transformation within the American historical profession was part of a larger "multicultural" turn across other disciplines that led to the ascendancy of African American studies, women's studies, and ethnic studies, as well as queer theory, critical race theory, postcolonial theory, and other similarly radical new ways of thinking about history and literature, politics and culture, and law and society, among other things. All of this laid the fertile intellectual, theoretical, and political terrain upon which our generation of scholars came of age.

I have written elsewhere about my own struggles to find my way as a graduate student in the 1990s, but as hard as that time was, in many respects it was a powerful incubator for the kind of scholar, writer, teacher, and troublemaker I would become.[13] I went to Columbia, principally, to study with Eric Foner, whose award-winning book *Reconstruction* made quite an impression on me as an undergraduate. I was struck by his thesis: "Black participation in Southern public life after 1867 was the most radical development of the Reconstruction years, a massive experiment in interracial democracy without precedent in this or any other country that abolished slavery in the nineteenth century. . . . The transformation of slaves into free laborers and equal citizens was the most dramatic example of the social and political changes unleashed by the Civil War and emancipation."[14] This, too, was nothing I had ever been taught. By placing Black people—and their ongoing struggle for freedom—at the center of the story of social, political, and legal transformations in the mid-nineteenth century, Foner helped to illuminate the unprecedented radical experiment in "interracial democracy" that flowed from the Civil War. I would later come to fully appreciate that his argument was indebted to—and helped to reinvigorate—W. E. B. Du Bois's pathbreaking *Black Reconstruction*, published a half century before, which had boldly challenged an earlier generation of racist Columbia historians, including William A. Dunning and John W. Burgess (after whom, respectively, our graduate student travel fund and library reading room were named). "One fact and one alone," wrote Du Bois, "explains the attitude of most recent writers toward Reconstruction; they cannot conceive of Negroes as men; in their minds the word 'Negro' connotes 'inferiority' and 'stupidity' lightened only by unreasoning gayety and humor."[15] Whereas Dunning and Burgess had considered Reconstruction to be a wholesale tragedy of errors, Du Bois characterized it as a "splendid failure," tragic only insofar as it did not go far enough to deliver on its radically transformative promises. As Columbia graduate students, we often talked about the "double revolution" in Reconstruction historiography—a *circular* revolution in the sense that the scholarship had returned to its Columbia roots, but also an *interpretive* revolution, a wholesale upending of the anti-Black racism and white supremacy so flagrantly on display in the original work of the so-called "Dunning School." Inspired by the work of Foner and Du Bois, I decided to write my master's thesis on the 1868 South Carolina Constitutional Convention, whose majority-Black delegation created the nation's first universal, tax-supported, racially inclusive public school system, which, as Du Bois rightly described, was "foremost a Negro idea."[16] It still brings me no small measure of joy that my initial travel and research for this project was supported by Columbia's "Dunning Fund."

As compelled as I was by my research on Reconstruction, and as convinced as I was that the Civil War and Reconstruction marked a dramatic "break" with earlier nineteenth-century antecedents, I was also curious to explore the *continuities* between the postbellum and antebellum eras, specifically, the history of the abolitionist movement, which had been my area of focus during my undergraduate years. After all, if Reconstruction was the first moment where Blacks and whites worked together in a political party at the state and federal levels, abolitionism was the first movement where they worked together in political protest. If Reconstruction represented an experiment with new practices of equal citizenship, abolitionism was the movement that first imagined the ideal of racial equality. If Reconstruction was a moment where the United States attempted to forge an interracial democracy from the ashes of slavery and white supremacy, abolitionism had posed the first sustained challenge to these things and helped to make emancipation possible. Even the rise of the Republican Party—both its moderates like Abraham Lincoln and its radicals like Charles Sumner and Thaddeus Stevens—was made possible by the abolitionist movement. Indeed, Lincoln would later "evolve" on issues of race and slavery precisely because of abolitionist pressure and the influence, in particular, of prominent Black activists like Frederick Douglass, Martin Delany, Harriet Tubman, and Sojourner Truth. In other words, abolitionism played an outsized role in the contentious politics that led to the Civil War, which led me to believe that a fuller accounting of the movement was necessary to make better sense of Reconstruction, the boldest attempt yet made to realize an abolitionist vision for American democracy.

The more I contemplated these matters, the more interested I became in writing my dissertation not on the constitutional politics of Reconstruction, as I had originally intended, but on the cultural politics of abolitionism. In a sense, I was returning to my undergraduate roots in research on antebellum Black writings. I came to see the abolitionists as America's first culture warriors—"passionate outsiders," to borrow a term from John Stauffer—who used print, oral, and visual culture as powerful weapons to stage one of the great social and political revolutions in American history.[17] My subsequent research centered on the "cultural work" of abolitionists as radical activists who were also artists of various kinds: poets, orators, pamphleteers, newspaper editors, literary publishers, songwriters, playwrights, painters, photographers, autobiographers, and novelists. Whereas other scholars had focused on the political and social dynamics of abolitionism, as well as the structure and strategy of the movement, I was more interested in how the abolitionists created a "culture of dissent," a broad political resistance rooted in expanding print, oral, and visual cultures and committed to the creation of a multicultural democracy based on the "first principles" of freedom and equality. I also wanted to trace the *long history* of American abolitionism—back to the Revolution and forward to Reconstruction—to insist that free, enslaved, and newly emancipated African Americans were the first and last abolitionists.[18]

While I was contemplating these things, two defining experiences transformed my life as an emerging historian. The first was my work at Columbia's newly established Institute for Research in African-American Studies, directed by Manning Marable, who arrived on campus from the University of Colorado at Boulder just as I was starting my graduate studies. One of the things I rarely talk about anymore is that I almost dropped out of Columbia. As a non-fellowship student initially, I had blown through my summer savings in a few short months during the fall of my first year. If I didn't find some way to make ends meet, I would not be able to stay in school. Encouraged by Professor Foner, who was on leave my first year of graduate school, I approached Professor Marable—who later insisted that we always call him Manning—because he had some fellowship money for graduate students studying African American history. After a short meeting, he hired me on the spot to be the managing editor of his new journal, *Race & Reason* (now *Souls*). I started immediately, as honored as I was horribly anxious, and I spent five years working under his brilliant and generous tutelage.

For some time, I was the only white person working at the Institute, during which I earned the nickname "Manning's white-hand man." To this day, I have never felt more valued, respected *and* challenged in a workplace in my professional life. In fact, I learned more working there than I did in all my graduate coursework—or ever since. I once described the experience this way:

> At the Institute for Research in African-American Studies . . . we became part of a vibrant community of scholar-activists who took Marx's challenge—to transform rather than merely understand and interpret the world—very seriously. But like DuBois before him, Manning's vision also drew deeply, even primarily, from the intellectual and political wellsprings of the black radical tradition. His Institute was a black space and a multicultural one, at once democratic and radical, scholarly and activist, critical and welcoming, privileged and public—and these were never contradictions. In this setting, with this charge, Manning taught us the most profound lesson of all: that it was as important to be *in* Harlem as it was to be *at* Columbia. In fact, from the Institute's windows, which deliberately faced uptown, he would frequently look out to Harlem, with a longing smile, a felt sense of responsibility to what he often referred to as "the world's most famous black neighborhood." Manning meant for his students to bridge the gap between the seminar room and the street, between theory and practice, between big ideas and the brutal realities of our present world. But he also saw beauty in the world beyond the academy, in the people whose lives and struggles and dreams he understood in his bones, and in the history and politics he sought to chronicle throughout his distinguished and tenacious career. Echoing DuBois, he insisted that all of us were "co-workers in the kingdom of culture." In Manning's presence, you felt like this was the highest calling of all.[19]

The Institute was both a home and a hub—for Black intellectuals and radical activists, people from across the university and throughout the city and world. It was in this special place that I learned the value of *praxis*—the political imperative of acting to transform the world based on what you know. The lessons I learned there still inform and drive everything I do.

The second defining experience that changed me was serving as a teaching assistant for Eric Foner's legendary course, "The American

Radical Tradition," a survey course on radical social movements from the American Revolution to the Civil Rights Movement. Another thing I rarely talk about any more is the fact that I taught that course for *free*, since my initial status as an "unfunded" history doctoral student in Columbia's grotesquely unequal system meant I was ineligible for teaching assistantships. If I was to teach—and I desperately wanted and needed to teach—I had to create my own opportunities. Professor Foner gave me my first shot, even as he was deeply uncomfortable with me teaching without compensation. (As grateful as I still am, to him and for the experience, the irony and injustice of all this has never fully escaped me.) My role was to help run the weekly discussion sections, during which I supplemented assigned secondary readings with primary sources related to the movements we were studying in the class, which I copied on the Institute's Xerox machine late at night from books I took out from the library. Throughout the semester, I tried to bring history alive through the speeches and writings of radical activists of various identities and ideologies. The students were enthralled with these documents, and they began to ask tough questions about the past and connect the dots to the present. I *loved* being in the classroom with them. By the end of the term, with a giant stack of photocopies piled on the floor of my office, I realized I had unwittingly created a compendium that could be useful to future iterations of the course. A year or two later, my fellow graduate student and friend John McMillian suggested that we approach Professor Foner with the idea of doing something with these documents. That conversation led to a meeting with a publisher at the New Press, and after several months of putting together a book proposal and gathering supporting materials—including endorsements from Professors Foner, Marable, and Zinn—we were able to secure a contract for what would become *The Radical Reader: A Documentary History of the American Radical Tradition*, my first book.[20] This experience confirmed for me a valuable lesson that I have kept with me all these years: teaching can be a productive catalyst for scholarly work—and vice versa. Nearly two decades later, I am proud to say that *The Radical Reader* has sold over ten thousand copies and has been adopted by high school and college classes throughout the nation. Not bad for a guy who used to hate history textbooks!

But a funny thing happened on the way to the Ph.D. At first, I was just frustrated by the insularity of academic life and yearned to engage a broader public, which led me to write a biweekly column, "Truth to Power," in the *Columbia Spectator*. Over time, my campus and community activism—on labor and racial justice issues, protesting police brutality and welfare reform, advocating for ethnic studies and better sexual assault policies—started to get in the way of my reading and research. Eventually, I threw myself into more teaching and advising, once I realized that a persistent proximity to students seemed to be the best source of fuel for my activist energies. But just as I was developing a reputation as a gifted teacher and trusted troublemaker, my scholarship was stalled, my academic "progress" and future "success" at risk. And then I got the call: to come home, back to Cambridge, and become the guardian to the "little brother" I had mentored in college, then a seventh grader who was starting to get into his own kind of trouble. I agonized over this for months, understanding the potential impact this might have on things, and then scheduled a meeting with Manning before I made my final decision. After hearing me out, weighing it all, and making me promise I would finish my Ph.D., he said this: "Go home and raise that young brother. We will be here and we will make sure you cross the finish line." It turns out, he was a man of his word, and so was I. It took me way too long, but I made it eventually. And Manning was the first person to call me "Dr. McCarthy." Now that he's gone, I hold that moment deep in my heart.

The intervening years, after leaving Columbia and coming back to Cambridge, were no straight line. It makes little sense to dwell too long on them now; they were long enough. But I'm forever grateful that Professors Foner and Marable made sure to introduce me to Professor Zinn as I moved back "home" to help raise my "young brother." In those years, Howard became a dear friend and mentor, another indispensable role model for the kind of person I still wanted to become. We saw each other regularly and he never ceased to inspire me. Still, those were the most difficult years of my life—helping to raise a teenager in my late 20s and early 30s and "coming out" as gay while doing so; getting "blacklisted" by Lynne Cheney a month after 9/11 and diving fully into anti-war activism;

teaching full time and delaying the completion of my dissertation; eventually moving to North Carolina and descending into a full-blown mental health crisis. In the midst of it all, my brother graduated from high school and started college. I started dating and fell in love with a man who would eventually become my husband. I won my first teaching award and earned the respect of fellow activists. I helped to launch an oral history project, bounced at a martini bar, and started therapy. And I finished my damn dissertation.

The one constant in the midst of it all—through these most difficult years, but also from that swing with my grandmother to the present day—is teaching. The one thing I love more than history is *teaching* history. First for free, then by necessity, and now by choice. I have had the great privilege, for fully half my life now, to be a history teacher. I have taught in the Ivy League and at public universities in the South, in prisons in upstate New York and through a community health center in Dorchester, Massachusetts. I have worked with educators in secondary schools, artists in theater and film, activists in human rights organizations, organizers in local non-profits, and policymakers at every level, in the United States and abroad. At Harvard alone, I have taught thousands of students in courses on "Stories of Slavery and Freedom," "American Protest Literature," "LGBTQ Protest, Politics, and Policy," "Arts of Communication," and "Race, Ethnicity, and Equity in Education," among others. I have had the opportunity to code switch, shape shift, re-invent myself, evolve and expand. There are very few things I love more than watching a student of mine encounter a historical document for the first time and realize that a portal to the past has opened, that their long mis-education is ending, and that something else is possible.

Historians have the responsibility, as best we can, to tell the truth about the past—and that includes our own. After all, as we know, history can help to illuminate the present and point a way to a better future. My past is messy, and my career has been unorthodox. Unlike some of my colleagues from graduate school, I am still a contingent faculty member, part of academia's permanent and proliferating underclass, with no prospects for promotion or sabbatical or tenure.[21] I hold my breath every spring, hoping that I will receive my annual renewal, the continuation of my employment and health care, in the mail before June expires. One of the reasons I have taught so many things to so many students in so many places, nearly every semester of every year since the mid-1990s, is simply because I have to. I still have books I dream of publishing—the long overdue manuscript on my laptop, my dusty old dissertation on abolitionism, that book on Lincoln—and they will remain unfinished for the time being, because I have other work I need to do right now. And yet, I'm one of the 'lucky' ones—a willing vassal in the academic Vatican of vicious exploitation and vindictive hypocrisy.

Still there's not one day that goes by that I do not mourn our colleagues and friends who languish—and perish—while precious few of us are anointed to flourish.[22]

Theirs, too, are unfinished stories of freedom.

NOTES

This chapter is dedicated to four Columbia historians who taught me more than they will ever know: Eric Foner, the late Manning Marable, the late Howard Zinn, and Dr. T.K. Hunter, our dear, departed Thea.

1. Manning Marable, *Living Black History: How Reimagining the African-American Past Can Remake America's Racial Future* (New York: Basic Civitas, 2006), 2.
2. Tawasentha has been translated variously as "tears" or "hill of the dead"; the Mohawk are one of the nations of the Haudenosaunee, or Iroquois Confederacy; and Hiawatha was an indigenous leader who cofounded the Iroquois Confederacy.
3. Timothy Patrick McCarthy, "Coming of AIDS," *Pangyrus* (2015), https://www.pangyrus.com/voices/coming-of-aids/
4. David Herbert Donald, *Lincoln* (New York: Simon and Schuster, 1996).
5. See also C. Peter Ripley, ed., *The Black Abolitionist Papers*, 5 vols. (Chapel Hill: University of North Carolina Press, 2015).
6. Frederick Douglass, "Oration in Memory of Abraham Lincoln" (1876), https://teachingamericanhistory.org/library/document/oration-in-memory-of-abraham-lincoln/.
7. Timothy Patrick McCarthy, "Antebellum America's 'Missing Link': Mulattohood and 'In-Betweenness' in the Early Black Novel, 1853–1862" (senior honors thesis, History and Literature, Harvard University Archives, 1993).
8. For more on protest literature, see Timothy Patrick McCarthy, "Afterword" in Robert Schenkkan, *Building the Wall: The Play and Commentary* (Arcade, 2017).

9. See Charles T. Davis and Henry Louis Gates Jr., eds., *The Slave's Narrative* (New York: Oxford University Press, 1991); William S. Andrews, *To Tell a Free Story: The First Century of African-American Autobiography, 1760–1865* (Urbana: University of Illinois Press, 1988); and James M. McPherson, *Abraham Lincoln and the Second American Revolution* (New York: Oxford University Press, 1992).
10. Howard Zinn, *A People's History of the United States* (New York: HarperCollins, 1980), 2.
11. Eric Foner, "Majority Report," *New York Times Book Review*, March 2, 1980.
12. Timothy Patrick McCarthy, ed., *The Indispensable Zinn: The Essential Writings of the "People's Historian"* (New York: New Press, 2012), xxi.
13. Timothy Patrick McCarthy, "Why I Write," in *Why We Write: The Politics and Practice of Writing for Social Change*, ed. Jim Downs (New York: Routledge, 2006), 27–38.
14. Eric Foner, *Reconstruction: America's Unfinished Revolution, 1863–1877* (New York: Harper Perennial, 1988).
15. W. E. B. Du Bois, *Black Reconstruction in America, 1860–1880* (New York: Free Press, 1998).
16. Timothy Patrick McCarthy, "When Slaves Became Citizens: Public Schools and Reconstruction Politics at the 1868 South Carolina Constitutional Convention" (M.A. thesis, Columbia University, 1996).
17. See John Stauffer, *The Black Hearts of Men: Radical Abolitionists and the Transformation of Race* (Cambridge, MA: Harvard University Press, 2002).
18. Timothy Patrick McCarthy, "A Culture of Dissent: American Abolitionism and the Ordeal of Equality" (Ph.D. dissertation, Columbia University, 2006).
19. Timothy Patrick McCarthy, "Honoring Manning," *Nation*, April 4, 2011, https://www.thenation.com/article/archive/honoring-manning/.
20. Timothy Patrick McCarthy and John McMillian, eds. *The Radical Reader: A Documentary History of the American Radical Tradition* (New York: New Press, 2003).
21. "Background Facts on Contingent Faculty Positions," AAUP https://www.aaup.org/issues/contingency/background-facts.
22. Adam Harris, "The Death of an Adjunct," *Atlantic*, April 8, 2019.

10

IN THE MATTER OF WORTH

The Value of Black Lives and the Law

T.K. HUNTER

Editor's note: T.K. Hunter died unexpectedly on December 17, 2018. She was unable to complete this essay but was working on it the weekend before she passed. We are publishing what she last saw. It is a historical analysis of the slave trade and the infamous *Zong* case as well as an effort to use history to frame the rise of the Black Lives Matter movement. It is also a meditation of a brilliant historian who conceptualizes various conclusions but hasn't settled on one. In this way, her notes have become a metaphor for the ways that slavery continues to shape the present. And even more, her notes to herself are a powerful, unique, breathtaking record of a Black woman who grappled with the history of slavery hours before her untimely death. This chapter further illustrates the point of this volume: we get to see the unfinished work of a historian who labored mightily to tell and teach these stories of freedom.

When the facile but urgent rejoinder "*All* lives matter" emerged in the run-up to the 2016 presidential election in an effort to simultaneously acknowledge the insistent "Black Lives Matter" phrase (which quickly had become a trending hashtag on Twitter in 2013, and served as the basis for a movement) employed to demand the attention of law enforcement personnel in particular and the American citizenry in general, it was met not simply with disdain, but fury. As a political strategy, it was gutless (perhaps it was meant to be so), as anyone with a passing knowledge of American history would realize: in the end, it landed more political candidates into hot water than not. While the insistence that "all lives matter" is an ethical and moral truth that few human beings would find fault with, in the face of American history and the contemporary American heritage—what we live with and can attest to in our twenty-first-century society—"all lives matter" is essentially a dodge. For some, the phrase's resonance with revered Enlightenment principles is a vindication of its earnest usage, but for those who are painfully aware of the countless ways in which American history has illustrated the failure of clergy, law enforcement, educators, politicians, and legal personnel to apply the Enlightenment-inspired phrase, it is something that in America we have yet to see happen. Truthfully, thanks to mid-nineteenth-century America's chief justice Roger Taney, the basic Americanness and the basic humanity of African Americans were fundamentally called into question. The fact that he was a slaveholder with a stake in the perpetuation and expansion of slavery is generally cloaked so that it appears that a chief justice of the highest court in the land was upholding the supposed neutrality of the law. But men have stakes in a wide range of ventures, and those stakes generally dictate their behavior.

Taney's verdict led all of America down the road to the 1896 case of *Plessy v. Ferguson* (and the fiction that "separate" could ever be equal when that separateness was administered by powerful white men), to the Jim Crow years (the systematic effort to reinstate the social, political, and economic hierarchy of slavery without the actual institution of slavery), and then to the mid-twentieth-century civil rights movement—one of *centuries* of natural rights/civil rights movements and for most Americans arguably the most prominent one.

And yet, in 2018 we continue to find ourselves still struggling for civil rights and ignoring searing truths. We are reluctant to face squarely the legacy that we live with in America daily: the lives of people of color in general and African Americans in particular are, quite simply, not valued. Naturally, white liberals will stand firm and swear that they are not bigoted, and that of course they value Black lives because . . . well, why wouldn't they? However, the reason they wouldn't is deeply insidious and has a history that one dare not discuss: the New World slave trade. That trade, because of its lucrativeness, privileged the buying, selling, and trading of the bodies and lives of Africans and people of African descent as *commodities* and not as people. The instances of brutality meted out against people of African descent when they fell afoul of the business of New World Slavery are legion and horrific, to be sure. In fact, we are encouraged to think of the physical reprisals in two opposing ways: either as if they were the product of aberrant behavior of slave owners, or as if slavery was chiefly about the physical suffering itself. But New World Slavery was not about punishment—diabolically creative punishments notwithstanding. New World Slavery was about the commodification of Africans and their bodies, for once transformed ideologically into merchandise, they could be traded, bought, and sold as merchants bought and sold metal or fabric. Activated by financial gain, a shift in thinking changed the living human beings with families, obligations, loves, hates—in short, textured lives—into nonentity objects by which individuals and companies profited. Their lives were utterly disposable, and in England they were regulated by a Board of Trade whose very name reinforced the nonentity status of Africans. The Black Lives Matter movement recognizes an American history of colonization that built a particularly American culture: one that developed systematic and systemic marginalization that had at its core the unspoken belief in the disposability of the lives of Africans and their descendants.

One of the most stunning examples of the disposability of Black lives that comes down to us can be found some 230 years *before* the Black Lives Matter movement was born in 2013, in the 1783 English court case *Gregson* v. *Gilbert*, more colloquially referred to as the *Zong* case. This was an "action on a policy of insurance, to recover the value of certain slaves thrown overboard for want of water" (3 DOUGL. 233—*Gregson v. Gilbert*, 629). The description is chilling in its matter-of-factness. The value of those Africans lay not in the outrageous circumstances in which their lives were stolen from them twice (once at the time they were sold away from family, friends, and all that was familiar, and again when the captain of a ship gave the order to toss them overboard like so much detritus), but in their tacit classification as objects that were simply considered a measure of someone's financial gain or loss. They could be claimed on insurance as inanimate objects—and they were.

Go to the Gregson v. Gilbert pdf →
http://www.commonlii.org/int/cases/EngR/1783/85.pdf
I'm considering this quote from the court report as the title of the essay:

> *". . . were obliged to throw overboard 150 other negroes" (3 Douglass 233, p. 629)*

The African trade was originally a legitimate trade in goods and favors between parties who, on equal terms, each gained what they wanted. But the interest in Africa shifted in character over the course of westward expansion across the Atlantic and the claiming of various lands by European countries. Those lands—especially the ones that were considered tropical—quickly became important for the production of sugar. For us in the twenty-first century, the cultivation of most crops is a mystery: we wouldn't have the first idea of what is involved in the creation of even a familiar commodity like sugar. Sugar, once the means of cultivation had been learned by the British, became a driving engine of the English economy over the course of the eighteenth century. Sugar production was labor-intensive—meaning that, effectively, there was no "downtime" in its production. Sugarcane, once harvested, needed to be processed immediately or else it would rot. (Tobacco, on the other hand, once harvested was hung in barns to dry, which meant that laborers on a tobacco plantation had a much different work cycle and work rhythm than those working on a sugar plantation.) Sugarcane, too, when processed, yields a variety of secondary and tertiary by-products. In other words, from the planting of a single sugar crop, a plantation could produce various grades of sugar—from the highly refined white sugar (shaped into a tall, solid cone in its eighteenth-century form, called a "sugar loaf"), to various grades of brown sugar, to molasses, to rum. While Britain initially employed its own white indentured servants and convicts as the laborers in the New World, the supply diminished over time: white indentured servants could manage to get word back home (even if they were not personally literate) to dissuade friends and family from following in their footsteps, noting that the promise of land acquisition and a new beginning on the other side of the Atlantic from Britain was spurious. And so with the gradual but steady loss of white indentured servants and convict laborers (who had been transported to the New World in lieu of being put to death for their crime in Britain), plantations—which were essentially factories in terms of producing commodities—needed to replace those laborers and to learn from the mistakes they made by using the previous labor forms. Convicts, while useful, could not be acquired dependably: crime came and went, and not every crime was a capital crime—the kind that made for transportation of convicts. White indentured servants themselves contributed to the gradual decrease of laborer prospects when they experienced a rude awakening: the New World and the promise of wealth and infinite possibilities were quite simply a lie. One can imagine the letters home saying "don't do it!" in an attempt to dissuade possible recruits. Indeed, a well-known letter from a young white indentured servant who was lured to the Virginia colony in the seventeenth century is a plea by the young man to his parents to get him out of the horrible situation he could not have imagined indentured servitude would be. Similarly, William Moraley, a British white indentured servant in the eighteenth century, was so shocked and disappointed by the *lack* of wealth that came his way by trying his luck in the New World that he returned home to Britain and wrote a brief chronicle of the "true adventures" he experienced as an indentured servant, hoping to catapult himself into fame and riches through the sale of his autobiography (http://www.virtualjamestown.org/frethorne.html; William Moraley, *The Infortunate: The Voyage and Adventures of William Moraley, an Indentured Servant*, ed. Susan E. Klepp and Billy G. Smith [University Park: Pennsylvania State University Press, 1992]).

Over the course of the eighteenth century, Africans had the dubious distinction of becoming the ideal labor force that replaced white indentured servants and convicts. They were to be found on the African continent in places that had established legitimate trading routes, and European traders found that they could exploit the internal conflicts among neighboring groups—in other words, language groups and kinship groups, kingdoms and various other types of societies engaged in battles and wars in which enemies were captured legitimately. Those conflicts were based upon local tensions—sometimes generational, sometimes not. But the key thing to understand is this: skirmishes, battles, wars, etc., tended to be lawful and just (as opposed to random and unjust), and so the losing side became captives, rightfully so. In short, according to the long-standing ethics of wars, those who were taken prisoner and made slaves were considered "captives of just wars." Their status as "slave" was considered *situational*, that is, as a result of having been on the losing side of armed conflict, as opposed to a condition that was considered *inherent* and eventually *generational*.

So why was it called a "trade," and what was being traded? It was an initially legitimate trade that became illegitimate. "The particular process of slave trading on the African coast depended on local geography. But it thrived best when there were good, proven relations—trust—between slave captains and local Africans. . . . The trading conducted by Liverpool's merchants was mutually beneficial" (Walvin, 22–23). The commerce included buying and bartering—again, both appropriate and reasonable methods of engaging in commerce. However, what was being traded? Money, cloth (linen, especially) were being traded and one more item: bodies. To be clear: for Africans who were conducting business, there was nothing wrong with trading linen for the ability to get rid of your local enemies who are potentially competing with you for power, territory, and the like or depleting your resources. Instead, because you cannot manufacture the linen cloth that you favor, the trade is value-free. Or so it appeared. Like the vast majority of human beings in the eighteenth century, people did not travel more than a few miles from their home, generally for their entire lives. Travel as we think of it today was not a leisure activity; travel was a frightening hardship that tended to occur in only extreme necessity. A local African trader would not know that by getting rid of his local enemies, he was consigning them to horrors beyond imagining: a sea change (in more ways than one) from a human being—with all that humanness entails—to something that was no longer judged worthy of consideration. Those who were sold to European traders were being unknowingly consigned to a different kind of bondage in New World Slavery. New World Slavery warped the existence of Old World Slavery based on captivity arising out of conflict, or what was described as "just wars," into something misshapen, exploitative, and devised to continue in perpetuity for the express purpose of financial gain.

It is not until one understands the *commercial success* of the various New World plantations and the nearly unfathomable amounts of money acquired by those who participated in some aspect of keeping those plantations thriving—regardless of whether they ever met an African, had any antipathy toward Africans, or even had a working idea of where the Caribbean was—that one can begin to see the African Slave Trade and New World Slavery in its true guise. Simply put, the trade had little to do with its participants considering morality or immorality; the trade was about financial gain. And what financial gain there was! The deeply intertwining nature of commerce AND SOMETHING ELSE—YOU NEED AT LEAST 2 THINGS TO INTERTWINE—made it clear: one could start out life as a lowly, local rope maker in a seaside town in England and over time become increasingly well-to-do, not because you were lobbying for the expansion of the buying and selling of human beings, but because sailing ships required a great deal of rope to rig the sails and to use in all aspects of running a ship: as far as the rope maker was concerned, all he was doing was making rope and noticing that the demand for rope kept growing. Indeed, almost all tradesmen in occupations that didn't have anything to do with slavery per se grew wealthier over time: chandlers, purveyors of comestibles, bakers, coopers, etc.—all of which were innocent enough trades. So, New World Slavery and the African Slave Trade by the end of the eighteenth century was, quite simply, a well-developed means for generating wealth, both for those who were part of slaving syndicates, such as William Gregson, one of Liverpool's major slave traders, and for those whose businesses supplied the needs of a seafaring economy (Walvin, 26). It was Gregson, that wealthy slave trader, who was at the center of the *Zong* massacre.

But how did the situation of the *Zong* come about? Perhaps one of the most fundamental ironies regarding the *Zong* slaughter was that it was engineered by a Briton during his country's colonial war that was being fought around the Enlightenment concepts of liberty and natural rights. In the North American colonies, British colonists balked against what they deemed unfair parliamentary initiatives to raise much-needed revenue after the successful conclusion to the Seven Years' War. White colonists chose to claim the language of liberty for themselves *politically* while people of African descent capitalized on that same language to point out the social, intellectual, and moral inconsistencies present in the colonies as long as the institution of slavery was alive. They wrote pamphlets, sermons, and letters to colonial legislatures—all of which were elegant arguments for the fundamental importance of natural rights: those rights argued as belonging to one by virtue of being born a human being. Natural rights were rights that belonged to all. (See Lemuel Haynes's antislavery manuscript "Liberty Further Extended"—Ruth Bogin, " 'Liberty Further Extended': A 1776 Antislavery Manuscript by Lemuel Haynes," *William and Mary Quarterly* 40, no. 1 [January 1983]: 85–105. See also Circular Letters to the Massachusetts Legislature, in Edward Countryman, *Enjoy the Same Liberty: Black Americans and the Revolutionary Era* [Lanham, MD: Rowman and Littlefield, 2012], 66.) And so in the midst of physical battles and intellectual battles in North America, a shore far from the African continent, William Gregson—uninterested in the Enlightenment ideology that guaranteed *his* liberty as he moved through life and facilitated his ability to begin as a lowly rope maker and eventually be catapulted to immense wealth—went about his business. With his liberty and natural rights, Gregson essentially stole the liberty and natural rights of all of the Africans he considered cargo. In the process, as he rose through the ranks—from rope maker to ship's captain, to merchant-partner in a Liverpool Slave Trading syndicate—Gregson grew in power and in his ability to abuse that power.

By 1781, when Captain Gregson was on the west coast of Africa, he had an opportunity to purchase the Dutch slave ship the *Zorgue*, which had been impounded (Walvin, 26). (In the American War for Independence, 1776–1783, England was effectively at war with her colonies and any European countries that offered material support to those colonies. Moreover, the English and the Dutch had been longtime maritime rivals, fighting a series of Anglo-Dutch Wars that effectively intertwined English and Dutch history for centuries; the fourth Anglo-Dutch War, 1780–1784, was contemporaneous with the American War for Independence, and as a result there was plenty of impetus on the part of Britain to do all it could to stifle the movement of goods and personnel throughout the Atlantic on Dutch vessels.) Upon acquiring it, he renamed it *Zong*, and so began the history of the infamous British ship (Walvin, 26).

The journey that the *Zong* began across the Atlantic in September 1781 would prove to be a disastrous one—both because, at the most basic level, it was a ship participating in the Atlantic Slave Trade, and because despite being a relatively small vessel that would generally only carry fewer than 200 people, Gregson and his men had packed 459 people—twice as many as prudent. Can we make sense of this set of facts as we shift back and forth between two truths that stand in tension with one another? The people on board the *Zong* were just that: people who, through no fault of their own, were swept up into a commercial venture from which they received no benefit. And yet, according to the Gregson syndicate and others like it, the people on board were not people: they were not mothers, fathers, brothers, sisters, cousins; they were not potters or builders or metalworkers; they were not selfish, generous, responsible, poetic, venal, patient, wise, or anything else that we associate with being human. According to the Gregson syndicate, they were objects of profit, commodities, and their lives and all of the complexities of human existence were suddenly no longer theirs (Walvin, 27).

And the profitability cannot be disputed. Economists, essayists, and the like were clear about the financial gain that Britain and her colonies (current colonies as well as the former North American colonies) enjoyed because of the commodification of Africans. "The Negroe [sic]

Trade on the Coast of Africa is the chief and fundamental Support Of the British Colonies and Plantations in America," declared a 1745 tract. This continued to be true, even as late in the eighteenth century as 1772, many decades after the African Slave Trade began for the British. Furthermore, it was patently clear that the importance of the trade was the *financial benefits* enjoyed by all who were touched by the trade—regardless of their participation in the actual enslaving of fellow human beings. "The African trade is so very beneficial to Great Britain, so essentially necessary to the very being of her colonies, that without it neither could we flourish nor they [the colonies] long subsist" (Walvin, 29).

But those advantages came with a cost—a cost that has implications and consequences that we continue to experience in present-day America. In order for the financial benefits to accrue, violence was built into the process—beyond capture, shackling, and dehumanizing. In addition to the basic expedient sundering of people from the lives that they knew, the crews of slaving ships had to be on the lookout for all attempts on the part of those unsuspecting Africans to resist their situation. In short, violence against Africans (and later, people of African descent) was *integral to the relationship*. It permeated the African Slave Trade throughout its existence. And, what's worse, the relationship built on power, violence, and the curtailing of liberty and rights was not limited to the Atlantic crossing itself: it continued and enlarged over the centuries so that slavery was present in America as part and parcel of the fabric of American society. Furthermore, the relationship conceived in power and violence did not simply magically disappear when the African Slave Trade ended. It was the *normalization* of the relationship of violence, power, and the curtailing of liberty and rights bound up in the trade that made African lives insignificant—despite the fact that, on the face of it, those lives represented substantial financial gain. One can see the inevitable ironies in the system: Africans and later people of African descent—both enslaved and free—because their lives were generally considered of little import—could be (and were) beaten for the sake of the terrorism that was integral to the assertion of power on the part of many white Americans. What is worse is that one need not have ever been a slave owner to have applied the actions of terrorism:

random threats of extralegal violence, insistence upon a hierarchy based solely on color, the application of violence to individuals who are part of society in order to "send a message" to others of that group, and, most importantly, the fear that the violence was specifically meant to generate. It quickly becomes clear that the violence and the devaluation of Black lives that were part and parcel of New World Slavery were perfected and endured well beyond the institution of slavery itself. And in a way, how could they not? Violence was the standard, along with the disregard first for Africans as they were being captured, then for African Americans—whether born into the American slave system or not. It was used to cement a relationship based on subjugation and fear. (Moreover, one need only consider the tenuous existence that free people of color experienced in America. As long as the institution of slavery existed in America, free people of color were considered slaves unless and until they could produce papers attesting to their freedom.) And it is patently clear that the legal end of slavery in the United States with the advent of the Thirteenth Amendment did not erase centuries of operational relationships: American history demonstrates that after Reconstruction many white Americans (not just southern white Americans) balked at the putative equality of people of African descent that accompanied the passage of the Fourteenth Amendment. In effect, much of the history of the United States after the Civil War details the numerous ways in which the United States, by custom and by law, attempted to keep the operational relationship of subjugation and fear healthy and thriving largely by the continuation of terrorism, seen most starkly in the workings of the Ku Klux Klan—though they were not the only ones to champion fear in order to sustain the subjugation of people of African descent. (Note: By this statement, I am not suggesting that the Klan only used terrorism against African Americans. The Klan has a shameful history of terrorizing homosexuals, relationships that were defined as "mixed," Jewish people, Roman Catholics, and so forth. In all cases the terrorist activities that were employed were in order to maintain a social, political, and economic hierarchy that excluded various marginalized groups.)

But the advent of the African Slave Trade to the New World and the development of New World Slavery carried with them numerous contradictions: abuse of power and the realization that one had to exercise restraint, the treatment of enslaved Africans as nothing more than items for trade and exploitation and the realization that it was a canny captain who treated his complement of Africans with care—essentially the better to guarantee that they arrived at their destination in good shape. Those internal tensions and contradictions can be considered hallmarks of the trade. "It was a business with a tendency to efface the moral sense, to rob the heart of every gentle and humane disposition, and to harden it, like steel, against all impression of sensibility" (Walvin, 45). When one considers the combination of the internal tensions that were integral to the trade, the power structures and their abuse, and finally that the trade was a business that eroded any sense of moral accountability as it privileged profits at all costs, the *Zong* incident becomes a little clearer. The steady and consistent immiseration of Africans was of little interest to those for whom profits prevailed.

In a way, William Gregson was emblematic of a rags-to-riches biography—quite unusual in British society in general, but increasingly a regular occurrence once the African Slave Trade was under way. Gregson's family beginnings were humble: his father was a porter (in eighteenth-century terms, one who moved and carried items), and in his early working life he was a rope maker. While his fortune over time would have grown substantially as he outfitted sailing ships with the nearly endless amounts of rope they needed, by entering into the slave trade directly, and being successful, he improved his fortunes dramatically. Slaving was a money-making business. Though his initial forays into slaving were not particularly auspicious, the failures did not deter Gregson. He continued, and over the decades following his initial 1744 failed outing, he became either investor in or owner of slaving ships. His prosperity, interestingly, paralleled Liverpool's prosperity and its ability to outpace Bristol as Britain's preeminent slave port (Walvin, 57–58). To recount the details of Gregson's decades of involvement in the slave trade, the various destinations in the New World where he sold shiploads of Africans, and his steadily growing fortune would require more time and space than this essay allows. Suffice it to say that he was a preeminent force in Liverpool slaving voyages over the course of the eighteenth century—from the early 1740s to the 1790s, when he turned over his business to his sons. Other Liverpool merchants did not come close to the number of slaving voyages Gregson's ships engaged in (152 between the years of 1750 and 1799), and only two surpassed the number of slaving voyages during that time: William Davenport and William Boats with 155 and 157 slaving voyages, respectively (Walvin, 60–62). It is a chilling truth in the form of a seemingly simple numerical calculation. And then there is the *Zong* ship.

We know the ill-advised choices made that contributed to the creation of the murderous circumstances that claimed the lives of hundreds of captive Africans who had been chained for months *before even setting sail into the Atlantic*—perhaps as much as an entire year (Walvin, 74). Those choices were a combination of the unexpected good fortune that sometimes occurs in war (at least for the party that gains the upper hand), such as the opportunity to have a slaving voyage that seemingly did not need to be put together from scratch, and the greed that was the lens through which the capture of the Dutch ship *Zorgue*, which would become *Zong*, was viewed. There were 244 Africans already on board the former Dutch ship, and the English captain Hanley, operating for the Gregson syndicate, valued those Africans at £30 sterling each—or approximately over $2,250 each in 2018 terms; they were insured for £8,000 sterling in 1781 British pounds (Eric W. Nye, Pounds Sterling to Dollars: Historical Conversion of Currency, accessed Friday, January 26, 2018, http://www.uwyo.edu/numimage/currency.htm). It is admittedly crass, not to mention pointless, to place a dollar value on human lives, but the measurement—an approximation though it may be—allows us to understand more tangibly the decisions based on financial gain. Furthermore, once the British finally set sail on August 18, five months *after* they had seized the ship, the *Zong* had 442 Africans all told; it was truly stuffed to the gunwales with human life.

On March 13, 1782

Ok. What do i want to say? I don't want to focus on the crowding, which then continues to lead us down the road to the immorality of the slave trade. We've been there and done that. What i want to focus on is when one's humanity is summarily dispensed with in the service of profit and power—not just short-term, but long-term. The profit that accumulates over the course of the existence of new world slavery builds power, the power then is perpetually positioned to reinforce profit, and profit reinforces the rationale for continued curtailing of liberty and rights; it is truly a vicious circle. . . . I also need to point out the irony: that while american colonists as britons press for their liberty and natural rights as "free born englishmen" gregson's syndicate and many like him systematically strip a segment of humanity of their liberty and rights—not just for the short-term. Once the commodification of africans and those of african descent supplanted their liberty and rights as human beings, the door was opened to endless egregious behavior by those who had stripped them of their rights and who had constructed a system that kept africans and those of african descent from their liberty and their rights in perpetuity. Forget the sentimental pleading of such works as "uncle tom's cabin" whose purpose was to tug on the heartstrings. Forget the handwringing over the diabolically creative brutalities to force compliance. Make no mistake about it: brutality was an integral part of systematic new world slavery. Brutality was an exercise of abusive power to force and to reinforce status, hierarchy, liberty (and the lack thereof), rights (and the lack thereof). But the handwringing focus on morality is, at the end of the day, a red herring. That is to say, it is easy to congratulate ourselves in 2017 on our supposed greater moral development (superiority?) compared with those in the past who held slaves or supported slavery. However, "morality" misses the crux of the matter: that a system of commodification was created for the express purpose of long-term financial gain and that in order for that system to function (according to their creators) the liberty and rights of a segment of humanity had to be curtailed in perpetuity—a curtailment that could only be accomplished by the continuing exertion of power that defined and reinforced status. Without that commodification of human beings, the zong incident (and others like it) could not have occurred.

> *"The slave ship was the human crucible which poisoned relations between black and white throughout the history of Atlantic slavery—and long afterwards."* (Walvin, 42. *This is an interesting quote from Walvin himself . . .*)

So, what is the

Jimmy says to play with the term/idea of "slave trade" and discuss what's being traded? Money for bodies but often in the most seemingly unobjectionable ways—because on the face of it, the trade is a legitimate trade: linen for the ability to get rid of your local enemies who are potentially depleting your resources. Instead, because you cannot manufacture the linen cloth that you favor, the trade is value-free. Or so it appears.

Not sure where to put this

The outrage we feel is clear and unsurprising—now. After all, it is easy to pass judgment on the actions of people from another time, and another place. What horrible human beings there were in the 1780s, we think. Could those people have been any more venal, any more self-serving at the expense of the lives of those around them? Who were those ruthless men, we wonder? Why would they pick on unsuspecting Africans who did not ask to be captured and thrust into chains as preparation for being divested of home, family, culture, opportunity, inheritance? How were such men able to sleep at night, and why were they not forever wracked with paralyzing, perhaps even redemptive, guilt? The horrors of New World Slavery (that is, slavery for the express/sole purpose of financial gain) and of the Atlantic Slave Trade (that is, the mechanism that systematically brought Africans to the New World involuntarily) are legion, and many of them can be recited—with the focus tending to be on the nineteenth-century American manifestation of New World Slavery, that is, the southern plantation, and some of the physical reprisals that have come to be a small part of our awareness of American history. However, by focusing on the nineteenth-century American manifestation of southern plantation slavery, we don't realize that we've placed our attention only on an expression *of the abuse of power required to* maintain *the institution, rather than identifying the imperatives for the basic devising, building, and expansion of the Atlantic Slave Trade.*

Somewhere in the essay toward the end:

At twenty-eight years old, Erica Garner is dead, sadly. She was the tireless champion of justice who sprang into action after the death of her father Eric Garner, who died at the hands of law enforcement officers who argued that their use of a chokehold on an unarmed, asthmatic man being detained for a misdemeanor (the sale of loose cigarettes) was crucial in his detainment. In that moment, when Eric Garner struggled for his life, insisting "I can't breathe" numerous times, officers did not relinquish their hold on him. At that moment, it seemed that for officers, the imperatives of policing and "making the collar" (i.e., being credited for subduing the suspect) protocols necessarily devised in the abstract took precedence over the real-time situation. Because of our American history, it is easy to believe that centuries of categorizing people of African descent as fundamentally problematic, dangerous, lazy, and disposable—though objectively the descriptions are contradictory—created a situation of long standing in which it was second nature for white men in a position of power, in this case law officers, to assume that Garner was inherently dangerous by virtue of the color of his skin and the neighborhood where he lived. And Garner was doubtless assumed to be problematic, lazy, and disposable by virtue of his sale of "looseies" (individual cigarettes) and the color of his skin. While selling "looseies" is indeed a crime (and is one primarily because it evades federal sales tax on tobacco), surely humane policing makes judgment calls regarding the order of magnitude of the alleged crime. But Eric Garner, again because of our American history, did not qualify for consideration on the "order of magnitude" scale: he died, literally for want of air. And Garner was just one in a long line of individuals and groupings who died because our American history demonstrates that deeply ingrained in our culture and our imagination is the dark, unspoken, and unacknowledged belief and the assumption that the lives of people of African descent are fundamentally and historically of less value than the lives of others.

The *Zong* case from 1783, terrifyingly, was not exceptional. In a sense, how could it be when New World Slavery (that is, slavery for the express purpose of financial gain) drove the economies of so many countries—including the American colonies before the Revolutionary War and the United States after independence was won? When human lives are bought and sold, and fortunes are made (so much so that those fortunes form the basis of family wealth and/or position that is inherited generationally and in perpetuity), and when organizations and cultural, political, and economic systems, even the law, create measures for preserving the continued disposability of people of African descent, it hopefully becomes easier to see, objectively, how and why the devaluation of black lives continues hundreds of years after an insurance case revealed that ship's captains, investors, and the like—all white men—felt no compunction about destroying the lives of men, women, and children who had been captured and forcibly removed from their homes in order to feed the insatiable desire for wealth. The solicitor general, Justice John Lee, had no hesitation in separating Africans from humanity: **"What is this claim that human people have been thrown overboard? This is a case of chattels or goods. Blacks are goods and property; it is madness to accuse these well-serving honourable men of murder. . . . The case is the same as if wood had been thrown overboard" (Gregson v. Gilbert)**. In 2017, we truly want to be shocked by *such an assertion—so much so that we are insistent that certainly no one believes that now. However, the point of the Black Lives Matter movement is to insist that we place our attention on a persistent truth that we would rather avert our gaze from: that we in the United States have a long history of categorizing people of African descent as separate and less than human so that their lives are easily forfeit and that it is a history that we continue to fail to acknowledge at our peril. In the current climate of balkanization that feeds fear and fear that feeds balkanization, as Americans we are hard-pressed to think in holistic terms: when the basic rights of one group are considered not worth protecting, then the basic rights of all groups will be similarly considered not worth protecting.*

TOWARDS AN ENDING

While various countries have acknowledged their part in the New World Slave Trade (notably Great Britain in 2006 under Tony Blair, who delivered a "historical expression of regret" for Britain's participation in the slave trade), the United States has, by contrast, done its best to avoid such admissions. (See Tristram Hunt's article in *The Guardian*, 26 November 2006. He was a Labour MP who in 2017 stepped down from Parliament to become the director of the V & A Museum.)

Blair was scheduled to say: "It is hard to believe that what would now be a crime against humanity was legal at the time."

The systematic and systemic disregard for Black lives continues to be possible because the law makes it so—but perhaps more important, it continues because the devaluation of Black lives is deeply integral to our way of thinking in America. Ostensibly one can point to a history of various civil rights laws, hoping to insist that the law protects everyone in America equally: certainly the Fourteenth Amendment makes it so. Or so it would seem. Nevertheless, often many steps are necessary before situations that flout such protection inscribed in law are eradicated.

12 MAY 2018

So, what do we take away from the recorded horror of the *Zong* case, knowing that there were countless other horrors that went unrecorded but that can be counted toward the steady normalization of the devaluation of Black lives?

It is hard for us in the United States, a country that was framed around liberty, rights, and justice, to be able to accept the very limited ways in which those ideologies were available and applied. Most people live with sanitized histories of their country, and Americans are no exception. How can we square the annual Fourth of July commemorations, and the way in which at core they bask in the righteousness of the condemnation of tyranny and the celebration of freedom, with centuries of slavery on American soil? How can we begin to realize that in American history, the institution of slavery was in existence longer than it has been formally dismantled? (If you take 1619 as the beginning of African slavery on American soil and 1863 as the end of the formal institution of slavery as a result of the Emancipation Proclamation, then slavery was in effect for 244 years. If you calculate the time between 2018 and 1863, the number of years comes to only 155 years *without* the institution of slavery. It is a staggering realization—particularly as we are taught, as Americans, to place American slavery as a category and a status into the distant past.) In addition, we are taught that once the category and status of "slave" ceased to exist, all was mostly well in America as we charted a course toward full liberty, equality, and prosperity—and what *wasn't* well received a course correction during the 1960s civil rights movement. And it is harder still for us in the United States to accept that violence against African Americans has been integral to the basic workings in the United States without white Americans feeling blamed and judged unfairly because, after all, most individuals have not been personally, overtly violent against Black Americans. But it is history, not opinion, that demonstrates the framework of violence that was built to "deal with" Africans and African Americans. And it is history, not opinion, that reveals the link between the commodification of Africans and African Americans and the alacrity with which violence is used to terrorize and control. And history, not opinion, demonstrates the countless ways in which violence against African Americans expanded and was perfected over the centuries of American history up to the present. How do we begin to look squarely in the face of this deeply disturbing fact: while we no longer have slavery in America, the ideological instruments and the legal instruments that were put in place to enforce the social and economic structures and benefits of a society based on slavery were never fully dismantled? Ideology is a tough one, because it is something that is simultaneously prominent and subtle, and it is its subtlety that is difficulty to dismantle. When consistent outrages against African Americans are constantly before us in contemporary life and thus prompt the insistent cry of Black Lives Matter, we MUST understand that cry not as an assertion that African American lives matter *more* than any other kind of lives, but as an assertion of our need to look history squarely in the eye and acknowledge that the ideological framework for the rationalization of violence against black bodies has not been dismantled and that until that framework is dismantled, we, as a country, cannot move forward in unity, liberty, equality, and prosperity. . . .

THIS MIGHT BE AN ENDING . . .

I WONDER IF I NEED TO EXPAND UPON WHAT I MEAN BY "VIOLENCE" AND POINT OUT THAT VIOLENCE IS BEING DONE BEYOND THE PHYSICAL . . . ?

Sadiya Hartman on Violence of the Slave Trade
Psychic violence keeps perpetuating itself.

EPILOGUE

Eric Foner: Historian of American Freedom

KATRINA VANDEN HEUVEL

The late, great novelist, essayist, and longtime *Nation* contributor Gore Vidal liked to call this country the United States of Amnesia. Even more so than in other places, our country has been formed not by what it chooses to remember of its own past but by what it chooses to forget. In such a country, in such times, simply to remember is itself a radical act. It is to refuse to submit to the blinders that the powers that be are always trying to slip onto the rest of us. It is to subvert, implicitly or otherwise, the tyranny of the present—to insist on expanding the realm of the possible. If all of this is true, and I submit that it is, then Eric Foner is one of the most dangerous men in America. And I submit that he is.

Eric's impact on the study of American history, and in particular, of course, on the study of the American Civil War and its aftermath, is impossible to measure. His work on the formation of the Republican Party, on the radicalism of Tom Paine, on Reconstruction, on American freedom, on Abraham Lincoln, on the underground railroad, and so much else will be read for decades, even centuries, to come. My own understanding and appreciation of our past—both the glories and the crimes—have been shaped to no small extent by the arguments Eric has put forward and by the stories he has told—stories he tells with good humor, cool passion, precision, and openness to argument.

Yet it is not Eric Foner—the widely influential People's Historian, Historian's Historian—whom I want to pay tribute to today. Others will speak to the importance of his field, shaping interventions in various debates.

I want to add something else. On top of his other laurels—the Bancrofts and the Parkmans and the Pulitzers—I suggest adding another distinction: Eric Foner has been one of the most indispensable political commentators in the United States in the last forty years. His public, political writing has never been a sideline or digression from his scholarly historical work. Both spring from the same deep commitment to a radical sense of justice. Eric is not interested in effacing the political in his own scholarship, or presenting his work as securely neutral products of mere curiosity about the past. He shows that another route is possible. We need not sever the connection between past and present. The best history, and the best politics, emerge from a dialogue between the two—and in his commitment to that dialogue, Foner has helped to shape a generation of American historians, dissidents, activists, journalists, and eminent figures.

This idea of Eric as political commentator may surprise those who first encountered Eric's work in the library, in journals like *Civil War History* or the *Journal of American History*. But many thousands of Americans first read him in the pages of a magazine whose first issue was published in 1865, that pivotal year in the life of this country when a group of abolitionists came together and decided they needed a magazine to continue their struggle for human freedom and equality in the age of emancipation. Inheriting the subscription list of William Lloyd Garrison's newspaper the *Liberator*—which shut down after Garrison declared its work was done—this new magazine would be dedicated to covering what an editorial in its very first issue called "the conflict of ages, the great strife between the few and the many, between privilege and equality, between law and power, between opinion and the sword." While remaining conscientiously loyal to its other mission, stated in the founding prospectus, to consider "the topics of the day . . . with greater accuracy and moderation than are now to be found in the daily press"—no "alternative facts" for this magazine, thank you very much—the weekly would nonetheless take sides in that conflict of ages, standing up for the many, for equality, for the rule of law, for opinion. The group gave the magazine a name to match their ambitions for the reconstructed United States: it was called the *Nation*.

Much has changed in 152 years, for both the nation and the *Nation*, as we like to say. But we continue to think of our mission as continuing the battle for emancipation, the battle for freedom. (Here, I am contractually obligated to note that *Battles for Freedom: The Use and Abuse of American History*, a collection of Eric's many articles and essays for the *Nation* over the last forty years, is available at thenation.com. The reviews are terrific.) In that battle, Eric Foner has wielded his pen like a sword. His first contribution to the magazine, exactly forty years ago, was a reconsideration of the case of Sacco and Vanzetti, fifty years after their tragic execution. "The tragedy of their case," he wrote, "lies not only in the injustice that was done but in the fact that their execution was one in a long train of events that seems to have driven their utopian vision out of American life." In 1993 Eric used the 130th anniversary of the Emancipation Proclamation to call for a "Third Reconstruction," following the first one in the 1860s, which he had already written about so compellingly, and the second in the 1960s. Nothing less was needed now, he wrote, than "a renewed national effort to address the racial divide that afflicts our society." Yet such an effort would require, Foner acknowledged, "the kind of moral leadership and political courage this generation is unaccustomed to in its presidents." A quarter-century after he wrote that dazzling essay, we're still waiting for that Third Reconstruction.

Thanks to the wisdom of the *Nation*'s editor/publisher Emeritus Victor Navasky, Eric joined the magazine's editorial board in 1996. He has been a wise board member, bringing history to bear when needed and interjecting a Foner-esque radical pragmatism into our discussions of movement and electoral politics, endorsement decisions, and various controversies. He has never failed to remind us that at a time when the old consensus has cracked open, the *Nation*'s "number one thing" must be to put forward an alternative view and vision. On the *Nation*'s 150th anniversary, over a series of Metro Diner breakfasts (one of our favorite hangouts), Eric guided me, and my editorial comrade Don Guttenplan, to themes, ideas, and readings that informed our special anniversary issue. He made sure I knew that the *Nation* had in fact been on the wrong side of some of the great battles—had been, in fact, the voice of plutocratic privilege and reactionary Republicanism for several of its early decades. (I had known—but in that U.S. amnesia spirit I had hoped to suppress remembering.) And his luminous contribution to the issue, "Freedom's Song," reminded us of how, over the *Nation*'s and the nation's history, each new generation of radicals and reformers has contested the promise—and the meaning—of freedom.

After the selection of George W. Bush by the Supreme Court in 2000, Foner the political commentator wrote, within weeks of the September 11 attacks, a powerful piece for the *Nation* called "The Most Patriotic Act." "Of the many lessons of American history, this is among the most basic," Foner cautioned.

> Our civil rights and civil liberties—freedom of expression, the right to criticize the government, equality before the law, restraints on the exercise of police powers—are not gifts from the state that can be rescinded when it desires. They are the inheritance of a long history of struggles: by abolitionists for the ability to hold meetings and publish their views in the face of mob violence; by labor leaders for the power to organize unions, picket and distribute literature without fear of arrest; by feminists for the right to disseminate birth-control information without being charged with violating the obscenity laws; and by all those who braved jail and worse to challenge entrenched systems of racial inequality.

He reminded us that, "at times of crisis the most patriotic act of all is the unyielding defense of civil liberties, the right to dissent and equality before the law for all Americans." It's hard to overstate how brave it was to write such things at a time when the drumbeat of war was ringing out all over the land. For his troubles, Foner found himself on a list of the most dangerous professors in America—an accomplishment for which I know he was rightfully proud. He was also rightly proud of being described, more recently, by the *Columbia Spectator* as a "general all-around cool cat." That would be in an article titled, "How Foner (Sort of) Feels the Bern."

Before I end, I would be remiss if I did not bring up that Eric has been unfailingly generous with his time, his words, and his counsel—and given his global fame, it is remarkable how unpretentiousness he is. He is also a masterful and speedy email correspondent, and often one of mordant wit. In one of his late-night emails, ostensibly about organizing a *Nation* event at the Schomburg, Eric asked in a postscript: "By the way, did you ever see *Lincoln the Vampire Hunter*? Totally absurd (Mary Lincoln and Harriet Tubman bring silver bullets to the Union troops at Gettysburg to defeat a vampire Confederate army) but oddly, it gives more of a sense of slavery than the Spielberg movie." There's one more article Eric has written for the *Nation* that I want to highlight, only because it exemplifies how unique and important his voice has been. In November 2015, just as Bernie Sanders was climbing in the polls, taking everyone, including himself, by surprise, Eric emailed me: "Thinking about the Democratic debate, if you or anyone else at the *Nation* has a way of communicating with Bernie, he needs to revise his approach when talking about radicalism and socialism. Forget about Denmark!" So, I asked Eric to pen an open letter to Bernie for the *Nation*. In it, he asked Sanders to stop appealing to the example of Denmark as inspiration for what he was proposing.

Instead, he suggested that Sanders ground what he was saying in American radical traditions, our own radical history: talk about abolitionists, Populists, feminists, Debs, the New Deal, the Great Society, King's critique of wealth and poverty and militarism in America, and refer to the Populists' Omaha platform of 1892, which sounds like it could be written today with its picture of inequality and a political system in urgent need of change. Eric asked Bernie to please talk about "our radical forebears here in the United States," because "the most successful radicals have always spoken the language of American society and appealed to some of its deepest values." Foner has spoken that language, too. And he has enriched it in invaluable ways. By telling the story of our most fundamental values—the story of American freedom, in the title of one of his greatest books—he has imbued them with new warmth, new rigor, and new importance. We are all in his debt.

CONTRIBUTORS

JIM DOWNS is the Gilder Lehrman NEH Professor of Civil War Studies and History at Gettysburg College. He is the author of *Sick from Freedom: African American Illness and Suffering During the Civil War and Reconstruction* (2012) and *Stand by Me: The Forgotten History of Gay Liberation* (2016). He is coeditor of *Connexions: Histories of Race and Sex in North America* (2016) and *Beyond Freedom: Disrupting the History of Emancipation* (2017).

ERICA ARMSTRONG DUNBAR is the Charles and Mary Beard Distinguished Professor of History at Rutgers University. She is the author of *Never Caught: The Washingtons' Relentless Pursuit of Their Runaway Slave, Ona Judge* (2017), which was a finalist for the National Book Award. She is also the author of *A Fragile Freedom: African American Women and Emancipation in the Antebellum City* (2008). She earned her B.A. from the University of Pennsylvania and her Ph.D. from Columbia University.

TIMOTHY PATRICK McCARTHY is an award-winning historian, educator, and human rights activist who currently holds a joint faculty appointment at Harvard's Graduate School of Education and the John F. Kennedy School of Government, where he is Core Faculty at the Carr Center for Human Rights Policy. He is also the Stanley Paterson Professor of American History in the Boston Clemente Course, a free college humanities course for lower-income adults and corecipient of the 2015 National Humanities Medal.

He has published five books with the New Press, including *The Radical Reader: A Documentary History of the American Radical Tradition* (2003) and the forthcoming *Stonewall's Children: Living Queer History in an Age of Liberation, Loss, and Love.* An honors graduate of Harvard College, he earned his Ph.D. in History from Columbia University.

MICHAEL GREEN is an associate professor of history in the University of Nevada, Las Vegas's Department of History. He earned his B.A. and M.A. at UNLV and his Ph.D. at Columbia University. His books on the Civil War era are *Freedom, Union, and Power: Lincoln and His Party During the Civil War* (2004), *Politics and America in Crisis: The Coming of the Civil War* (2010), and *Lincoln and the Election of 1860* (2011). His works on Nevada include *Las Vegas: A Centennial History* (with Eugene Moehring, 2005); *Nevada: A Journey of Discovery*, a middle school textbook (2004); and the oral history of a longtime Nevada attorney and politician, *A Liberal Conscience: Ralph Denton, Nevadan* (2001). The University of Nevada Press published his college-level textbook *Nevada: A History of the Silver State* in 2015.

ELIZABETH A. HERBIN-TRIANT is an associate professor in the Department of History at the University of Massachusetts Lowell. Her publications include *Threatening Property: Race, Class, and Campaigns to Legislate Jim Crow Neighborhoods* (Columbia, 2019), as well as scholarly articles in the *Journal of Southern History* and *Agricultural History*. She is working on a new book project that examines northern complicity with slavery through the example of Lowell, Massachusetts, home to textile factories that wove cotton grown by enslaved people into cloth. She earned her B.A. from Harvard College and her Ph.D. from Columbia University.

T.K. HUNTER received an M.A. from Hunter College and a second M.A. and a Ph.D. from Columbia University. With interests in the Black Atlantic, law, liberty, and slavery and studies regarding the question of rights, Dr. Hunter wrote book reviews, articles in law journals, and various essays and was a consultant for the nationally aired PBS/WGBH history documentary *Africans in America*. She was also the recipient of a variety of awards, including a University of Glasgow, Scotland Fellowship and an Andrew W. Mellon Fellowship. Dr. Hunter taught through the

Department of History and the Black Studies Program at City College in New York City. She was a Rifkind Center Seminar Fellowship winner for 2017–2018.

APRIL E. HOLM is an associate professor of History and the associate director of the Center for Civil War Research at the University of Mississippi. She is a historian of the nineteenth-century United States with an interest in border states, sectionalism, emancipation, and the Civil War and Reconstruction. Her work concerns the intersection of the moral and religious with the political. Her first book, *A Kingdom Divided: Evangelicals, Loyalty, and Sectionalism in the Civil War Era*, was published by Louisiana State University Press in fall 2017. She is currently researching a project on provost marshals and civilians in the occupied border region. She received her Ph.D. from Columbia University in 2010 and spent a year as a Schwartz Postdoctoral Fellow at the New School and the New-York Historical Society before joining the faculty at the University of Mississippi.

KELLIE CARTER JACKSON is Knafel Assistant Professor of Humanities in the Department of Africana Studies at Wellesley College. She is the author of *Force and Freedom: Black Abolitionists and the Politics of Violence* (2019) which won the James J. Broussard Best First Book Prize and was a finalist for the Frederick Douglass Prize. She is also coeditor of *Reconsidering Roots: Race, Politics, and Memory* (2017). Carter Jackson's essays have been featured in the *Atlantic*, the *Washington Post*, the *Los Angeles Times* and other major news outlets. Carter Jackson also sits on the board for *Transition Magazine*.

MATTHEW TAYLOR RAFFETY is a professor of History at the University of Redlands. He earned his B.A. from Williams College and his Ph.D. in American History at Columbia University. A historian of the early American republic, his research interests include legal, gender, and maritime history and questions of citizenship. He also works on the history of sport. His book, *The Republic Afloat: Law, Honor, and Citizenship in Maritime America* (2013), examines violent crimes on American ships before the U.S. Civil War. He appeared in the feature documentary *Stolen Seas* (2012) on Somali piracy. He is currently working on a book-length project about American merchants and diplomats running amok in 1830s Cuba.

KATRINA VANDEN HEUVEL is editorial director and publisher of the *Nation*. She served as editor of the magazine from 1995 to 2019. A frequent commentator on U.S. and international politics for ABC, MSNBC, CNN, and PBS, her articles have appeared in the *New York Times*, the *Los Angeles Times*, and the *Boston Globe*, and she writes a weekly column for the *Washington Post*. Vanden Heuvel is also the author of several books, including (with Stephen F. Cohen) *Voices of Glasnost: Interviews with Gorbachev's Reformers*, and *The Change I Believe In: Fighting for Progress in The Age of Obama* (2011).

ASHLI WHITE is an associate professor of History at the University of Miami. She specializes in early American history, with particular attention to the connections between North America and the larger Atlantic world. Most of her research has concentrated on the political, social, and cultural history of the age of revolutions. White's first book, *Encountering Revolution: Haiti and the Making of the Early Republic* (2010), explores the far-reaching impact of the Haitian Revolution on the early United States. This book won the Gilbert Chinard Prize for 2011 from the Society for French Historical Studies and the Institut Français d'Amérique. Her current book project analyzes the circulation of objects associated with the age of revolutions, and in support of this work, White has received fellowships from the National Endowment for the Humanities, the Omohundro Institute, and the American Philosophical Society Library, among others. She is also associate curator for the exhibition *Antillean Visions: Maps and the Making of the Caribbean*, which opened at the Lowe Art Museum in spring 2018.

INDEX

CPSIA information can be obtained
at www.ICGtesting.com
Printed in the USA
LVHW021940181021
700737LV00002B/4

9 780231 192576